"So Much Generosity"

An Appreciation of the Fiction of Nicholas Cardinal Wiseman, John Henry Cardinal Newman, and Monsignor Robert Hugh Benson

By
Michael D. Greaney

© 2013 Universal Values Media, Inc.

© 2013 Universal Values Media, Inc

3800 Powell Lane, No. 823
(Tel) 703-243-5155 • (Fax) 703-243-5935
(Eml) onceandfuturebooks@yahoo.com
(Web) www.benson-unabridged.com

All rights reserved. No part of this edition may be reproduced, stored in a retrieval system, or transmitted, in any form, or by any means, electronic, mechanical, photocopying, recording or otherwise, without the prior written permission of Universal Values Media, Inc.

International Standard Book Number: 978-1-60210-002-2

Library of Congress Control Number: 2010940347

Cover design by Rowland L. Brohawn

Table of Contents

I. The Stage is Set 1
   Nicholas Patrick Wiseman 15
   John Henry Newman 23
   Robert Hugh Benson 33

II. The Novels of Wiseman and Newman 45
   1. Fabiola 47
   2. Loss and Gain 55
   3. Callista 65

III. The Fiction of Robert Hugh Benson 73
   1. The Short Stories 75
      The Light Invisible 77
      A Mirror of Shalott 83
   2. The Early Historical Novels 87
      By What Authority? 89
      The King's Achievement 95
      The Queen's Tragedy 101
   3. The History of Richard Raynal, Solitary 107
   4. The Conversion Stories 119
   5. The "Sensational" Novels 127
      The Sentimentalists 129
      Lord of the World 133
      The Conventionalists 139
      The Necromancers 145
      The Dawn of All 151
   6. The Holy Blissful Martyr, Thomas à Becket 159
   7. The Contemporary Novels 175
      A Winnowing 177
      None Other Gods 187
      The Coward 195
      An Average Man 203
      Initiation 213
      Loneliness? 223
   8. The Later Historical Novels 235
      Come Rack! Come Rope! 237
      Oddsfish! 249
Index 255

I. The Stage is Set

The late Dr. Ralph McInerny, noted author of the "Father Dowling" mystery novels and a host of other fiction and non-fiction works, once commented that the trouble with so much "Catholic fiction" is it's so good, it's bad. By that, of course, he meant that the characters were so saccharine and artificially holy that the novel or story, however well or poorly written, was already a failure due to the fact that it lacked the necessary link to reality. A good rule of thumb to follow in fiction is for the author to place extraordinary people in ordinary situations, or ordinary people in extraordinary situations; there must be something with which the reader can identify, some connection with "real life."

A Change in Moral Absolutes

This creates a problem for authors of works of fiction within western culture as it has developed over the past several centuries. The civilization founded on the heritage of Greece and Rome has, to all intents and purposes, abandoned a philosophy derived from the natural moral law based on God's Nature/Essence (self evident in His Intellect), and shifted to a private interpretation of whatever someone has decided is God's Will. This has severed the connection with the moral absolutes reflected in human nature, to say nothing of the world around us.

Western society was once "Catholic" in the religious sense of the term as well as the philosophical and political, being based on universal — catholic — acceptance of the precepts of the natural moral law. Western culture has, however, largely forsaken the natural law basis of civilization common to Catholicism, Judaism, Islam, and any other religion or philosophy that partakes of what Anglican apologist C. S. Lewis referred to as the "Tao," or "the Way." The West has for the most part abandoned the universal or "catholic" principles that necessarily provide the framework within which humanity defines proper conduct as well as principles of right and wrong. Consequently, there is no common ground on which the popular culture, and those who hold by the basic tenets of sound philosophy can meet.

This makes it all the more surprising that the works profiled in this book, composed by such luminaries as Nicholas Patrick Cardinal Wiseman, John Henry Cardinal Newman, and Monsignor Robert Hugh Benson, enjoyed not just acceptance as good literature, but, to a significant degree, popular acclaim. The suggestion intrudes that, despite all the effort and the centuries of human suffering that have gone into trying to change humanity into something other than what is, it is an exercise in futility to try and transform the moral absolutes that define humanity as human.

If, as Aquinas, Maimonides, and Ibn Khaldûn taught, human nature is a reflection of divine nature, and divine nature is, by definition, unchanging and unchangeable, then any attempt to change the basic principles of the natural moral law is doomed to failure. As the poet Horace reminded us, "You can chase Nature out with a pitchfork, but she always comes back." We would otherwise have to assert that God is at humanity's command, not the other way around, or that God does not exist.

The basic problem, and one that is addressed either directly or peripherally in every one of the works profiled in this book, is the nature of humanity itself — what it means to be truly human. It's a long story, but I'll try to condense it. This may be difficult, but necessary, for the shift in understanding of what it means for something to be *true* is at the heart of most of our social, political, and even economic problems today.

A Meditation on the Manichees

While the roots of the problem go back millennia, today's problems can be traced directly to a split that occurred within the three major monotheistic religions approximately 800 years ago. The philosophy of Aristotle had just been "rediscovered" in Europe, along with the principles of Roman law. The trouble with Aristotle, however, was that a number of critical texts had been corrupted and transmitted to the west through Muslims who, to put it charitably, were less than orthodox in their beliefs even as Muslims. They had been heavily influenced by the doctrines of the Manichees.

From the standpoint of monotheism, Manichaeism is a heterodox belief that arose soon after Christianity, originating in Persia in the third century. As an organized religion, Manichaeism has an elaborate and "dualistic" cosmology describing the struggle between a good, spiritual world of light, and an evil, material world of darkness, or two gods, equal and opposite, one good, and one evil. Human history is a record of the struggle by means of which light is gradually removed from the world of matter, and returned to the world of light from whence it came. Evil results from the impure mixture of light and darkness.

Naturally, oversimplifications crept in when these doctrines influenced monotheism. The material world became viewed as inherently evil, while the spiritual world contains the only good. The world is therefore becoming increasingly evil over time as light is removed and the world becomes less spiritual and more material. Individuals are faced with the choice of giving in to their material wants and needs and deliberately helping evil to triumph, or of denying materialism and assisting light by abjuring the world around us.

Aside from the idea that a creation of an all-good Creator can be inherently evil (bad enough, as it calls the goodness of God into question), the problem from the monotheistic point of view is that Manichaeism defines a supreme being out of existence. Having two gods equal in power, locked in eternal conflict, necessarily means that the attributes assigned to God by Judaism, Christianity, and Islam, *e.g.*, omnipotence, omniscience, perfection, immutability, and so on, no longer apply. God ceases be a god, or is a god only because some people have decided that he is; man creates god.

That being the case, whatever we worship ceases to command our obedience because it is the right thing to do, that is, is consistent with nature and is thus "true." From a Manichaean orientation, this is because nature, partaking of the material world, is unalterably corrupt, and cannot be the standard of behavior or measure of right or wrong. Instead, something that we believe to be a god commands our obedience because he (or, more usually, those who claim to speak for him) has the power to force us to do "his" will . . . as those who claim to speak for the god interpret it.

Ultimately we don't need a god or gods at all. The only thing we need is whatever somebody has decided is a statement of his will[1] — and that, as also becomes obvious, is subject to a vote among believers. Truth ceases to be true, and becomes, instead, whatever happens to be expedient to meet the wants and needs of the moment.

Within a Manichaean or Manichaean-influenced system, principles are constantly in a state of flux as people continually redefine truth in order to get what they want, rather than conform themselves to truth in order to become more fully what they are. Naturally, this leads to constant acrimony as people who believe in absolutes come into conflict with those whose only absolute is that there are no absolutes. As G. K. Chesterton analyzed the essential difference between the two positions,

> It is no good to tell an atheist that he is an atheist; or to charge a denier of immortality with the infamy of denying it, or to imagine that one can force an opponent to admit he is wrong, by proving that he is wrong on somebody else's principles, but not on his own.[2]

In other words, no two people or parties can ever come to an agreement when they are speaking different languages, even if they are using the same words. The sounds may be the same, but the meanings attached to those sounds are completely different, depending on the definitions — or lack thereof — being used.

---

[1] "What we have been saying would have a degree of validity even if we should concede that which cannot be conceded without the utmost wickedness, that there is no God, or that the affairs of men are of no concern to Him." Hugo Grotius, *De Jure Belli ac Pacis Libri Tres*, Prolegomena, II.

[2] G. K. Chesterton, *St. Thomas Aquinas: The "Dumb Ox."* New York: Doubleday, 1956, 95.

Problem Solved?

Superficially, the idea of equal and opposite forces of good and evil simplifies a problem that has troubled Jewish, Christian and Islamic philosophers and theologians for centuries. That is, how can an all-good God permit evil to happen? How can "bad things happen to good people?" The quick (and correct) answer to that is, "free will."

The exercise of free will, however, is not a deliberate choice between good and evil, as the Manichaean orientation would have it. Rather, free will consists of deciding freely whether to submit one's will to that of God, of making the ultimate Good your own personal good, or putting your own will above everything else. Contrary to Manichaean theology, no person, sane or insane, deliberately chooses evil knowing it to be evil but, as Aristotle explained, because the evil seems good to him. This creates a paradox and raises the question, What is "good"?

Aristotle explained that, as well. "Good" is that at which all things aim. If someone instead strives for evil, it is because he believes it to be good. The ultimate good for humanity is to become more fully human. Man becomes more fully human by acquiring and developing virtue, a word that, while literally "male-ness," signifies "human-ness." Because acquiring and developing virtue is the highest good, it is what makes man truly happy; "pursuit of happiness" and "the acquisition and development of virtue" are equivalent concepts.

Faith and Reason

That does not, however, completely answer the question. Leaping forward a few centuries from Aristotle, Aquinas explained that "good" is what we as human beings can discern in our nature that matches or is a "reflection" of God's Nature. Discerning the reflection of God's Nature in human nature, however imperfectly or incompletely, is the job of reason. According to Aquinas, then, "good" is whatever the general consensus of humanity has perceived as consistent with human nature throughout the ages. Because human nature is a reflection of God's Nature or Essence, self-evident in His Intellect, the existence of God and certain attributes of His Nature — the natural moral law — can therefore be discerned by the use of reason alone, without faith.

Does this mean that faith is unnecessary, or that such things as the Torah, the Bible, or the Quran are fables or lies adopted for expedience, or useless encumbrances used by knaves to pull the wool over the eyes of fools? Of course not. The holy books of any religion, while written by believers for believers, embody what adherents of a particular faith believe has been revealed to them, and which they accept on the basis of faith. Something is not true because it is in a holy book, but has been put in the holy book because believers already accept it as true — including the precepts of the natural moral law discerned by reason. It surprises some people who take the Bible as the sole rule of faith for Christianity to discover that "the Bible" as we know it did not even exist for nearly four centuries after Christ.

What happens, however, is that when people define or redefine what is true in a holy book or any other source in a way different from the definition used by whoever composed the text,[3] not only is conflict inevitable, but resolution by reasoned argument becomes impossible. As Chesterton explained,

> The principle stands, or ought always to have stood established; that we must either not argue with a man at all, or we must argue on his grounds and not ours. We may do other things *instead* of arguing, according to our views of what actions are morally permissible; but if we argue we must argue "on the reasons and statements of the philosophers themselves."[4]

All holy books — as well as all legal codes, for that matter — give specific applications of the natural moral law; they express someone's idea of how to apply the precepts of the law in specific circumstances. *They are not them-*

---

[3] See, *e.g.*, the analysis of the United States Constitution in Michael D. Greaney, *Supporting Life: The Case for a Pro-Life Economic Agenda*. Arlington, Virginia: Economic Justice Media, 2010.

[4] Chesterton, *op. cit.*, 95-96.

selves the law, that is, the *principle*. As Heinrich Rommen explained, "the natural law lays down general norms [principles] only."[5] This fact cannot be stressed enough, especially in our day when Modernism, a form of intellectual Manichaeism, pervades not only the culture, but almost every aspect of individual life as well.

What the intrusion of Manichaeism into the three great monotheistic religions did was to change the basis of the natural moral law from God's Intellect, to God's Will — or, more accurately, to someone's idea of what constitutes God's Will. This is a very "iffy" avenue by which to approach truth. If we are strong enough to bully others into accepting our views, or clever enough to persuade them, contrary to reason, that our interpretation of God's Will is the correct one, then we can, in effect, get anything we want. As Rommen pointed out,

> With Duns Scotus (d. *cir*. 1308), and with the principle of the primacy of the will over the intellect so much emphasized by him, there began inside moral philosophy a train of thought which in later centuries would recur in secularized form in the domain of legal philosophy. The principle that law is will would be referred in legal positivism, as well as in the theory of will in jurisprudence, to the earthly lawmaker (self-obligation).
>
> For Duns Scotus morality depends on the will of God. A thing is good not because it corresponds to the nature of God or, analogically, to the nature of man, but because God so wills. Hence the *lex naturalis* could be other than it is even materially or as to content, because it has no intrinsic connection with God's essence, which is self-conscious in His intellect. For Scotus, therefore, the laws of the second table of the Decalogue were no longer unalterable. The crux of theology, namely, the problem of the apparent dispensations from the natural law mentioned in the Old Testament and thus seemingly granted by God (the command to sacrifice Isaac, Raphael's apparent

---

[5] Heinrich Rommen, *The Natural Law*. Indianapolis, Indiana: Liberty Fund, Inc., 1998, 59.

lie, Osee's alleged adultery, the polygamy of the patriarchs, and so on), was now readily solved. Yet St. Thomas, too, had been able to solve such cases. Now, however, an evolution set in which, in the doctrine of William of Occam (d. *cir.* 1349) on the natural moral law, would lead to pure moral positivism, indeed to nihilism.[6]

Reason and the Preeminence of the Intellect

Some people might protest that our conclusions as to the content of the natural law based on reason are no more valid than the conclusions based on a human understanding of God's explicit commands delivered in a holy book or revealed to a prophet. Are not both, ultimately, mere opinion?

No. While the process of discerning the precepts of the natural law from the general consensus of all mankind does not meet the requirements of *deductive* reasoning, it does meet those of *inductive* reasoning, an equally valid way of proceeding. Basing the natural law on what we discern by reason alone is therefore not mere opinion that depends on acceptance of something by faith, but an argument supported by evidence that can be examined objectively.

Correlating what is said in a holy book regarding the precepts of the law, with the general consensus of humanity as to what is right and wrong allows us to interpret that which we believe to be God's Will with a high degree of certainty. Why? Because we can then judge the rightness or wrongness of a proposed act on the basis of something other than someone's mere word.

As members of a particular religion we can — and must — believe as firmly as ever that God did, indeed, command such-and-such a thing, but we must not accept anyone's interpretation of what we believe God has mandated if it appears to go contrary to reason. In ethics — moral philosophy — the Intellect is preeminent over the Will. Believers in any religion with what Catholics call a "well-formed conscience," that is, a sense of right and wrong consistent with the precepts of the natural moral law,

---

[6] *Ibid.*, 51-52.

have the right to an explanation from proper authority when something appears to go contrary to reason, and the duty to demand it if an explanation is not forthcoming.

My Will, Not Thine

Shifting the basis of the natural moral law from Intellect to Will means, in the end, abandoning what we can prove to be right by the use of reason. We are then free to surrender to our own desires by claiming that we have been granted special insights as to the meaning of God's Will. Inevitably, these are insights that we accept not on the basis of reason, but of faith. Our "vocation," that is, our "calling" in life, that which God wants us to do, becomes a simple projection of our own will and desires, concerning the goodness of which we, not God, are the best judges.

Anything or anyone that comes into conflict with our desires must be ignored, rejected, or attacked. Rather than being a part of nature (and thus Nature), we set ourselves above such matters and assert a superior spirituality above the material (and thus evil) world. In a frenzy of Manichaean madness, "right" and "wrong" become eternally changeable, depending on what we want, based on our will alone. As Chesterton characterized the situation,

> What is called the Manichean philosophy has had many forms; indeed it has attacked what is immortal and immutable with a very curious kind of immortal mutability. It is like the legend of the magician who turns himself into a snake or a cloud; and the whole has that nameless note of irresponsibility, which belongs to much of the metaphysics and morals of Asia, from which the Manichean mystery came. But it is always in one way or another a notion that nature is evil; or that evil is at least rooted in nature. The essential point is that as evil has roots in nature, so it has rights in nature. Wrong has as much right to exist as right.[7]

Out of this philosophy come virtually all the attacks on the natural moral law that are so pervasive today. Natu-

---

[7] Chesterton, *op. cit.*, 106.

ral rights that, within an orientation that bases the natural moral law on Intellect, define us as human persons, become changeable at the will of whoever is strongest or has the most power. Liberty (freedom of association), private property, the pursuit of happiness — even life itself — all become subject to redefinition, which in natural law is the same as abolition. Man, as C. S. Lewis put it in the title of one of his collections of essays,[8] is abolished, becoming something less than human in the process.

The bottom line is that a Jew, Christian, or Muslim who accepts the Aristotelian "take" on his or her religion as analyzed by Maimonides, Aquinas, or Ibn Khaldûn, respectively, necessarily has a different outlook on truth than is common today, especially in distinguishing right from wrong. An Aristotelian Jew, Christian, or Muslim assumes as a matter of course that when someone does evil, it is because he or she is under the impression that it is good; that he or she is mistaken about what constitutes virtue. It is the sin that is to be hated, not the sinner. The sinner is someone to be pitied and instructed to have a better idea of right and wrong, that is, on how to be more consistent with God's Nature — truth — reflected in human nature. Punishment may be necessary on occasion, but the ultimate goal at all times should be the rehabilitation and redemption of the sinner.

A Manichaean, or a Jew, Christian, or Muslim with a Manichaean orientation, however, necessarily operates on a different assumption. Anyone in this paradigm who does evil or who understands right or wrong in a different way, is presumed to have deliberately chosen evil over good — at least as the Manichaean or Manichaean-oriented Jew, Christian, or Muslim defines good. "Good," however, ceases to be something discernable by reason.

Instead, "good" becomes completely subjective, the judgment of whoever or whatever has the means and the willingness to coerce others into accepting the new definition of good. Someone becomes a "bully for God," so to speak, promoting a sort of "muscular" Judaism, Christian-

---

[8] C. S. Lewis, *The Abolition of Man*. New York: Harper Collins, 2001.

ity, or Islam through intimidation, threats, and coercion whenever persuasion fails — as it inevitably must, not being supported by reason. Ultimately, murder is justified for the crime of disagreeing or obstructing the will of one who believes at some level that he speaks for God or sits in His place — "Is there not one that will rid me of this troublesome priest?"

The Cause of Catholic Emancipation

The three authors who wrote the novels and other fiction profiled in this book, Nicholas Patrick Cardinal Wiseman, John Henry Cardinal Newman, and Monsignor Robert Hugh Benson, all professed a form of Christianity — Catholicism — that rejects the Manichaean orientation as the basis of society. Among the many reasons why the Catholic Church rejects Manichaeism is that Manichaean philosophy manifests itself in civil society in the centralizing of all political, economic, and financial power in the State or a tiny private elite that controls the State — a sort of "triumph of the Will" over reason. Accepting the Manichaean orientation and abandoning the natural moral law based on Intellect as the foundation of the social order inevitably leads to the development of the totalitarian Nation-State as the "normal" form of civil organization, and socialism as the required economic organization.

It was in England where much of the philosophy of the totalitarian Nation-State developed. This began in a "big way" with the political philosophy of Sir Robert Filmer and Thomas Hobbes, both strong supporters of the Established Church of England. Filmer was, in fact, chief theologian for James I Stuart, and tailored both his theology and his political theory to meet the king's requirements.

It comes as no surprise, then, that membership in the Catholic Church, even adherence to Catholic customs in the practice of one's religion (candles, incense, *etc.*), was viewed by many people as being tantamount to high treason. Within this framework, no one could be both a good Catholic and a good citizen, a claim that has also been levied against Jews and, both in the early days of Christianity and today, other Christian groups.

These views persisted even after "Catholic emancipation" in the United Kingdom. This was largely achieved in 1829 as a result of efforts spearheaded by Daniel O'Connell, the "Great Emancipator." O'Connell linked civil rights for native Irish Catholics (especially freedom of religion) to the effort to repeal the 1800 "Act of Union"[9] that made Ireland officially part of the United Kingdom instead of a separate kingdom under the same ruler. The passage of the Catholic Relief Act in 1829 removed most disabilities from Catholics, although leaving in place the legal requirement to pay tithes to the Anglican Church and the prohibition against any Catholic becoming king, queen, or royal consort.

What the Catholic Relief Act did not remove was the violent prejudice many of the English still had (although markedly less intense by then in many quarters) against "popery" and "papists." For centuries the English had been taught as a matter of public policy that Catholics were natural traitors to England and everything English. Even the support of the Duke of Wellington, a national hero, and Lord Grenville, one of the most prominent political leaders of the day — as well as the reluctant support of Sir Robert Peel, soon to be Prime Minister — could not legislate popular acceptance of Catholics as fellow citizens, and Catholicism as a legitimate expression of the virtue of religion.

How, then, can we understand just how the works profiled in this book were not only published, but, by all measures, outstandingly successful? The authors themselves were, to a greater or lesser degree, seen either as notorious, or (at the very least) slightly suspect for being not just Catholics, but Catholic priests, the archetypical villains of the nation for centuries. Wiseman was suspect for being a "foreigner" (his parents were Anglo Irish who had settled in Spain for business reasons), and Newman was a traitor for being a convert to Catholicism. Of the

---

[9] Actually two separate acts, the Union with Ireland Act 1800 (1800 c. 67 39 and 40 Geo 3), an Act of the Parliament of Great Britain, and the Act of Union (Ireland) 1800 (1800 c. 38 40 Geo 3), an Act of the Parliament of Ireland (which thereby legislated itself out of existence), both of which took effect January 1, 1801.

three, Benson was the most widely accepted during his lifetime, although, of course, still somewhat suspect for being a convert.

Still, the change in attitudes from the attacks on Wiseman and Newman, to the general acceptance, even popularity of Benson seems almost miraculous. The transformation — we might almost say transubstantiation — occurred within a society that had (and has) a basic orientation directly at odds with the philosophy that guides the Catholic Church, and saturated with the idea that Catholics and Catholicism are somehow the enemies of society. Understanding how that happened is, in part, the reason for this book.

The Plan of the Work

Understanding the cultural context of the novels and short fiction of Wiseman, Newman, and Benson, however, is actually the smaller part of what I hope to accomplish. The main purpose is to encourage the reading public to become acquainted (or reacquainted) with the novels and short stories themselves, and gain an appreciation of them as works of literature that offer profound insights into the human condition, whatever one's faith or philosophy.

All of the essays in this book were written as forewords to the works they critique. For that reason I tried to avoid "spoilers" about the plot — or at least no more than was necessary to give what I considered a full and accurate appreciation of both the authors' intent and how we should understand it.

As the pieces were intended to stand alone, a little redundancy was unavoidable. Rewriting for a greater degree of continuity would have involved completely redoing the pieces to the point where they constituted new works.

That, however, is of little or no relevance to the purpose of this book. While I edited the essays for continuity and elimination of redundancy to a limited extent, I also thought it best to leave some of the apparent redundancies in to demonstrate the essential consistency of the work of the three authors, as well as Benson's literary relationship to the two earlier English Catholic writers, Nicholas Patrick Wiseman, and the recently beatified

John Henry Newman. All three sought to present the truths of the Catholic faith in popular form within the unique religious and cultural milieu of England.

Had that been their only goal, however, their novels and other works would not only have virtually no interest for the modern reader of any faith, but would have had almost no appeal to their contemporaries, Catholic, Protestant, or any other sect or religion. Whether they intended it or not, all three authors also — or primarily — took as their essential theme something much deeper and more profound than the tenets of a particular faith, however deeply held. Their works touched, in varying degrees, on the universality — the "catholicity," if you will — of the human condition, regardless of specific philosophy, religion, or lack of either.

By studying the works of these men, perhaps we can come to learn how to present truths, whether religious, political, or economic, to an audience to which those truths are alien or even hostile concepts.

Nicholas Patrick Wiseman (1802-1865)

In his first letter to the Corinthians, St. Paul tells us we must be "all things to all men."[10] Nowhere is this more evident than in the spectacle of a Cardinal of the Catholic Church turning popular novelist. At first glance surprising, on reflection it makes sense. If Christ came to save the entire human race, then no elite or select group can possibly have a monopoly on the ability to become a Christian — or fully human, for that matter. The "good news" (the meaning of "gospel") should be preached in a way that gets the message across to people in language that they will understand. If people are reading novels — as they did for entertainment in nineteenth century England — then novels are one way to reach them.

The Pitfalls of Popularity

There is, of course, a danger in using popular culture to communicate with people. It usually takes an extraordinary individual to be able to communicate effectively, and not succumb to the allure of celebrity. Many "televangelists" of today appear to start out with the best of intentions, and yet easily surrender to the temptation of hypocrisy inherent in showmanship. It is, of course, possible to avoid the pitfalls of popularity and celebrity status — Fulton Sheen seems to have been a case in point — but it is not easy, nor, for most people, is it a temptation that they should risk. Entertainment folklore is full of stories of "stars" who ultimately destroyed themselves by becoming the very thing they believed they wished to become, and found out that it wasn't what they wanted at all. The danger is even greater when we add religion to the mix, to say nothing of politics.

In that sense, failure can be more in keeping with what we as humans are to become than success. Of course, "failure" must be understood in purely worldly or materialistic terms. As Robert Hugh Benson was to explain in

---

[10] Corinthians, 9:19-23.

some of his novels, that which the world declares to be the most abject failure can, instead, be a glorious triumph: "Then his head sank once more and the Failure was complete."[11]

Take, for example, the only novel written by Nicholas Patrick Cardinal Wiseman, *Fabiola, or, The Church of the Catacombs*. It's a bit harsh, not to say untrue to claim that Wiseman's novel was a "failure." By normal standards, it was a considerable success, certainly outlasting the productions — one in particular — it was written to counter. Unlike the writer who writes in order to become a celebrity — as the writer's joke has it, someone more concerned with being a famous author than with getting anything written — Wiseman did not follow up his early success with more novels. No, he had accomplished what he had set out to do, and then set aside his pen. His novel gives sufficient evidence that he could have developed into a very successful and popular writer — but that was not his goal.

Rather, Wiseman was concerned with defending that which he believed to be true, the teachings of the Catholic Church, against unfair and unjust attacks. As one of the more effective media by means of which this attack was delivered was the popular novel, Wiseman selected the novel as the proper form for the most effective response. A faithful follower of any religion would certainly agree, both with Wiseman's assessment of the situation, and his decision to use popular media to present his case.

Wiseman's Prominence

Wiseman had made a name for himself long before he decided to write a novel. Before the age of thirty he had become one of the most prominent scholars in the Catholic Church, attaining a number of prestigious posts in the world of Catholic academia. Anticipating Pope Leo XIII's emphasis on the philosophy of Aquinas, Wiseman was a champion of faith and reason, countering the wild emotionalism that suffused Christianity, both Catholic and Protestant, during this period. In his lectures "On the

---

[11] Robert Hugh Benson, *None Other Gods*. London: Hutchinson & Co., 1911, 360.

Connection Between Science and Revealed Religion," Wiseman argued on the side of the Thomist position that apparent differences between the findings of science and the teachings of revelation are necessarily susceptible to reconciliation without either faith or reason having to "surrender" anything.

Wiseman took the opportunity during a visit to England in 1835-1836 to present the Catholic position in a number of venues, impressing many members of the Oxford Movement with his learning and grasp of the issues. Notable among the people whom he influenced was John Henry Newman, at this time one of the leading lights of the Movement, although Newman's conversion to Catholicism was still a decade in the future.

Among his activities, Wiseman delivered a great many lectures that highlighted the similarities of Catholicism with the Church of England, but without "softening" any of the differences. To one critic who complained that certain Catholic practices and ceremonies bore a strong resemblance to pagan practices, Wiseman boldly agreed — and then pointed out that many Christian *doctrines*, not just practices, accepted by both Catholics and Protestants, were also prefigured in paganism. In the mid-twentieth century, C. S. Lewis also made a practice of pointing this out, notably the belief in a dying god who comes back to life in the Spring of each year, and who becomes in some mysterious fashion the food of believers.

Wiseman founded the *Dublin Review* in 1836. He had a twofold purpose in mind. The first was to invigorate the English Catholics by bringing them into the mainstream of Catholic thought and the latest theological and liturgical developments. Operating within a legal and social climate that made them second-class citizens, the practice of English Catholicism had tended to be something one did on the sly or with an extremely embarrassed air, with anything explicitly Catholic deemphasized as much as possible. Catholic "chapels" rarely had steeples, for instance, while the role of the papacy was not well understood by many English Catholics.

The second purpose of the *Dublin Review* was to make certain that the Catholic Church kept up with developments in the Oxford Movement, in which Wiseman had expressed great interest. As a profound historical scholar and sound theologian, Wiseman probably had a very good idea where the Movement would inevitably lead people — as, in point of fact, it did — even if they didn't realize it themselves. He may have wanted to prepare the Catholic Church in England to be ready to receive a flood of converts once people argued themselves into becoming Catholic. Despite Wiseman's expressed hope of a rapid return of England to Catholicism, however, the flood never materialized. This was despite the fact that the progress of Catholicism in general, the Oxford Movement, and Newman's 1852 "Second Spring" sermon would have persuaded people much less optimistic than Wiseman.

In 1840 the pope consecrated Wiseman a bishop and made him "Coadjutor" to Bishop Thomas Walsh, the "Vicar-Apostolic" of the central district. Wiseman was also appointed president of Oscott College near Birmingham. It was due to his efforts that Oscott became a center of learning for English Catholicism. It was also during this period that matters came to a head in the Oxford Movement, and a number of clergy converted to Catholicism, most notably John Henry Newman. While this was considered a great advance for the "Catholic Cause" in England, it also put a heavy financial burden on Wiseman. Most of the converts had lost their incomes, and he assumed personal responsibility for their maintenance.

In 1846 Bishop Walsh was appointed Vicar-Apostolic of London, bringing Wiseman along with him as his Coadjutor. When Walsh died early in 1849, Wiseman was promoted to Vicar-Apostolic. Wiseman was thus the obvious candidate to be installed as the first Cardinal Archbishop of Westminster when Pope Pius IX reestablished the hierarchy in England on September 29, 1850.

Why a Novel?

This, then, was the background against which Wiseman wrote his novel. The immediate circumstances, however, are somewhat less complex. Frankly, a significant number of English people did not view the progress of "popery" with equanimity. The mere fact of the Catholic Relief Act of 1829 was bad enough. The Oxford Movement and the consequent conversions of a number of England's leading intellectual lights added insult to injury. What really tipped the scales, however, was the official reestablishment of the Catholic hierarchy in England. This was considered an outrage.

That being the case, it was inevitable that anything Wiseman said would be misinterpreted, taken the wrong way, or twisted completely out of context — and so it was. When traveling to Westminster to take up his new duties, people threw manure at his carriage. It is a tribute to Wiseman's diplomatic skills that he was able to smooth things over as much as he did. In this he was helped not a little by Pius IX's liberalism and reforming zeal.[12]

Wiseman's efforts did not, however, call a halt to the bigotry and prejudice, although he could probably rightfully claim that by 1852, due to his work, many English people were more than willing to "live and let live" as far as the Catholic Church was concerned, especially after the self-sacrifice of the Catholic nursing sisters in Crimea became known a few years later. The doctrinaire anti-Catholics, however, were still smarting from the "defeat" they had suffered at the hands of the Oxford Movement, especially after so many of its leaders, the core of the religious intelligentsia in England, became Catholic.

Consequently, in 1853 the reactionary elements in the Church of England began to go on the offensive — and "offensive" is the term that best describes their efforts, as far as a number of English Protestants were concerned. Many elements in the Church of England itself as well as the general public were, if not persuaded of the rightness of the Catholic position, at least convinced that the old style bigotry and the traditional shrill rallying cry of "No Popery!" were in bad taste as well as contrary to the English concept of fair play. In 1853, however, Charles Kings-

---

[12] The story of "Pio Nono," a play on words of his name in Italian, is a complete fabrication. Pius IX was the liberal darling of Europe's reformers until he refused to use Papal troops to support the liberal revolutions. As a result, the liberals excoriated him and invented stories to his discredit, such as the myth that he shook his head and muttered, "No, no," to every proposal to liberalize.

ley, an Anglican clergyman with decidedly radical views (among other things, he was a convinced socialist) published his novel, *Hypatia*, a vicious and thinly disguised attack on the Catholic Church.

The novel was personally offensive to Wiseman and even the members of the Oxford Movement on at least two grounds, aside from the vitriol with which Catholics and anyone "tainted" with "popery" were attacked. One, the history was very bad. Kingsley's research consisted primarily of extemporizing what he thought *should* have happened, and picking and choosing support for his position, rather than verification of facts and development of a theory or argument supported by empirical evidence.

Two, and more importantly, Kingsley's theology and reasoning were at least as bad as his history. Having accepted the Manichaean orientation, he typically characterized all Catholics, especially the clergy, as knowingly and willfully participating in evil in order to destroy England and Christianity ("God is an Englishman, probably educated at Eton"). Catholics, as far as Kingsley was concerned, were inveterate liars and hypocrites, the spawn of Satan, determined to bring everyone in the world down to eternal damnation by whatever means necessary, the more depraved, the better. This was proved (at least to Kingsley's satisfaction) by the fact that Catholics and many members of the Church of England disagreed with his radical ideas. They were therefore, at one and the same time, both knaves and fools. These others were deliberately choosing evil when the truth was patently obvious to Kingsley who, evidently without realizing it, was thereby putting himself in the place of God.

As a novel was the chief means by which the Catholic Church was attacked, Wiseman reasoned that a novel was the appropriate vehicle in which to present the truth. Since the attack was based on distortions of history and theology, corrections had to be incorporated into the plot. Since, without false modesty, Wiseman could reasonably be said to be the leading authority in England on Catholic history and theology, he was the obvious person to make the effort.

Fortunately Wiseman was a competent writer, and the novel he produced, *Fabiola*, is well crafted and readable. If not great literature, it did the job it set out to do: present the Catholic side of the issues in fictional (or semi-fictional) form, refuting the hysteria of Kingsley with calm recital of the truth. As such, *Fabiola* is an important link in the chain of events that led to the acceptance (as far as it goes) of Catholicism in England and, from there, in the United States. It enjoyed a very wide readership, and was translated into ten languages.

After *Fabiola*

The publication of *Fabiola*, of course, was a minor incident in Wiseman's career, and must be regarded as such. It would hardly be worth mentioning if our object in this book was not to gain an appreciation of the role that literature has played in presenting principles of the natural moral law as the basis of a just society. After the book's publication, Wiseman went on to much bigger and better things.

By assisting the Liberal Party at critical moments, he was able to solidify Catholic support and, in exchange, gain more concessions for Catholics, particularly in the matter of education, social welfare, and the position of Catholic chaplains in the military. He was able to report in 1863 that there were three times as many Catholic clergy in England as there had been in 1830, that houses for women religious had increased by a factor of ten, and that houses for men religious had gone from none to fifty-five in number.

Ironically, in his later years he received more opposition from English Catholics than from Protestants for his support of the papacy and advocacy of liberal views. The last two years of his life were marred by illness and the move to a less liberal position for the sake of expediency.

Nevertheless, Wiseman was held in increasing regard, even admiration by both Catholics and Protestants. After he died on February 16, 1865, there were signal popular marks of respect paid during the funeral procession.

John Henry Newman (1801-1890)

The recent beatification of John Henry Cardinal Newman by His Holiness Pope Benedict XVI — two weeks ago as of this writing — leaves very little left to say about the man. What remains can better be learned by reading Newman's own spiritual autobiography, the stunning *Apologia Pro Vita Sua*. Newman composed the work over a period of weeks to meet a vicious attack by none other than our old acquaintance, Charles Kingsley. As described by Philip Hughes in the introduction to a popular edition of the *Apologia*,

> The actual writing of the *Apologia* was a real feat of scholarly industry — 562 pages in ten weeks, a ten weeks that saw the book planned and revised, and revised again, and published. It was the method of publication — i.e., by weekly parts — that forced the pace, and Newman worked daily "from morning to night, hardly having time for my meals." One day he was at it for sixteen hours at a stretch, and, when writing Part III, his diary notes, "At my *Apologia* for 22 hours running."[13]

Such a feat was probably made possible by the fact that Newman wrote, as Father John Hardon put it, "in a white heat," with the result that it revealed "the inner soul of Newman as nothing else he spoke or wrote. In eloquent prose, he tells the story of his religious change from early childhood to where years of study and prayer finally led him to 'the one fold of Christ,' the Catholic Church."[14]

What Newman did in his *Apologia* was present the justification for his conversion to Catholicism to ordinary English people, using reason and logic to counter Kingsley's hysteria. Kingsley had expected people to accept his calumnies against the Catholic Church and his animad-

---

[13] Philip Hughes, "Introduction," *Apologia Pro Vita Sua*. New York: Doubleday Image Books, 1956, 25.
[14] John A. Hardon, S.J., *The Catholic Lifetime Reading Plan*. New York: Doubleday, 1980, 124.

versions on Newman's character without question, presuming his own bigotry and *avant garde* approach to religion to be an accurate barometer of public feeling.

Kingsley could not have been further off the mark. Newman defended himself against Kingsley's unfounded accusation that Newman was a liar to such good effect that Kingsley was completely discredited. Disgusted at Kingsley's tactics and outraged at his obvious unfairness in attacking a man who had been retired and out of the public eye for years, the ordinary people of England rallied to Newman's defense. Catholicism in England gained a degree of prestige that it had not enjoyed for centuries. When Newman died in 1890, he was widely mourned.

The Perverse Enmity of Kingsley

What, however, caused Kingsley to indulge his obsessive, even psychotic hatred of the Catholic Church in such a fashion when, had he been more astute, he would have seen that his actions could not help but be self-defeating?

The standard account of events is fairly straightforward, although, frankly, still leaves much of the "why" unanswered. On December 30, 1863, Newman received a copy of the January 1864 issue of *Macmillan's Magazine* from an unnamed correspondent. The magazine contained a review of James Anthony Froude's anti-Catholic *History of England*, volumes seven and eight, a polemical work that would probably be little remembered today if the review, signed only with the initials, "C. K." hadn't occasioned the scandal that followed. On pages 216 through 217 the anonymous reviewer made several statements regarding the Catholic Church, most of them intemperate, and one to which Newman took particular exception:

> Truth, for its own sake, had never been a virtue with the Roman clergy. Father Newman informs us that it need not, and on the whole ought not to be; that cunning is the weapon which Heaven has given to the saints wherewith to withstand the brute male force of the wicked world which marries and is given in marriage. Whether his notion be doctrinally correct or not, it is at least historically so.

To put it more briefly and in a more modern idiom, "C. K." asserted, one, that Newman claimed that truth is not a virtue, and, two, that the Catholic clergy are, despite what their religion might teach, pathological liars.

Newman wrote a letter to the editors, pointing out that "C. K.," concerning whose real identity he was completely in the dark, did not reference any specific words spoken or written by Newman by means of which Newman had conveyed such a notion. Far from demanding reparation or even apology, however, Newman contented himself with going on record as protesting the statement as slanderous (actually libelous, as it appeared in print), and left it at that, appearing to consider the matter closed. As Newman explained,

> I should not dream of expostulating with the writer of such a passage, nor with the editor who could insert it without appending evidence in proof of its allegations. Nor do I want any reparation from either of them. I neither complain of them for their act, nor should I thank them if they reversed it. Nor do I even write to you with any desire of troubling you to send me an answer. I do but wish to draw the attention of yourselves, as gentlemen, to a grave and gratuitous slander, with which I feel confident you will be sorry to find associated a name so eminent as yours.

Less than a week later (possibly after being raked over the coals by the editors of *Macmillan's* for having embarrassed them in so public a fashion), Newman received a letter from the Reverend Charles Kingsley. Far from either apologizing or providing Newman with proofs of his assertions, Kingsley simply reasserted that what he said was true. Kingsley made a vague reference to a sermon that Newman had preached while still an Anglican, and insulted Newman again by intimating that Newman's denial of Kingsley's claim that all Catholic priests are liars was itself a lie.

Newman's extraordinarily calm and reasoned response to Kingsley's provocative letter was to point out, again, that Kingsley had failed to cite any specific words or phrases that could possibly be construed to mean what Kingsley asserted they meant. Newman also expressed his amazement to find out that the author of the review was Kingsley. It seems apparent from the lack of any references to the two men ever having met, corresponded, or interacted in any way, that Newman was completely baffled as to why Kingsley should not only single him out, but continue to insist on maintaining the truth of a demonstrably false assertion.

Kingsley's Psychology

In any event, Newman's soft answer failed to turn away Kingsley's wrath. Accounts of Kingsley's character by his friends and sympathetic historians all go on at great length that he was always the kindest of men, that to give pain to others was unthinkable to him.

The problem with these character witnesses, however, is that the uniformly high level of praise, even the repetition of certain phrases, suggests that Kingsley's friends and acquaintances might, like ladies in Shakespeare plays, be protesting too much. Seemingly inevitably, Kingsley's alleged kindness is never mentioned without it being followed by a rather gargantuan implied "but," describing his quick temper, sloppy research, hasty generalizations, and the disjointed nature of his thinking.

A less suspicious writer than I would be tempted to put down the high praise meted out to Kingsley by those who knew him as partaking of a fear that, should his friends and acquaintances fail to praise him adequately, they would be the next targets of his wrath. He had, after all, developed the habit of attacking anyone who disagreed with him on almost any subject, and appeared to attach great importance to the public's adulation and praise of him.

Before going after Newman, Kingsley had written a book slamming the American existentialists Ralph Waldo Emerson and Henry David Thoreau, even though their thought could easily be reconciled with Kingsley's innovative theology of what became known as "Muscular Christianity," such as it was. The thought intrudes that the "muscles" of Kingsley's Christianity were used more often to bully others than to defend truth. Why Kingsley failed to attack Orestes Brownson isn't quite clear, unless perhaps he decided that Brownson's conversion to Catholicism at about the same time as that of Newman had been enough of a punishment of the apostate third of the American existentialist trio.

In any event, having revealed himself, and in receipt from Newman of a demand for proof of his assertions, Kingsley seems to have gone berserk. A battle ensued, with Kingsley continually escalating the conflict and increasing the stakes, as it were, painting himself into a corner from which he refused to extricate himself, which he could easily have done with a simple apology and a retraction.

After the exchange of a few more letters in which he took an increasingly insulting tone, Kingsley published a reiteration of his allegations against Newman in *Macmillan's Magazine*, having the gall to call it an apology. Newman responded by pointing out that simply making the same accusations all over again in different words was hardly an apology. Newman then infuriated Kingsley by explaining Kingsley's lapses in logic as well as basic truthfulness, and reiterated the fact that Kingsley was not proving his case, simply making additional unproved allegations.

More letters ensued, Kingsley making his increasingly hysterical claims, and Newman responding by explaining, once again, that making additional accusations does not prove previous accusations. Newman also attempted to disengage from the bizarre controversy, repeating that, having presented his denial and demanded proof that was not forthcoming, he considered the matter closed. To ensure that his denial became as public as the accusation, Newman published the correspondence — with Kingsley's explicit permission — as a short pamphlet.

Kingsley went almost insane with fury. Clearly he had not expected Newman to take his permission to make the correspondence public at face value, evidently considering it as something of a schoolboy dare. He immediately wrote and published his own pamphlet, *What, Then, Does Dr. Newman Mean?*, repeating every accusation he had made previously, and adding a host of others, most of them as ill-considered as they were ludicrous. As Hughes described the reaction of one editor friendly to Kingsley, Richard Holt Hutton of the *Spectator*,

> The title of one of Kingsley's own books, *Loose Thoughts for Loose Thinkers*,[15] Hutton said, described only too well the author's own habitual way of going on; and he wrote of "the ordinary steeplechase fashion in which he [Kingsley] chooses not so much to think as to splash up thought — dregs and all . . . in one's face." Of Kingsley's pamphlet, Hutton spoke most severely: it "aggravates the original injustice a hundredfold"; and he castigated Kingsley for allowing himself "a perfect licence of insinuation."[16]

Perhaps most revealing, Hughes related that,

> Kingsley, preparing the pamphlet *What, Then, Does Dr. Newman Mean?*, wrote to a friend "I trust to make him and his admirers sorry that they did not leave me alone. I have a score of more than twenty years to pay, and this is an installment of it.[17]

Unfortunately for anyone attempting to discern the reason for Kingsley's exaggerated animus against Newman, the statement doesn't appear to make too much sense. First, there is the self-pitying tone. "Leave me alone"? The entire situation was, from start to finish, entirely Kingsley's own creation. Kingsley had only himself to blame for any discredit or pain he suffered after attempting to inflict the same on Newman.

Second, there is the reference to Newman's "admirers." Newman had enjoyed a somewhat limited renown as the principal writer of the Oxford Movement, and certainly a degree of notoriety after the publication of "Tract 90" that attempted to demonstrate a congruity of doctrine between the Council of Trent and the "Thirty-Nine Articles" that define the official position of the Church of England.

But "admirers"? By all accounts, Newman, while personally affable and enjoying the company of other indi-

---

[15] The book Kingsley wrote attacking the American existentialists.
[16] Hughes, *op. cit.*, 26.
[17] *Ibid.*, 24.

viduals as much as they enjoyed his, had never been popular with the public at large, and many of his friends had done a "fast fade" when he converted to Catholicism. The few friends left to him after his conversion he cherished highly, so much so that latter day revisionists have attempted to manufacture a scandal out of it. In consequence, Kingsley's reference to "admirers" comes across as another expression of his manipulative self-pity.

Third and finally, there is the claim that Kingsley had "a score of more than twenty years to pay." Kingsley was forty-four in 1863, making him either in or just out of his teens "more than twenty years" previously, the approximate date of Newman's conversion. By all accounts, the two men had never met or interacted in any way prior to Kingsley's anonymous cheap shot at Newman in the January 1864 issue of *Macmillan's Magazine*.

The Real Reason?

There does not, therefore, appear to be any satisfactory way to explain Kingsley's hatred of Newman, or even the gratuitous insult that started the whole thing. A general malice against Catholics and particular converts to Catholicism seems too weak an explanation in light of the incredible hatred expressed by Kingsley toward a man he appears never to have met or interacted with previously.

Only one thing suggests itself, and I have absolutely no evidence to substantiate the possibility. Having entered that caveat, however, I believe that the possibility may have some merit. I repeat, of course, that this is mere supposition. I believe it to be plausible, but have no way of proving it.·

It surprises many people to learn that Newman was a novelist — and, despite the fact that his output consisted of exactly two works of fiction, an outstanding one. Newman's novels, *Loss and Gain*, published in 1848, and *Callista: A Sketch of the Third Century*, written soon after

---

· As this book was going to press, I came across an article drawing the same conclusions, but more deeply researched, suggesting strongly that jealousy over Newman's *Callista* was, in fact, the source of Kingsley's animus. *Vide* Susan Dorman, "*Hypatia* and *Callista*: The Initial Skirmish between Kingsley and Newman," *Nineteenth-Century Fiction* Vol. 34, No. 2 (September 1979): 173-193.

Loss and Gain but not published until 1855, strongly suggest that, had his vocation been that of popular novelist, he would have rivaled the authors of the early nineteenth century for which England is so justly renowned.

It may, however, come as less of a surprise to learn that Charles Kingsley was also a novelist and, despite his lack of sound research and the polemical tone that suffused his works, rather popular. His novel-length fable, *The Water Babies*, still enjoys the status of a minor classic despite a deplorable incidence of racial prejudice against the Irish and a rather shallow moral philosophy, while *Westward Ho!*, a bombastic anti-Catholic/anti-Spanish historical fantasy set in Elizabethan times, is occasionally found on lists of books that people should read, but for which they never seem to find the time. The novel's chief claim to fame is that a town in Devon is named after it, being the only place-name in England incorporating an exclamation point.

We have already seen how Kingsley's historical novel *Hypatia*, an explicit attack on Catholics, called forth a response from Cardinal Wiseman: *Fabiola, or, The Church of the Catacombs*. Wiseman's novel, however, while competently written and generally considered superior to Kingsley's production, was clearly the work of an amateur. I have not been able to find that Kingsley even reacted to the publication of Wiseman's novel, possibly considering the work of an obvious amateur no threat to his fame as a writer of inspirational and uplifting fiction.

It may be, however, that Newman's *Callista* had a different effect on Kingsley. (Again, I stress that this is pure supposition.) Newman's second novel was already written when *Hypatia* appeared, but Kingsley's screed may have inspired Newman to take *Callista* off the shelf, give it a final polish, and send it to the printer — a decision for which generations of readers should give Newman (perhaps even Kingsley) more thanks than appears to have been the case.

Comparing Newman's and Kingsley's novels, it is immediately and painfully obvious that *Callista* is the work of a true professional, written with a specific and explicitly stated purpose in mind. In contrast, Kingsley's effort is not only ramshackle, but written with an extremely interested and definitely ulterior motive. *Hypatia* virtually drips with malice.

It is thus possible — and I raise it as no more than a possibility — that Newman's publication of a clearly superior novel in response to Kingsley's inferior production hurt Kingsley's pride on several levels. First and foremost, there would have been jealousy that another writer was able to enter the lists of authors of "early Christian romance" and outdo Kingsley so spectacularly. Newman met Kingsley on Kingsley's chosen ground and beat him on it.

Second, to someone of Kingsley's hasty temper and ill-considered judgment, it probably looked as if Newman had written *Callista* specifically to make Kingsley's novel look shoddy — which it did. Having come to a conclusion about something, Kingsley was not the sort to test his hypothesis and find out whether Newman had, in fact, written *Callista* to "attack" Kingsley. That is impossible, as *Callista* was written before *Hypatia* was published. All Kingsley had to do was ask in order to ascertain the truth. That, however, was not his way, and it may not even have occurred to him to do so. Accepting the Manichaean orientation, however unconsciously, Kingsley's belief in something and its usefulness for his purposes, not any objective facts or empirical evidence, was what made something true for him.

Third, and finally, such an "insult" as Newman's publication of a novel in Kingsley's chosen field would have caused a great deal of self-pitying reflection on wrongs, real or imagined (mostly the latter), that Newman had inadvertently inflicted on Kingsley since Newman's conversion. Citing a "score of more than twenty years" suggests that Kingsley may have been obsessed with Newman. This might have been caused by too much brooding over the imagined slight. It would have been made worse by the invention of crimes to justify putting so much time and effort into hating a man whom he had never met.

Kingsley's Victory

If it was, in fact, the case that the publication of *Callista* was the source of Kingsley's bizarre obsession with Newman, Kingsley, in a sense, lost the religious battle but won the literary war. For all their faults (and they are many), Kingsley's novels are, relatively speaking, today better known than the better-written fiction by Newman.

Had Kingsley not attacked Newman, Newman would very likely have faded into obscurity. His work, while vitally important in the development of the Church of England and the reestablishment of the Catholic hierarchy in England, is not something to which people today attach any importance — when they think about it at all. Few people other than historians of the Church of England, a rather elite group, would even have heard of the Oxford Movement were it not for the connection with Newman.

Thus, the irony is that Kingsley's injustice to Newman brought Newman into the public eye and kept him there. Newman's response to Kingsley is considered one of the finest "spiritual autobiographies" ever written, rivaling in some respects the *Confessions* of St. Augustine. Further, although Newman was in his sixties when he wrote the *Apologia* and considered himself retired from public life, Kingsley's attack launched a whole new phase in Newman's career. In worldly terms, Newman was, to all intents and purposes, a failure before Kingsley decided to score off him. As a direct result of Kingsley's attack, Newman became the most noteworthy convert of the nineteenth century in the English-speaking world. Newman's handling of the situation gave immense prestige to the Catholic Church.

Kingsley did, however, succeed in his efforts against *Callista* — if that was indeed his aim. Newman's *Apologia* so far overshadowed his other works, especially his fiction, that many people are not even aware that Newman wrote novels, or are, at best, only vaguely aware of them. This is unfortunate.

Newman's two novels, *Loss and Gain* and *Callista*, are literary gems. They give more than a suggestion that he could have been one of the leading novelists of his day, even given the competition from Dickens, Lever, Thackery, Scott, Trollope, and a host of others. Newman's talents, however, turned in other directions, as his recent beatification by Pope Benedict XVI makes clear.

Robert Hugh Benson (1871-1914)

Robert Hugh Benson, who wrote half a century after Wiseman and Newman published their novels, is the only one of the three who made popular fiction a centerpiece of his ministry. In common with the others, however, Benson appeared to regard fiction, however insightful or well crafted, as secondary to his mission in life. Wiseman sought to show that faith and reason, especially in their aspects of religion and science, are not in opposition. Newman worked tirelessly to present the full truths of the Catholic faith to both Catholics and Protestants, principally by adhering to the motto he chose as Cardinal: "Heart Speaks to Heart."

Seeking a Calling

For his part, Benson seemed suffused with a sense that he was constantly seeking and yet not finding the particulars of his true calling, his "vocation." This meant exploring the multitude of ways in which people work to try and discern God's Will for themselves, a search unique to every person, yet based on universals about the human condition. What binds Benson to the other two authors whose works I am examining in this book is the feat of successfully presenting a specific body of truths within a society that, in large measure, either rejected those truths as hostile to their being and way of life, or to the whole concept of what it means for something to be true.

Benson was by far the most *popular* writer of the three. Wiseman might be more learned, Newman a better writer and more profound scholar, but Benson spoke more to the task to which every human being is set: becoming more fully human not only by conforming one's self to God's Nature, but also by fulfilling God's particular plan for each individual. This is why the English satirist Evelyn Waugh remarked in his essay on Benson that appeared as an introduction to the 1956 Regnery edition of *The History of Richard Raynal, Solitary*, that Benson's work was chiefly concerned with the question of vocation.

The fact that Benson felt himself constantly in search of his own vocation did not mean that he could not help others in their searches. Perhaps he felt that others might profit from his struggles. It might even be construed an advantage to have a man who evidently felt something at loose ends to use his possibly more highly developed sense of vocation to discern that of others — except when those others were clearly making no effort to help out in the matter, and, in fact, obviously believed that the task of seeking a vocation didn't even have any meaning. This latter group Benson saw exemplified by the upper classes of English society, the milieu with which he was, by nature and by nurture, most familiar.

A constant theme running through much of Benson's fiction, especially the later, "contemporary" or "mainstream" novels, was the loss of the sense of purpose on the part of the English upper classes. It seemed to Benson that, on the whole, the purpose of the upper classes was to have no purpose. He may have struggled with finding his particular vocation (he was never in doubt about his vocation in general), but he appeared to have little sympathy for people who not only didn't bother to search for their vocations, they didn't seem to feel that there was any need to do such a thing.

The nineteenth century may have been the twilight of an upper class in England that retained even a vestige of *noblesse oblige*. This faded quickly by the end of the century, however, and within fifty years would infect the United States as well. When Benson wrote, the rich in America were still flexing their muscles, so to speak, wondering where this new class that technology had enriched far beyond what could be attained by human labor fit into the scheme of things.

The Last, Best Hope of Mankind

From a number of hints (and pointedly demonstrated by the Heckers in *Initiation*) Benson appears to have considered Americans the hope of humanity in some fashion — a view in which Pope Leo XIII seems to have concurred. We have only to read *Rerum Novarum*[18] with its emphasis on

---

[10] Leo XIII, *Rerum Novarum* ("On Labor and Capital"), 1891.

widespread ownership in the means of production, a condition that still marked American society, to see the importance that the pope placed on a property-based economic order.

If any doubt remains, reading *Testem Benevolentia Nostrae*, "Concerning New Opinions, Virtue, Nature, and Grace with Regard to Americanism," issued in 1899, should put those doubts to rest. The "Apostolic Constitution" praises American political and social institutions highly, but warns of the application of such otherwise admirable principles to the discernment of religious truths and the natural moral law. These are not something subject to a democratic vote or to change at the will of the majority or the strongest will — a clear warning against the dangers of Manichaeism.

With respect to Benson's analysis, it appears that he saw the chief spiritual difference between England and the United States in how the upper classes viewed themselves and their respective purposes in life. Possibly to over-generalize, the American upper classes tended to have purpose, while the English seemed to exist merely to take up space.

In the late nineteenth and early twentieth centuries, for example, the term "old money" in America did not mean vast wealth. Instead, it identified a class that, while it might pursue "genteel" trades, still felt compelled to *do* something. A man or (especially) a woman of the upper class was expected to engage in some useful occupation, all the better if it was something that offered no compensation other than the sense of a job well done and filled a social need. The "socialite" of the mid-twentieth century was a pale imitation of her purpose-driven nineteenth century sister, while the celebutants of the twenty-first century seemingly exist only to drift from one meaningless activity to the next.

Men of that class might enter politics but, on the whole, politics was something that "the best people" avoided as dirty. Theodore Roosevelt was an anomaly — yet even there, true to the "code" of his class, he entered politics to carry out the socially useful task of trying to reform what had become a very rotten system.

To someone of Benson's mindset, with his constant worry about whether or not he was doing God's Will, the contrast of the American upper classes of his day (at least as he perceived them) and the English upper classes as he personally experienced them could not have been more striking. The typical member of the "Upper Ten Thousand" (as the ruling and social elite was termed) seemed to have as its sole object the condition of being absolutely idle, and of serving no useful purpose whatsoever. Benson saw the ancient tradition of *noblesse oblige*, which was long believed to justify the presumably exalted position the upper classes enjoyed, as replaced with arrogance and pride, with the belief instilled at a very early age that the rest of humanity was made to serve their every whim.

The Effect of the Reformation

Benson appeared to be convinced that the change had begun when England abandoned Catholicism during the Reformation, cut itself off from the Catholic culture of Europe, and crafted an idiosyncratic religion that brought out the worst in the English people. Of course, the social, political and, above all, economic forces that laid the groundwork for the Reformation in England and elsewhere had been laid long before the Reformation. The Reformation could reasonably be said only to have accelerated a process that was already underway, aimed at the economic disenfranchisement of ordinary people.

Not being concerned with economics, nor very much with politics, Benson concentrated on the explicitly religious and social issues involved in the Reformation and the social and religious results of what he regarded as tantamount to a religious earthquake or tsunami. This did not detract any from his main theme of vocation, although it sometimes resulted in a few misstatements concerning the correct application of the precepts of the natural law within the field of political economy . . . to which the typical reader of Benson's novels would be more than justified in shrugging his or her shoulders and saying, "So what?"

In any event, whatever the goodwill or justification of the Reformers, Benson took as one of his themes the sea-change that had taken place when the basis of the social order shifted from the Catholic understanding, to the Protestant understanding. Ironically, there is evidence that Benson himself accepted some of the precepts of the new order, particularly with respect to the transmission of political sovereignty, but not enough to affect his basic premise.

The most significant change was, as I hinted previously, a shift in basing the natural moral law on Will rather than Intellect. In England as well as in other places, the Reformation was based on the theory that the State, not the Church was supreme in matters of faith and morals, that is, in matters relating to the meaning of revelation and the interpretation and basis of the natural moral law. Consequently, what was regarded as "true" became subject to political expedience instead of what could be accepted on the basis of faith or discerned by reason. If the State required that God, His Will, or even His Nature — truth itself — be redefined in order to meet some need or want of the ruling elite, then it must be so.

This was, essentially, the basis of the totalitarian philosophy detailed by Thomas Hobbes in *Leviathan* and other works, and which was eventually taken as the essential political philosophy of the modern Nation-State, as well as the economic and financial system. The State is supreme in all things, whether by divine right or the will of "the people," or some other authority, real or imagined — it doesn't matter, as long as the State can justify its absolutism in some fashion.

Democracy's Last Gasp

In the latter half of the nineteenth century, at a time when the last vestiges of *noblesse oblige* were rapidly disappearing from England, the totalitarian Nation-State philosophy of Hobbes was updated and presented by Walter Bagehot in *The English Constitution* (1867). This was followed in 1873 by *Lombard Street*, in which Bagehot applied the political philosophy expounded in *The English Constitution* to the financial markets of the City of London.

Briefly, Bagehot's premise in *The English Constitution* was that the real power in England was vested in the House of Commons, which was controlled by the Upper

Ten Thousand through manipulation of the "rotten borough" system. Under the rotten or "pocket" borough system, large population centers sometimes had less than a dozen eligible voters, who could easily be controlled at very little expense. Everything else, from the queen, the Prince of Wales, the House of Lords, and even *Magna Charta* was "dignified," rather than "expedient," *i.e.*, so much window dressing to keep the stupid masses more or less contented and in their place.

Bagehot applied these principles to the money and credit system in *Lombard Street*, still considered by many authorities to be the first, if not the last word in sound principle for the financial markets. All money, instead of being created by accepting a bill drawn on the present value of existing and future marketable goods and services ("discounting and rediscounting") as the medium of exchange, is instead created by the State by fiat.

Instead of the amount of money in the economy being determined by the present value of existing and future marketable goods and services in which the issuer of the money has a private property stake, private property is effectively abolished. This is done by having the State back the money supply with the present value of future tax revenues — in which it does not have a private property stake. In more understandable terms, the State redefines money from "anything that can be accepted in settlement of a debt," to "whatever the State says it is." By asserting and maintaining control over money and credit, the State establishes absolute power.

As a number of rather astute individuals have pointed out over the centuries, power tends to corrupt. Absolute power corrupts absolutely. As far as Benson was concerned, the corruption that began with the Reformation in England had reached its inevitable conclusion by the end of the nineteenth century. The upper classes of England had a doom hanging over their heads, although Benson was never able to explain in any definite way the exact nature of the catastrophe he saw coming.

I could, of course, go on at great length as to why, although I believe Benson's intuition was correct, his reasoning was a little off. That, however, is not the point. The fact is that Benson understood, in however distorted a fashion, that something was seriously wrong with the world. He correctly identified the underlying cause (abandonment of the sound moral philosophy taught by the Catholic Church and other reason-based systems[19]) and the fact that something had to be done if the world was to avert disaster — discern and live up to one's vocation to the best of one's ability. The rest is detail, with which we may or may not agree. Such is Benson's skill as a novelist, however, that we don't have to agree with the details. Wisely, Benson presented his ideas in fictional form, and we can suspend any disbelief we might have while we are entertained, and certainly run the risk of learning something about the world, other people, and, most of all, ourselves.

Benson Was Born . . .

In C. S. Lewis's apocalyptic novel, *That Hideous Strength*, one of the characters, a college professor, excuses himself from something-or-other by saying he has to go home and begin the dreary and wearying task of correcting and grading a pile of undergraduate essays on Jonathan Swift, all beginning, "Swift was born . . ."

With that barb in mind, I've tried to avoid relating too obviously the fact that Benson was somehow catapulted into this world in 1871, coincidentally (in light of the renown of his own "future war" novel, *Lord of the World*) the same year in which Sir George Chesney published the novella that began the "future war" subgenre, *The Battle of Dorking*. "Dorking" is a town in England, so no comments or asides are necessary or welcome.

---

[19] Significantly, in his apocalyptic future war masterpiece, *Lord of the World*, Benson has the western "Christian" nations abandoning every vestige of the natural moral law along with Christianity, while the sole remaining catechumen (someone receiving instruction to enter the Catholic Church) at the end of the book is an obviously sincere Muslim. This suggests that Benson viewed orthodox Muslims who accept the Aristotelian/Thomist understanding of the natural moral law as closer to the truth than apostate or heretical Christians who reject it.

Robert Hugh Benson was a son of the Anglican Archbishop of Canterbury. He converted to Catholicism and was ordained a priest in 1903. He was a member of the famous Benson literary clan, whose members included such luminaries as horror writer Arthur Benson and E. F. Benson of "Lucia" fame, both brothers of Robert.

Benson, however, managed to surpass all his siblings in quality of output, if not quantity in the shortest period of time. His writing career lasted just short of eleven years before his untimely death in 1914 at the start of World War I. Benson wrote twenty novels and short story collections, four plays, a volume of poetry, and countless articles and books on theology and apologetics for ordinary people.

Some of his short stories are considered horror classics, although the extremely rare collection *A Mirror of Shalott* is thought to be apocryphal by some authorities. It was, however, in the field of satire that Benson excelled. Evelyn Waugh greatly admired him, and credited Benson with an enormous influence on him. Waugh used some of Benson's devices in his own, much blacker, satires. *Lord of the World*, for instance, may have inspired Waugh's surreal masterpiece, *Love Among the Ruins*.

Arthur Christopher Benson, an accomplished author in his own right, and who seems to have been closest to Benson of all his family, succinctly described his youngest brother in his book, *Hugh: Memoirs of a Brother* (1916), by commenting, "I think of him as always larger than his books." There have been many commentaries on Benson's life and work since his death of complications from pneumonia resulting from overwork, but none more heartfelt or, from the perspective of a family member, more insightful than Arthur's brief tribute.

Arthur's personal reminiscence is all the more valuable in that, with one possible exception, it came from the individual who knew Benson best. The exception was Benson's beloved nurse, Beth. Arthur's memoir is a valuable resource for people who want to understand Benson. While respectful and certainly a labor of love, *Hugh* helps strip away the patina of false reverence that has managed to layer itself on Benson and his writings. It would have startled Benson's family (and possibly embarrassed him terribly) to find out that some recent enthusiasts have republished a number of his works of fiction in the form of illuminated texts! Benson regarded his fiction primarily as a way to make extra money, as well as give a Catholic perspective in fictional form to counter some of the dreadful anti-Catholic stereotypes prevalent in the popular fiction of his day, but above all, as we have seen, to explore the concept of "vocation," one's calling in life.

Paradoxically, Benson refused to take his novels or short stories seriously, and yet took them very seriously indeed. This seems to have shocked some of his more fervent admirers as well as baffled his biographers. When he discovered that some readers were taking his satiric "future war" science fiction novel *Lord of the World* as prophecy, he expressed amazement, In response, he quickly turned out a novel that he felt would correct that misimpression: *The Dawn of All*. When some enthusiasts began taking this later "counterblast" as Benson's blueprint for an ideal society, the author was appalled, and continued to insist that his readers were getting it all wrong. They were trying to put too much on to something he regarded almost as an idle pastime. As Arthur expressed it,

> Neither do I think that his books emanated from a high artistic ideal. I do not believe that he was really much interested in his craft. Rather he visualized a story very vividly, and then it seemed to him the finest fun in the world to spin it all as rapidly as he could out of his brain, to make it all alert with glancing life. It was all a personal confession; his books bristle with his own dreams, his own dilemmas, his own social relations; and when he had once firmly realized the Catholic attitude, it seemed to him the one thing worth writing about.

However a reader views Benson's fiction, Arthur's memoir would prove an invaluable — and fascinating — guide to the man behind the writing. It presents a different perspective on an author whose merits may at times be obscured by a misguided reverence, but within limits. Fortunately those very limitations are invaluable to non-

Catholics who may otherwise be "turned off" reading Benson's novels because of the encrustations of veneration that have managed to get piled on to them.

Arthur excelled in explaining Benson as a person, but failed badly when attempting to understand his brother's conversion to Catholicism. Arthur tended to speak in unconsciously denigrating terms that betray a deep lack of appreciation of both his brother's motives, and the Church to which Benson converted. Paradoxically, this gives Arthur's recollections their particular value. Non-Catholics reading some Catholic enthusiasts' descriptions of Benson, or reviews of some of his novels from a "Catholic" point of view, will in all likelihood be repelled. Some of Benson's fans, in fact, make some errors about their hero's early life that, to someone who knew him as a younger brother with whom he played and (at times) fought, are laughable:

> In a friendly little memoir of him, which I have been sent, I find the following passage: "In his early childhood, when reason was just beginning to ponder over the meaning of things, he was so won to enthusiastic admiration of the heroes and heroines of the Catholic Church that he decided he would probe for himself the Catholic claims, and the child would say to the father, 'Father, if there be such a sacrament as Penance, can I go?' And the good Archbishop, being evasive in his answers, the young boy found himself emerging more and more in a woeful Nemesis of faith." It would be literally *impossible*, I think, to construct a story less characteristic both of Hugh's own attitude of mind as well as of the atmosphere of our family and household life than this!

Not that Arthur himself managed to get everything right. He was, after all, a faithful member of the Church of England, and several times mentioned that he simply did not understand why or how his favorite brother converted to Catholicism. The non-Catholic would doubtless find much sympathy with Arthur when he read, "I do not wholly understand in my mind how Hugh came to make the change."

In attempting to understand, Arthur mentioned that he studied *Confessions of a Convert* at some length. The book he should have read, however, is *The Religion of the Plain Man*. The former is intensely personal (although not to the degree to which modern readers have become accustomed), so much so that it does not adequately explain Benson's thought processes in reaching his decision. *The Religion of the Plain Man*, however, is much more objective, and answers many of the questions Arthur raised in his memoir.

To gain the best perspective on Benson, then, it would be very useful to read both Arthur's short memoir and the "official" biography by Reverend C. C. Martindale — if you can find a copy. Each one supplies what the other lacks in attempting to gain insights on Benson's complex — that is to say, ordinary — personality. As Arthur commented,

> "It is impossible to select one of his moods, and to say that his true life lay there. His life lay in all of them. If work was tedious to him, he comforted himself with the thought that it would soon be done. He was an excellent man of affairs, never "slothful in business," but with great practical ability. He made careful bargains for his books, and looked after his financial interests tenaciously and diligently, with a definite purpose always in his mind. He lived, I am sure, always looking forward and anticipating. I do not believe he dwelt at all upon the past. It was life in which he was interested. . . . He had a supreme power of casting things behind him, and he was far too intent on the present to have indulged in sentimental reveries of what had been."

We are left with the impression of a man greatly loved, but seeking more to love. It is difficult to see how anyone could want a better memoir than that.

II. The Novels of Wiseman and Newman

1. Fabiola (1853)

The tragedy of many great novels is their relegation to the category of "influences" and "required reading" when they should be considered "entertainment," however artistic, inspirational, or educational. This fills up the category quickly, so that other novels, while not great, are still well worth reading as genuine influences and, in the proper context, required reading, tend to get ignored. A case in point is *Fabiola, or, The Church of the Catacombs*, by Nicholas Cardinal Wiseman.

Wiseman was a competent writer as well as a profound scholar. *Fabiola*, while his only work of fiction, is well-plotted, coherent, and holds up reasonably well more than a century and a half after its first publication. It enjoyed good sales for eighty years or more, and proved its basic quality by outlasting any possible novelty value as a book written by a prominent member of the Catholic hierarchy.

Even the usual amateur's mistakes, while present, are minimized. Yes, the book tends to get a little didactic in tone. That was, after all, the reason for writing the book in the first place, and Wiseman was not practiced enough in the art of fiction to make it more subtle. There are also frequent changes of "voice" as the narrator shifts back and forth from simply describing events and the characters' thoughts and actions, to addressing the reader directly. Finally, "surprise" twists in the plot are signaled well in advance — as they should be — but Wiseman makes it obvious in a trifle heavy-handed manner that he is alerting the reader to something astounding that will be revealed shortly. In consequence, the twists are mildly startling, but the reader is far from surprised.

On the other hand, Wiseman succeeded in making saints and martyrs of the early Church a bit more human than is usually the case. Even Heinryk Sienkiewicz, one of the greatest masters of what we might, for want of a better term, call "Catholic fiction," wasn't quite able to overcome his evident awe of the heroes of his religion. Sienkiewicz tended to make historical saints, as opposed to his fictional saints, a trifle two-dimensional in his otherwise splendid *Quo Vadis*. Wiseman, operating within the Catholic hierarchy (and maybe it had something to do with hearing confessions), seems to have been fully aware that great saints are, above everything else, great human beings first, having acquired and developed more of that virtue that defines us as human.

So why would a Cardinal of the Catholic Church undertake to write a novel, however competently written, anyway, and Wiseman most of all? As the man selected to reestablish the Catholic hierarchy in England on September 29, the "Feast of St. Michael the Archangel,"[20] 1850, shortly after Catholic Emancipation, Wiseman certainly had more serious things to worry about. Not the least of these worries was the almost hysterical hatred directed against the Catholic Church in general, and Wiseman in particular.

This animosity, in fact, appears to have been the justification for writing the novel — although Wiseman gave a slightly veiled account of the circumstances of its composition and publication. As he related in the "Preface,"

> When the plan of the *Popular Catholic Library* was formed, the author of the following little work was consulted upon it. He not only approved of the design, but ventured to suggest, among others, a series of tales illustrative of the condition of the Church in different periods of her past existence. One, for instance, might be called "The Church of the Catacombs;" a second, "The Church of the Basilicas;" each comprising three hundred years: a third would be on "The Church of the Cloister;" and then, perhaps, a fourth might be added, called "The Church of the Schools."
>
> In proposing this sketch, he added, — perhaps the reader will find indiscreetly, — that he felt half inclined to undertake the first, by way of illustrating the proposed plan. He was taken at his word, and urged strongly to begin the work. After some reflection, he consented; but with an understanding, that

---

[20] Now the Feast of the Archangels.

it was not to be an occupation, but only the recreation of leisure hours. With this condition, the work was commenced early in this year; and it has been carried on entirely on that principle.

Not addressed in the Preface is *why* the plan of the "Popular Catholic Library" was formed. The story is a trifle ugly.

Anti-Catholicism in the England of the nineteenth century was not the "anti-Semitism of the intellectual." There was nothing intellectual about it. The Catholic Church was, as all good English men, women, and children knew from their cradles, the enemy of England. All of its members were either dupes or tools of a foreign prince, and natural born traitors to everything good and decent, *i.e.*, English.

Catholic Emancipation was bad enough — who knew what those papists would do if they could hold public office and enter the professions without restriction? (Voting was not much of an issue, as most Englishmen did not have the franchise under the infamous "rotten borough" system, in which some large urban areas had less than a dozen qualified voters.)

To have a foreign prince foisted on them with the provocative title of "Cardinal Archbishop of Westminster" was an obvious attempt to engage in "papal aggression" as a first step in the conquest of England and the imposition of Catholicism as the State religion in place of the Church of England. There was something sinister and (of course) *Jesuitical* about the whole business. The Yeomen of the Guard could expect to find kegs of gunpowder under the Houses of Parliament at the opening of the next session — if the papists didn't try something worse. The streets of London would run red with the blood of a new crop of Protestant martyrs.

It was within this atmosphere of fear and loathing that Charles Kingsley, a minister of the Church of England, decided to strike a blow at the pretensions of the papists. In 1853 he published *Hypatia, or, New Foes With an Old Face*. Ostensibly an "early Christian romance" of the sort typified by Edward Bulwer-Lytton's *The Last Days of Pompeii*, Kingley's work was a scarcely veiled attack on

Catholicism, filled with misrepresentations, half-truths, and outright fabrications.

Kingsley, as even his best friends admitted, was both hasty and hot-tempered, to say nothing of being prone to judge others in the harshest possible terms for the crime of disagreeing with him. Typically putting the worst possible interpretation on the actions or even imagined thoughts of anyone he regarded as an enemy — whether or not he had ever even met them or had any hard facts to go on — Kingsley also had the deplorable habit of stretching the truth past the breaking point when he felt that he had discerned someone's *true* motives for anything he imagined they might have done. His friends generally agreed that Kingsley, while never knowingly or consciously telling an outright lie, was never able to admit a mistake, and managed to twist events to fit his preconceived notions. Kingsley's friends also admitted that they were rarely, if ever, able to persuade him to depart from a course of action, no matter how ruinous or embarrassing to Kingsley it might ultimately prove to be.

As the head of the Catholic Church in England, the chief object of Kingsley's venom (at least for the time being), Wiseman may have felt it far more prudent that he write the first response in order to prevent a literary war from erupting as Catholic and anti-Catholic writers vied to see which could get in the last word, or deliver the most devastating insults. There was also the additional, and possibly greater motive that Wiseman needed something that he felt would educate the novel-reading public in the true history of the Catholic Church, but in a way that did not attack or play to people's prejudices directly.

This was an extremely non-confrontational way to counter the arguments of Kingsley and others who claimed that the Church of England was the true church, and it was the Church of Rome that had broken away from the body of the faithful. By showing that specifically Catholic practices were of long-standing — especially those that the Church of England most detested — Wiseman cleverly made the case for the Catholic Church against the claims of the Church of England, while specifically mentioning England only once, and that in a brief and rather esoteric discussion concerning grave inscriptions. The persecution of the early Christians, clearly Catholics, by the State and members of the established State (pagan) religion out of mindless bigotry and clearly interested motives — usually the acquisition of wealth by any means necessary — drew obvious parallels with the situation in England, but in a way that excited the reader's sympathy instead of drawing his ire.

That Wiseman succeeded is obvious. As noted, *Fabiola* enjoyed good sales for more than half a century after its first publication, while few people today even know of *Hypatia*, except, perhaps, as a historical curiosity. Many people simply group its crudely disguised Victorian prurience and vitriolic anti-Catholicism with *The Awful Disclosures of Maria Monk* and similar productions. The publication two years later of John Henry Newman's *Callista*, an extraordinarily well-crafted novel, was an even more effective counter to Kingsley's screed — although it didn't stop Kingsley from carrying out his anti-Catholic activities at every opportunity.

Kingsley may even have taken *Callista* as directed specifically at him, particularly in that he later claimed already to have had a special animus against Newman, a convert to Catholicism, and whom in consequence (as we might expect) Kingsley regarded as a traitor both to England and the established church. This would have been unjust even for Kingsley, for Newman began writing *Callista* soon after completing *Loss and Gain* in 1848. At best, the publication of Kingsley's *Hypatia* may have provided an excuse for dusting off the manuscript and getting it published, but not the inspiration for its composition.

As for *Fabiola*, after filtering out the antiquarian proofs of the historicity of the Catholic Church (interesting, even fascinating at times — but not well-integrated into the story), the plot is relatively straightforward. The twists that Wiseman inserted do not really advance the story, although a more experienced novelist would have been able either to disguise this better, or figured out a way to make them seem important, if not integral to the plot. This, in addition to the fact that there are just a few too many known saints thrown into the book, give it something of the air of "Close Encounters of the Holiest Kind." Fortunately, however (as noted above), Wiseman makes them more human than is usually the case, so it works pretty well.

Fabiola is the indulged daughter of Fabius, given every advantage, even an advanced education — something probably shocking to mid-Victorian sensibilities. People of the day tended to forget the learned and saintly women who flourished during late Classical times and into the Catholic Middle Ages . . . and no doubt one of the reasons Wiseman gave the girl a superior education. In that sense, *Fabiola* might also be taken as a counter to the Victorian productions that advocated the emancipation of women, but on such terms as to de-feminize them. Thanks in large measure to devotion to the Virgin Mary, discouraged after the Reformation in England as "Mariolotry," the Catholic Church is credited with giving women a much greater status than they had enjoyed in most pagan societies, in the language of one commentator, "taking Eve out of the Pit and putting her on a pedestal."

The girl, however, feels that something is missing in her life, and she grows increasingly discontented. Losing her temper one day, she brutally attacks her devoted slave, Syra, who (as we might expect) is secretly a Christian. The injury Fabiola inflicts shocks her to such an extent that a gradual transformation begins. Toward the end of the novel, when nearing the inevitable (from a fictional standpoint) conversion, Fabiola reflects that every decent person she has known has turned out to be a Christian.

Fabiola is, of course, exceptionally wealthy, which makes her the prey of numberless pagan fortune hunters, among them Fulvius and Corvinus. Corvinus has been dismissed from school for bullying and fighting, blaming both his teacher, Cassianus, and a fellow student, Pancratius, both secretly Christians, for the punishment. Corvinus — possibly a Roman version of Kingsley? — has a particular hatred of Pancratius, and persecutes him unceasingly in an effort to get Pancratius to betray his coreligionists so that Corvinus can collect the reward for turning the Christians in. Demonstrating Corvinus's vileness, he manages to trick the remaining students into murdering Cassianus. Pancratius saves Corvinus's life soon afterwards, although no reform or conversion ensues.

Fulvius, too, is revealed to be engaged in hunting Christians for fun and profit, although with a bit more reason than Corvinus — while appearing to be a wealthy idler, Fulvius is deeply in debt. He overcomes his self-loathing for what he believes to be the only method left to him to recoup the family fortune, using every trick in the book to betray Christians to the authorities.

Fulvius and Corvinus enter into a plot to obtain both Fabiola's money and that of her beloved cousin, Agnes (yet another secret Christian), but Fulvius is betrayed in turn by Corvinus, who is convinced that he will end up with both fortunes and the hand of Fabiola. The imperial edict obtained for Corvinus to that effect by his father turns out to be worthless, however. It so happens that Agnes's estate is entailed and therefore not subject to confiscation. The estate went to Fabiola immediately upon the death of Agnes. (Whether the intricacies of Roman law really permitted such a thing is not entirely clear.)

Fabiola, of course, is ultimately converted to Christianity, but the story continues with a brief epilogue. Fulvius escapes his creditors and leaves Rome, seemingly forever. Fabiola, however, settles both Fulvius's debts and those of Corvinus (for which she receives no thanks). Fifteen years later Fulvius returns, having mended his evil ways and converted to Christianity. He has become a holy hermit in the desert, but has obtained permission to return to Rome and settle his debts. When he finds out that they were settled by Fabiola years before, he reveals his history to her in what Wiseman seems to have considered a series of shocking revelations, but which are pretty tame by modern standards, as well as being signaled well in advance of the actual disclosure.

Overall, the story comes across to modern readers unfamiliar with the background that occasioned its writing as fairly innocuous entertainment, edifying, if not as thrilling as it might have been. We have only to compare the most intense scenes in *Fabiola* to the description of the chariot race in *Ben Hur* to see how exciting a "Biblical epic" can be. The novel is well worth reading, however, and not just because it is an "influence" or is an interesting historical curiosity.

There was a European film version of *Fabiola* made in 1949, but it bears very little resemblance to the novel. It was dubbed and released in the United Kingdom in a much-truncated version as *The Fighting Gladiator*, possibly in an effort to avoid offending any remaining fans of Charles Kingsley, who probably wouldn't have recognized anything in the film version of the story in any event.

2. Loss and Gain (1848)

No one would think, from a brief outline of the plot of Jane Austin's *Pride and Prejudice*, that the novel was worth reading by anyone other than the most fanatical *aficionada* of genre "Regency Romances." A single rich man rents a house in the neighborhood, bringing along his even richer and equally unmarried (but unfortunately arrogant) friend. A flighty mother throws her far-too-numerous marriageable daughters into the fray, of which only the two elder siblings appear to have any brains or character. The characters meet various difficulties on the road to marital bliss, including the rescue, by the misjudged friend, of one of the daughters from a potentially disastrous social situation. Everybody gets married and lives happily ever after.

Come to think of it, that would make pretty dull reading for anyone.

Of course, anyone who has ever actually read *Pride and Prejudice* knows full well that the minimal plot is only there to provide the stage on which the characters exercise extraordinary wit and cleverness to present the author's insightful, sometimes barbed observations on early nineteenth century England. Even that limits analysis of Jane Austin's genius to a single level. A deeper understanding of her work reveals incisive commentary on the human condition that applies to any time and place.

A similar superficial glance at John Henry Newman's *Loss and Gain* would reveal the outline of an incredibly dull story. The son of a Church of England minister goes off to Oxford. While there he has a few deep conversations and a large number of shallow ones regarding religion. As the novel can be taken as Newman's fictional treatment of the Oxford Movement, the conversations revolve around the similarities and differences between the Church of England and the Catholic Church. Eventually the young man argues himself into becoming a Catholic, and ends up ostracized from polite society.

Dull stuff, no? And made even more dull by the fact that a lot of the terminology and even the concepts are unfamiliar to modern readers. For example, Newman has his characters employ a lot of Latin "tags" in conversation, and does not forebear to use them himself. Why? Because that's the way students at Oxford spoke when Newman was one of the leading lights of the Oxford Movement. The effect is to recreate the atmosphere, if not actual events, of the time.

Then there's the whole matter of the "Oxford Movement." The general public of the 1840s might not know all the theological and historical fine points involved, but they knew about the Movement. They considered it revolutionary, in both the best and worst senses of the term.

The Movement was an initiative by a group of "High Church" Anglicans (which needs a little explanation itself!) who, through historical investigation, set out to prove that the Church of England was the same institution established by the Apostles. It derived its name from the fact that most of its members were at Oxford University, notably John Henry Newman, who at that time was a "fellow" of Oriel College at Oxford, and Vicar of the University church of Saint Mary the Virgin, and who did most of the writing.

"High Church" versus "Low Church" is an Anglican concept regarding how far one has "Catholic views" or sympathies, and how far these are incorporated into church services by the adoption or rejection of the externals of Catholic worship. At one end of the spectrum, a High Church adherent may hold every belief and doctrine of the Catholic Church except for papal supremacy, making him, in Catholic terms, a "schismatic" rather than a "heretic." At the other end of the spectrum, a Low Church adherent is extremely careful about participating in anything that smacks of Rome, whether it be externals such as vestments, candles, incense, and so on, or doctrines such as the Real Presence.

Members of the Movement were sometimes called "Puseyites" (not always as a compliment) after one of their other leaders, Edward Bouverie Pusey, Regius Professor of Hebrew at Christ Church, Oxford. They were also called "Tractarians," from the series of religious "tracts" they produced, mostly from Newman's pen, called "Tracts for the Times," issued from 1833 through 1841. Notable members of the Movement included John Keble, Archdeacon Henry Edward Manning, Richard Hurrell Froude, Gerard Manley Hopkins, Robert Wilberforce, Isaac Williams, and Sir William Palmer, a number of which ended up converting to Catholicism.

The Movement started in response to an inevitable consequence of having an "established" church, that is, a religion set up as a recognized and official branch of the State, with the Head of State in place as the head of the religion. The "Reform Act" passed by parliament in 1832 resulted in a State decision to reduce the number of bishoprics in the Church of Ireland, which was at that time the branch of the Anglican Church established in Ireland.

This made sense from a political point of view. Maintaining a diocese and the administrative structure thereof is an expensive proposition. Prior to the Catholic Relief Act of 1829, the Church of Ireland *officially* counted all Irish subjects as members of the church, and taxed them accordingly for its support. The reality was that for centuries English policies in Ireland had eroded the tax base by causing widespread poverty, and few Irish attended services in the national church, preferring their own illegal Catholic religious services.

This decision and some others that came out of the Reform Act caused outrage in High Church circles. It was viewed as a secularization of the Church by subordinating the presumed religious needs of the Irish, who probably couldn't care less since they didn't attend Anglican services anyway, to political expediency. (This was just after Catholic Emancipation, and membership in the Catholic Church was only newly legal.) John Keble labeled the proposal a "national apostasy" in a sermon he preached at Oxford in 1833. Opponents of the reform quickly organized and condemned religious liberalism, or the belief that all religions are equally true, which, logically, also means that all religions are equally false. On a more proactive note, they began investigating the historical origins of Christianity to support their position.

Naturally these historical investigations forced them to reconsider the relationship among all the various Christian bodies, particularly that of "the Church of Rome" and the Church of England. In consequence, they developed the "Branch Theory." According to this theory, Anglicanism, Orthodoxy, and "Roman Catholicism" form the three visible branches of the one invisible Catholic Church.

This explains, in part, why there is such an insistence on the part of Anglicans even today that the body that refers to itself as the Catholic Church is actually the *Roman* Catholic Church. As far as that institution having the pope as its head is concerned, the "Roman Catholic Church" properly applies only to the Catholic Church of the diocese of Rome, Italy. Both the Catholic Church and the autocephalous Orthodox Churches reject Branch Theory, considering each other "schismatic," or breaking the unity of the Church without denying any essential doctrines. (Denying essential doctrine would make a church "heretical.")

This Branch Theory led John Henry Newman to write *Tract 90: Remarks on Certain Passages in the Thirty-Nine Articles* in which he postulated that the doctrines of the Catholic Church, as defined by the Council of Trent (1545-1563), were fully compatible with the "Thirty-Nine Articles" of the Church of England. The Thirty-Nine Articles, incorporated into the Book of Common Prayer, define certain doctrines to be held by the Church of England, especially as they relate to those of the Catholic Church. They posit a *Via Media*, a "middle way" between what England's sixteenth century reformers regarded as the extremes of both the continental Protestants and the "popery" of the Catholic Church. Adherence to the Thirty-Nine Articles was a test for public office. This made it impossible for any Catholic to run for parliament. The Articles were enforced by the State until the Church of England was "disestablished."

Newman's arguments were so convincing that he ended up convincing himself. He converted to Catholicism in 1845, causing a storm of fury and outrage. Other members of the Movement didn't go quite as far as Newman, but Anglican clergymen with "Catholic views" were frequently denied promotion, and even parish assignments, or "livings." This backfired on the religious and political establishment, because this left the "Anglican Catholic" clergy free to engage in the social work that had been neglected since the Reformation. This in turn led to a measure of acceptance of Catholicism — both Anglican and "Roman" — among the lower classes that had formerly been strongly anti-Catholic. It even resulted in the formation of Anglican religious orders in a somewhat artificial attempt to restore an important feature of pre-Reformation English life. Certain Catholic practices were introduced into Anglican religious services that, as we might expect in an established church, caused a number of lawsuits.

Ironically, it was this same lack of official response to the terrible conditions that resulted from the Industrial Revolution (aside from the inadequate and horrifying "Poor Laws") that led Karl Marx to write *The Communist Manifesto* and provide immense evidence for his monumental *Capital*. It also provided impetus for the establishment of the Christian Social Union and the radical (Anglo-) Catholic Crusade. These agitated for the just wage, reform in the system of property renting ("rack-renting," or numerous levels of subletting before being rented to the ultimate tenant, still being common), concern for infant mortality, and industrial conditions, among other things. All of this flew in the face of Malthusian concepts of scarcity, which had by this time become economic, political, and even religious orthodoxy for the greater part of the establishment.

The backlash naturally focused on John Henry Newman, because of his writings and the effect of *Tract 90*, but especially his conversion, the most visible and obvious target. The reaction ranged from cries of "Treason!" to "How *could* you?" He answered members of both groups with his *Essay on the Development of Christian Doctrine*, which he published soon after his conversion. This did not, however, explain his position to the great mass of ordinary people, who were confused, hurt, and puzzled by

Newman's act, but who would be unlikely to read the *Essay*, any more than popular adherents of Adam Smith, Thomas Malthus, or Karl Marx have managed to work their way through *The Wealth of Nations*, *An Essay on Population*, or *Capital*.

Consequently Newman turned to popular entertainment. In his day, that meant the novel. This was still a relatively new venue, but one with acceptance in virtually all levels of society, especially with the new literacy that was springing up. Novel-reading had supplanted play-going, just as movies would displace novels in the next century, and television subsequently take over from the movies. (That's oversimplified, of course, but this is not the place to get into a detailed analysis of the evolution of popular entertainment.) Nearer our own day, Archbishop Fulton Sheen proved himself even more adept than Newman at using the popular media to explain some extremely complex subjects.

Newman could not have picked a better vehicle for his purpose. Had he not been one of the greatest theologians of the nineteenth century, *Loss and Gain* and *Callista*, the story Newman began almost immediately after completing *Loss and Gain* (although not published until 1855), give more than ample evidence that he could very easily have rivaled Dickens and Thackery, to say nothing of Trollop or Charles Lever, and won a secure place as one of English literature's greatest novelists. Newman's prose is more fluid and concise than that of Dickens (Newman wasn't paid by the word), while his understanding of both political and religious life in England in the nineteenth century leaves Trollop in the dust.

Perhaps one way to draw an analogy would be to say — somewhat misleadingly — that Newman's fiction manages to combine the wit and cleverness of Jane Austin with the socio-religious insightfulness of Allesandro Manzoni, without Austin's "diversion" into purely social commentary, or Manzoni's epic scope. That does nothing to disparage the genius of either of the two comparisons, for the goals of each of them were different from that of Newman, and each accomplished the set goals with a brilliance that has never been equaled. Manzoni's *The Betrothed* (the usual translation of *I Promessi Sposi*) holds a place in Italian literature comparable to that of Dickens, Thackery, Trollop, Scott, and a number of others, combined. It has, unfortunately, suffered at the hands of the Italian academic establishment by being almost universally regarded as "required reading," thereby removing virtually any incentive to read it for pleasure.

Similarly, the English-speaking Catholic educational establishment has typically regarded Newman's two novels as books that *should* be read . . . and relegated them to a distant second behind non-fiction works such as *Tract 90*, *Essay on the Development of Christian Doctrine*, and (above all) his monumental *Apologia Pro Vita Sua*, a work that rivals any work of fiction in its profundity and even entertainment value. If even Catholics regard the novels in that light, how likely is it that non-Catholics would ever pick up a copy?

Thus we have a "double tragedy," as it were. Catholics don't read Newman's fiction because they haven't gotten around to it — and take the "backwards" approach of assuming that his non-fiction will lead them to his fiction, which was contrary to Newman's evident intent. Non-Catholics don't read the novels, well, because they are "Catholic novels" written by a Catholic for a Catholic audience, as Newman himself stated.

This is like saying that Miguel de Cervantes's masterpiece, *El Ingenioso Hidalgo Don Quixote de la Mancha*, should only be read as a remedy by individuals who have succumbed to the distortions of chivalry that dominated the sixteenth century, or as evidence by those who wish to hold such aberrations up to ridicule. That should, logically, make *Don Quixote* a bestseller among members, enemies, or critics of the Society for Creative Anachronism, and mean that the book holds no interest for anyone else.

In *Loss and Gain*, however, once we get past the special language and the topical references, we discover an extraordinarily entertaining work of fiction. Like all good fiction, it is firmly grounded in some aspect of truth. With uncommon wit and an astonishingly deft touch Newman delineates types of characters and at the same time endows them with personality. We are tempted, along with commentators on Jane Austin's works, to declare that no real person ever spoke with such cleverness, but the artistry with which Newman and Austin handle their characters leads us to question that conclusion. The characters are very real at the same time we recognize them instantly as archetypes.

Newman's skill in both fiction and non-fiction led his critics to accuse him of being a "Jesuitical serpent," leading faithful Anglicans into the Catholic fold by the deception made possible by his wit and cleverness. This was even more unfair than the cries of "treason" and exclamations of dismay that accompanied his conversion. The motto that years later he chose as Cardinal, "Heart Speaks to Heart," was in effect simply a statement of how Newman expressed himself at all times, whether preaching, writing non-fiction, or as a novelist.

Individuals such as Charles Kingsley saw Newman's sincerity as just another Jesuitical trick. When opportunity arose, they didn't hesitate to accuse Newman of dishonesty. Charles Kingsley especially (identifying himself only by the initials "C.K.") in the specific incident in 1863/64 that called forth the *Apologia Pro Vita Sua* — maintained in a popular magazine that, "Father Newman informs us that truth for its own sake need not be, and on the whole ought not to be, a virtue of the Roman clergy."

After some back-and-forth in which he was continually bested, Kingsley again accused Newman in public of being a liar, with the clear intent of discrediting the Catholic Church in general, and Newman in particular with the British public. (The heroic patriotism displayed by nursing nuns and the Catholic clergy during the Crimean War, 1853-1856, as in the American Civil War a short time later, had caused many people to re-think their prejudices against Catholics and their Church.) In response, Newman wrote his *Apologia Pro Vita Sua* with incredible speed. Rather than play to centuries of prejudice, as Kingsley had done, Newman appealed to the common Englishman's sense of fair play and justice — something that the English upper classes had been in the habit of denigrating.

Newman made his case with logic and reason, but from which he did not remove emotion. In consequence — and to Kingsley's utter astonishment — Newman gained the sympathy of all but the most intransigent of bigots. In this he helped clear the way for a number of highly-visible conversions in the late nineteenth and early twentieth centuries, most notably that of Robert Hugh Benson, who, as a son of the Anglican Archbishop of Canterbury, could otherwise have expected to be greeted with even more shrill cries of horror and protest than those that assailed Newman.

With Newman's intellectual background, we could expect his fiction to be both tedious and concerned with esoteric minutiae. Esoteric minutiae certainly appear to be there in plenty, but it is only the backdrop against which the story is played out. Astonishingly, we come to realize that Newman is relating a romance, not, perhaps, precisely in the style of Sir Walter Scott (whose work Newman greatly admired), or in the more modern understanding of the term, but a romance nonetheless.

Literature was to Newman "the autobiography of mankind," presented in a manner in which the author's and the characters' — and the readers' — hearts could speak to one another. Unlike the more extreme of the Romantics he did not jettison reason, the classics, or (most importantly) Christianity, but integrated them into a completed picture of the human condition. The "romance" that he relates in *Loss and Gain* and again in *Callista* is not the typical "boy meets girl" (or "girl snags boy") type of production, however. It is of a soul moving itself closer to God — a romance that should appeal to all people of all faiths. It is that, and not the specific circumstances that surround the novel's creation or even the fact of its explicit Catholicism, that makes this novel a classic, to be read and enjoyed by anyone.

3. Callista (1855)

In 1855 John Henry Newman, who had previously shocked the Anglican establishment by converting to Catholicism in 1845, managed to do so again with the publication of his second novel, *Callista*, a historical romance set in early Christian times. Part of Newman's object was doubtless to counter the sort of production so prevalent then, and which reached its climax in the "Biblical Epic" phase of Hollywood in the 1950s. There is also a hint that the publication of *Callista* may have been intended to counter Charles Kingsley's anti-Catholic tirade, *Hypatia: New Foes with an Old Face* (1853), although Newman's novel was written before that of Kingsley.

At least one authority has written an article attempting to prove that Charles Kingley's deep-rooted animosity against Newman was the result of Newman's *Callista* being a much better novel than Kingley's *Hypatia*, and for giving the impression that the Teutonic "race" was not inherently superior to the decadent Semitic and Mediterranean "races." Citing an article by Susan Dorman,[21] the writer stated,

> Dorman argues that the battle lines of the 1864 Kingsley-Newman controversy were drawn a decade earlier in the two ideologically opposite novels, Kingsley's *Hypatia* and Newman's *Callista*. ". . . it is clear that the seed of the 1864 conflict which culminated in Newman's personally triumphant *Apologia Pro Vita Sua* is deeply rooted in the philosophical antithesis between the novels *Hypatia* and *Callista*" (193). Dorman also suggests that the criticism Kingsley received from Pusey for his novel's alleged immorality, and his subsequent humiliation, strengthened his resolve not to be humiliated afresh years later

---

[21] Dorman, *op. cit.*

but to make a strong attack on Newman in his 1864 pamphlet.[22]

In general such novels promoted a very superficial understanding of both theology and history. They usually gave the impression that the only thing necessary to be a "Christian" was to be a good and decent man (or woman)... more or less. God might test you with some trials and tribulations (or there wouldn't be much of a plot), but there would be the necessary happy ending, with the handsome hero and the beautiful Christian maiden riding off into the sunset, or whatever it was that Romans did in those days. All that nasty and unpleasant martyrdom and death was ignored.

Almost without exception, these novels and plays assumed any one of the many Protestant positions as a given. Being works of fiction, events could be tailored to support or conform to any theological or political claim. From the point of view of one of the most intellectual English converts to the Catholic Church in the nineteenth century, these stories were both bad theology and bad history — as Newman himself said, to know history is to become Catholic.

Needless to say, many of these novels were also just plain bad stories. The most enduring of the bad stories has been *The Last Days of Pompeii*, by Edward Bulwer-Lytton. Bulwer-Lytton, of course, is the man famous for penning the immortal opening line of *Paul Kelver*: "It was a dark and stormy night."

There were, however, good stories as well. In a sense these were worse than the bad ones. Few people were taken in or convinced by Bulwer-Lytton's cardboard characters, although the book and dramas based on it have enjoyed a longevity that historians, theologians, and even critics are hard put to fathom, any more than anyone really understands the popularity of "reality TV." On the other hand, *Ben-Hur: A Tale of the Christ*, by General Lew Wallace of Indiana, later territorial governor of New Mexico and official nemesis of Billy the Kid, was well-written with good characterization and — with the exception of

---

[22] http://www2.bc.edu/~rappleb/kingsley/KHypatia.html.

some historical blunders (such as the fact that the Romans did not use galley slaves in their navies) — extremely plausible.

The assumption common to every single one of these epics was one that would be completely unacceptable to a man who had argued himself into the Catholic Church by examining its historical claims. That is, the impression was always given (or stated outright) that Jesus had not established a visible Church. Christianity was not, therefore, initially a *religion*, but a *movement*, a spontaneous outburst of feeling and belief due to the memory of the teachings of an extremely wise man named Jesus with special powers of some kind — so wise that His followers soon began to think He was divine. This also makes the willingness of the early Christians to die for their beliefs and refusal to apostatize utterly incomprehensible. In a movement, death is a defeat, a tragedy. In a religion, it is a victory.

The idea of Christianity as a movement instead of a religion was the premise of Lloyd C. Douglas's *The Robe*. Part of the plot involved a Roman Tribune who decided to go about preaching the Good News, captivating people and converting them by impressing them with the truth and beauty of Jesus' teachings. The book (and, presumably, the author) completely ignored the fact that wise men and philosophers in every day and age had taught the same thing. What made the Christian message different, and which Saint Paul and others stressed above everything else, was that the Person who taught these things had been crucified — and on the third day rose from the dead.

It was this and nothing else that took the ancient world by storm. All of the pagan religions had myths about the god who died and rose again, bringing about the rebirth of the world. The problem was that these events happened in the "before time" and not within human reality at all. None of them affected people directly or personally. Baldur, Osiris, Mithras — all of them — were always undergoing death and rebirth, but not in our world; they were usually construed as symbols of fertility instead of reality.

In the case of Jesus, however, you had an Individual who had been executed as a common criminal, with His death duly noted in the records. These and the census records mentioned in the Gospel of Luke were maintained in Rome until the early fifth century when Alaric's Goths burned the hall of public records during the sack of the Eternal City in 410 . . . after which began the claims that neither the census nor the crucifixion had taken place. This Person had been observed among the living after His death, as attested to in writing by numerous witnesses — one of which was a Roman citizen and a lawyer, Paul of Tarsus.

The teachings of Jesus were thus important not because He was a nice guy, a wise man, or even a really good stage magician, but because they were a direct public revelation from God Himself, as proven by His resurrection. Only a god, after all, can raise Himself from the dead. Aside from the miraculous and mystical teachings, the teachings were (as we noted) nothing that had not been said many times before. What made the "good news" of the Gospel specifically *good*, and seized the imagination of the ancient world, though, was the fact that here was a proven way to release mankind from the burden of sin. If someone can raise Himself from the dead as announced, He can certainly deliver on a promise to forgive sins.

This was the clincher, so to speak. As C. S. Lewis noted in one of his essays, no one can read any of the ancient authors without soon coming to the realization that they were suffused with a sense of sin. By sacrificing Himself on the cross, Jesus redeemed mankind from the slavery of sin, and made virtue not only possible, but the optimal, even wisest choice. This is embodied in "Pascal's Wager" addressed to agnostics: if God exists, you gain everything by believing. If He does not, you have lost nothing.

Rejecting the miraculous and mystical elements in the Good News or downplaying or ignoring the divinity of the God-man had, however, been fashionable for quite a while by the time Newman wrote *Callista*. It is not an invention of the twentieth or even twenty-first century. Further, it was crucial to Protestant claims that Christianity as a way of life or a movement be carefully separated from

Christianity as a divinely instituted religion, and that the teachings be stressed at the expense of the miraculous elements. The English upper classes were much more concerned with an orderly and prosperous life in this world for themselves, than with a possibly ephemeral heavenly reward for others. Besides, a truly well-bred God wouldn't come back from the dead after all the trouble and expense of a public execution and funeral. It isn't *done*.

That such a belief would lead eventually to diminishing or dismissing Jesus's claims to divinity would be obvious to someone like Newman. Since one of the vehicles that spread this attitude was bad popular fiction, Newman seems to have decided that the best way to counter it was with *good* popular fiction — a novel that assumed as a given that Jesus was God-made-man, that He established a visible Church as the instrument for conveying both His message and to provide His sacramental priesthood with the means of ministering sanctifying grace to the faithful, and that He was crucified, died, and was buried, rising to live again on the third day.

These assumptions are embedded in *Callista*, and all the more powerfully so for being implicit rather than stated. That, however, only took care of part of Newman's goal. The other was to give Catholics inundated with distortions of the history of the early Church a more realistic and accurate picture of the times. It was for that reason that Newman may have called this novel a "sketch" instead of a "tale" or a "story."

Newman stressed over and over the fact that he wrote the novel for Catholics. The first edition in 1855 was announced as being a novel "from the Catholic point of view." In 1888 he made his point much stronger, declaring that *Callista* was "specially addressed to Catholic readers, and for their edification."

Of what did this "edification" consist? Newman being who he was, he seems to have tried to supply the Catholics of his day with counter-arguments to the attacks that had been made against them since the Reformation. Both of the major arguments are still with us today, and the answers in *Callista* are equally valid — and not just for Catholics.

The first is familiar to many American Catholics, as it has been to English Catholics for centuries. That is, no one can be a good Catholic and a good citizen. This is, in substance, the same accusation made for centuries against the Jews, and in our day increasingly against Muslims and even Christian Evangelicals. There are even some Catholics who, apparently without a hint of irony, continue to assert that Jews, because they are Jews, cannot be good citizens, understand the natural law, or a host of other claims that don't really make sense. With respect to Catholics, however (Newman's particular concern) it remains a mystery how this claim can be made with a straight face in view of the centuries of good citizenship seen on the part of the inhabitants of the "Catholic" nations of the world, as well as the countless Catholic lives that have been sacrificed in defense of non-Catholic states.

The second should be even more puzzling to any religious believer, regardless of his or her particular faith. That is, all that "ritual" and "dogma" isn't necessary. All you need to do is just be a good fellow, don't lie, cheat, or steal (too much). Behaving like a gentleman or a lady is much more important than any specific religious belief . . . which only makes for unpleasantness anyway. Don't rock the boat. Go along to get along. Those espousing such "indifferentism" seem oblivious to the fact that when religious belief is shunted aside or put into its own special box and trotted out for an hour on Friday, Saturday, or Sunday, the moral codes based on those beliefs — and all moral codes are, ultimately, based on some form of religious belief — very soon find their way into mothballs as well.

With all this, someone who has never read *Callista* would end up thinking that it must be a very dull book indeed. After all, who wants to read a thinly disguised lecture on the fine points of Anglican v. Catholic theology? (Well . . . every reader of Newman's earlier novel, *Loss and Gain*, 1848, one of the most barbed, insightful — and amusing — examinations of the Anglican claims ever written, that's who.)

The impression that *Callista* is simply a Catholic version of a Bulwer-Lytton potboiler has probably prevented more people from reading it than any other cause. Yes, there are Catholic romances in that vein, at least one of which, Henryk Sienkiewicz's magnificent and panoramic *Quo Vadis?* is justifiably considered a classic, and a thrilling story — and it doesn't avoid all that unpleasant stuff like death and martyrdom. A good translation of *Quo Vadis?* — the one by Jeremiah Curtain, the Irish folklorist, was personally approved by Sienkiewicz — is well worth the effort to locate, and is almost guaranteed to be read more than once.

So what has prevented *Callista* from also being enjoyed to this degree? For one thing, the cover art of at least one popular paperback edition probably hasn't helped matters any. Coincidentally, it dates from the same period as the Hollywood Biblical Epic phase. The cover depicts a "typical" early Christian maiden in a typical "stained glass" pose with an appropriately "holy" expression on her face. I showed a friend of mine a copy of that particular edition, whereupon she exclaimed that her father had had that same edition, and had always urged her to read it.

"And did you?"

"No. It looked too boring."

This is unjust. *Callista* does not follow the established pattern of an "early Christian romance." It blazes a new trail, one that few writers have dared to follow. There is, of course, a happy ending . . . but it is not "happy" in the sense that many of today's readers would understand or appreciate without first grasping the basic idea that underpins every sentence of the novel: that Jesus is God and rose from the dead. Nothing that happens in the book makes sense unless we realize that all the characters are either acting in accordance with that belief, or in opposition to it.

Then there's the fact that Newman's most famous book, his *Apologia Pro Vita Sua*, is a spiritual autobiography . . . whatever *that* might be, a typical novel-reader might ask. His *The Idea of a University*? A treatise on higher education. Bor—ing. And here's a winner: *Tract 90: Remarks on Certain Passages in the Thirty-Nine Articles.* Ouch. *Essay on the Development of Christian Doctrine?* Yow. Why don't you just shoot me? *The Dream of Gerontius?* That's, like, poetry, isn't it? Read that stuff in high school. Didn't like it. *Grammar of Assent?* Sounds like an English textbook. Yawn.

When classics of literature can be dismissed so easily, we obviously have one more charge to level at the academic establishment. Someone isn't doing his job if the great works of western civilization are known only to be avoided. Yet all of these works, and more besides are not only intelligently and thoughtfully written, they are also entertaining, all the more so for the two novels Newman wrote that were explicitly intended as entertainment. As the Reverend John A. Hardon, S.J. said in his *Catholic Lifetime Reading Plan,* "The more than forty volumes of Newman's published works contain many sermons, several religious novels, and hundreds of letters. They are all superbly written. His motto as cardinal, Heart Speaks to Heart, was taken from St. Francis de Sales and reveals the secret of his genius as a man whose soul was always in tune with the Spirit of God."

Ultimately, *Callista* is a novel written by a Catholic for Catholics — although Newman being Newman, he couldn't help but turn out a work of literature that appeals to audiences far removed from the questions he examined and the belief system he explained. It can — and should — be read as a well-written and exciting story, certainly much better than a great deal that is churned out today. It also has the advantage of reinforcing an essentially sound orientation to life, a benefit to anyone, regardless of his religious belief or affiliation. There is no reason to cheat yourself out of a good story simply because you may disagree with the religious beliefs of the author or have a prejudice against anything written before you were born. Read it anyway; besides which, you may find that you don't disagree quite as much as you thought you did. You might even learn something, and you will certainly be entertained.

III. The Fiction of Robert Hugh Benson

1. The Short Stories

The Light Invisible (1903)

A Mirror of Shalott (1907)

The Light Invisible

The Light Invisible always seemed to me a beautiful book. It was in 1902 that Hugh began to write it, at Mirfield. He says that a book of stories of my own, *The Hill of Trouble*, put the idea into his head — but his stories have no resemblance to mine. Mine were archaic little romances, written in a style which a not unfriendly reviewer called "painfully kind," an epigram which always gave Hugh extreme amusement. His were modern, semi-mystical tales; . . . . it was the first book in which he spread his wings, and there is, I think, a fresh and ingenuous beauty about it, as of a delighted adventure among new faculties and powers.[23]

For some reason, Robert Hugh Benson didn't share the generally favorable opinion of his first and, according to some authorities, one of his best works: the themed short story collection, *The Light Invisible*. As his brother Arthur related,

. . . he says that he personally came to dislike the book intensely from the spiritual point of view, as being feverish and sentimental, and designed unconsciously to quicken his own spiritual temperature. He adds that he thought the book mischievous, as laying stress on mystical intuition rather than Divine authority, and because it substituted the imagination for the soul. That is a dogmatic objection rather than a literary objection; and I suppose he really disliked it because it reminded him later of a time when he was moving among shadows.[24]

---

[23] A. C. Benson, *Hugh: Memoirs of a Brother*. New York: Longmans, Green and Co., 1916, 177-178.
[24] *Ibid*.

Martindale quoted a letter that Benson wrote, and then comments at some length on his own theory as to why Benson took *The Light Invisible* so much in aversion.

> I dislike, quite intensely, *The Light Invisible*, from the spiritual point of view. I wrote it in moods of great feverishness, and in what I now recognize as a very subtle state of sentimentality; I was striving to reassure myself of the truths of religion, and assume, therefore, a positive and assertive tone that was largely insincere.[25]

According to Martindale, the above passage concludes "by professing an entire disbelief that anyone *could* really like the book, and had to be given a list of confessedly 'right people' who *did*."[26] (Emphasis in the original.) Martindale conceived the idea that Benson was "worried" that what became almost his most popular book during his life had more success among Anglicans than Catholics.

A better guess might be that Benson may have felt that he put just a little bit too much of his own self-doubt and personal struggle into the structure (as opposed to the theme) of the book. This seemed to be on his mind from the very beginning, as a matter of fact. As Martindale related,

> Slightly nervous as to how his book's religious color might affect the reputation or the feelings of the Mirfield Community, he wrote a complete volume of his own 'under an ingenious pseudonym that I do not believe anyone will guess.' He signed himself simply *Robert Benson*, reviving the unused *R* and dropping *Hugh*. He even on one occasion allowed it to be surmised that Mr. A. C. Benson had written the stories.[27]

This worry about self-revelation and, indeed, that of vocation consumed Benson. The question of vocation, Evelyn Waugh remarked in his "Introduction" to *Richard Raynal*,

---

[25] C. C. Martindale, S.J., *The Life of Monsignor Robert Hugh Benson, Vol. I*. London: Longmans, Green and Co., 1916, 178.
[26] *Ibid.*
[27] *Ibid.*, 170-178.

was a theme that pervaded all of Benson's fiction and quite a bit of his non-fiction as well. It was certainly a lifelong struggle, as Martindale noted in his biography of Benson.

Generally this struggle over Benson's particular calling (the meaning of "vocation") was projected onto his fictional characters. Possibly, however, Benson felt that in *The Light Invisible* he did not put enough of a screen between himself and his readers. The result, especially to someone as sensitive as Benson proved to be, could have been an extremely uncomfortable degree of self-revelation. Paradoxically, this self-revelation might account for the book's popularity.

In reference to Martindale's apparent misinterpretation of Benson on this point, that is, advancing the theory that his dislike of *The Light Invisible* was due to its popularity among Anglicans, this may not be a tenable position. Benson, while convinced that the fullness of truth could be found in the Catholic Church alone, never denied that other Christian — even non-Christian — churches and religions had at least some measure of the truth. Many of his most sympathetic characters (and some of the best drawn) are not Catholic. For the rest of his life he expressed the greatest respect for the Church of England, into which he had been born and in which he was raised.

So how are we to assess *The Light Invisible*? Is it worth reading, or should we respect the author's apparent wishes and disregard it? Aside from the fact that Benson never repudiated the work and seems to have kept his seemingly adverse opinion of it within a very small circle, its continuing popularity should speak for itself. After all, at least two of Benson's contemporaries, one each from the Anglican and the Catholic communions, seemed to agree that the book is well worth the minimal effort required to pick it up. We also, however, have some modern evidence of its worthiness, and from a very good source.

Father John A. Hardon, S.J., "specially recommends" *The Light Invisible* in his book, *The Catholic Lifetime Reading Plan*.[28] The *Reading Plan* is a list of one hundred

---

[28] New York: Doubleday, 1989, 133.

authors and their most important works designed to serve as a guide for Catholics seeking to enrich their cultural and spiritual lives. Hardon gives primacy of place to *The Light Invisible* among the books by Benson he recommends.

The collection is long enough to enjoy as a full meal in itself, yet short enough to whet the appetite for more — and there was a great deal more to come. Benson's conversion seems to have provided the inspiration for a series of rapidly written yet hard-hitting novels that, nonetheless, never fail to entertain. There were to be, ultimately, eighteen novels, two short story collections, four plays and a volume of poetry — to say nothing of his significant output of non-fiction — and all this in the space of barely ten years.

This works out to approximately three major books per year. This is in addition to lecture tours, preaching, missions, a large correspondence (handwritten), and attempting to organize a religious community. However anyone looks at it, this is an impressive record for someone who seems to have been constantly worried whether he was doing what God wanted of him.

Had he not died at a relatively young age, Benson would doubtless have continued to struggle with the problem of vocation. Despite the fact that he excelled at writing fiction, he, like his contemporary Sir Arthur Conan Doyle, had a low opinion of his work that had the most popular effect. Martindale related an amusing, yet revealing anecdote.

> "Why don't you take more trouble over your novels?" a friend once asked him. "If a thing's worth doing at all, it's worth doing well."
>
> "I totally disagree," he energetically exclaimed. "There are lots of things which are worth doing, but aren't in the least worth doing *well*."[29]

That remark is a striking revelation of Benson's lifelong internal conflict over the problem of vocation. He seemed at times to be the quintessential amateur. With the sole

---

[29] Martindale, Vol. I., 386.

exception of his priesthood, he never seemed to take things as seriously as other people thought he should. Part of this, of course, is the still-lingering attitude that clergy aren't supposed to do anything except pose in stained-glass attitudes for the benefit that their good example gives to others — an attitude that Benson continually lambasted. Some of his clergymen characters seem to work very hard to make themselves caricatures by constantly posing and pontificating. They only succeed in sounding pompous — though never sanctimonious or hypocritical, even the Protestants among them. Benson avoided the trap that many Catholic writers fall into, of assuming that Protestant clergy are as hypocritical as their fictional Catholic counterparts are presumed to be by some Protestant authors.

Benson was, in spite of his opinion that some things were not worth doing well — or, perhaps, because of it — a fairly good artist, an excellent organizer and administrator, a gifted orator and, of course, a superb writer, possibly even a great one. Treating only one thing as worth serious consideration, his vocation, he was able to achieve a high degree of natural unaffectedness in everything else — at the cost of a lifelong struggle to understand the only thing that truly mattered to him: his priesthood.

The Light Invisible is thus valuable not only because it is an excellent work of literature. It displays to a marked degree the most significant aspect of the author's life — determining in exact specifics precisely what life is supposed to be about.

A Mirror of Shalott

Critics who don't like a certain type of story should never comment on them. If the critic tries to be fair, he will distort the picture in an effort to "give the Devil his due." If he follows his natural inclination, he will end by castigating the story more for its virtues than for its faults.

A case in point is Robert Hugh Benson's collection of macabre short stories, *A Mirror of Shalott*. The book seems to have suffered more from his admirers than from his harshest critics. While the book contains some of the most chilling horror stories ever written, Benson's readership did not, by and large, care for that sort of thing. The stories were considered "out of character," especially for an author in Holy Orders.

Consequently, the collection slipped into semi-oblivion, albeit achieving a certain "cult status" among horror story *cognoscenti*. Among others, while the existence of a collection was "rumored," it was considered virtually apocryphal, rooted in the occasional reprint of the magazine version of "Father Girdlestone's Tale" that appeared in various anthologies over the decades. It's existence is, however, fully confirmed, and is available.

There is, however, still one mystery connected with *A Mirror of Shalott*. It's not quite clear who had the original idea, but at one point Benson, his sister Margaret and a friend were planning on collaborating on a collection of horror stories. As Martindale related, "The idea of the whole book was, to picture forth 'the world within the world,' or, if you will, 'the soul within the world.'" Martindale continued,

> Collaboration between Hugh Benson and anyone else was, I believe, an impossibility [why? — ed.], and the plan fell through. The ideal survived, however. In ghost stories, he argued, the "real thing" expresses itself as far as possible in a certain medium. They are the translation of the supernatural into the natural, and therefore only analogical to any true statement, even, of fact. Spiritual events undoubtedly

(any Christian will admit) occur; *how* they occur, not we with our brains dependent upon matter for their imagery can define; whether individual portents have occurred — well, you must decide for yourself upon the evidence.

Due to various objections by publishers to whom the project was submitted (one wanted all the stories rewritten to reflect an "Egyptian" setting), "the plan," as Martindale said, "fell through." It was to include "Mr. Percival's Tale," "My Own Tale" ("Mr. Benson's' very weird story"), and something called "The Music of the Other World. Nuremberg." of which Martindale declared, "I can find no trace and no explanation."

There thus exists the possibility of a "long lost" and hitherto unknown short story by Robert Hugh Benson someday surfacing. It is entirely within the realm of possibility that this hint given so briefly by Martindale might spur a "treasure hunt" by Benson's admirers, resulting, if nothing else, in a renewed interest in this long- and unfairly neglected author.

What, however, are we to think of *A Mirror of Shalott* as it now stands? On the surface, it appears at first glance to be the typical "themed" collection so popular at one time, and probably originally inspired by *The Canterbury Tales*. A group of persons, more or less diverse, are gathered together, usually for some reason unrelated to the eventual topic of the collection. To pass the time, they agree to tell stories, a common theme being an absolute requirement in these productions.

In the case of *A Mirror of Shalott*, the group consists of Catholic clerics, gathered in Rome at a thinly disguised Church of San Silvestro (according to Martindale). To pass the time (of course) after dinner each night, they agree to tell stories on successive nights. The chosen topic, due to a discussion they presumably have at the beginning of the collection, is unexplained paranormal experiences each one has had. The reader is put in the position of deciding whether the event really happened. There is really nothing more to say about the book, unless one wants to indulge in the fruitless game of trying to determine the author's "real" motives in writing such creepy fiction, instead of simply enjoying them.

One thing about the stories that struck me is the resemblance, both in setting and the general theme of the stories, to Taylor Caldwell's equally unappreciated themed collection, *Grandmother and the Priests* — well worth reading if you can locate one of the rare copies.

Like his earlier collection (*The Light Invisible*) and unlike virtually all the rest of his fiction, *A Mirror of Shalott* contains virtually no satire — if any at all. All of his known short stories make the point and, instead of moving on, stop there. To some readers, fixated on "explanation," this can be irritating, especially those who like to engage in endless speculation about things that don't really matter. The "point" of these stories is, however, the feeling of horror itself, not an involved explanation of the events that caused the feeling. Some things are better left unsaid.

This apparent attitude on the part of Benson seems to have irritated Martindale, he apparently being of the opinion that a story must have a more obvious point. To modern readers more used to unexplained horrors, however, it should prove exceptionally popular. Who, after all, cares where the ghost miners came from? The point is that they were there, and scared the reader as well as the characters in the story.

In *A Mirror of Shalott* we have a horror classic — minor at this time, perhaps, but a classic nonetheless. It should provide a welcome anodyne to the impersonal horrors of an increasingly alienated world to read some very personal frights.

2. The Early Historical Novels

By What Authority? (1904)

The King's Achievement (1905)

The Queen's Tragedy (1906)

By What Authority?

I can hardly say how much I was delighted with him. His enthusiasm as a Catholic and his humility as a raw convert were equally touching. He then began to consult me on the book he was writing on the Elizabethan persecution. I took him to Oscott, and he was greatly delighted with the treasures preserved there — the old vestments, the chalices, missal, altarstones, &c., of penal days. He poured out the details of the book, as it was shaping itself, and eagerly seized on any points that would be of use to him. In the end it was settled that I should read and correct the proof-sheets and do my best to help him to secure historical accuracy. But before that I used to get (after he left us) sheets of questions, full of historical puzzles, often beyond my wit to answer.[30]

In *By What Authority?* Robert Hugh Benson took great pains to get the historical details of Elizabethan England absolutely accurate. Then, as now in so many fields of scholarship, the temptation was simply to take what "everybody knows" (or which the presumed scholar simply suspects with no proof) and report it as established fact without verification.

By What Authority? was Benson's first novel. It followed hard on the heels of *The Light Invisible*, that attractive and strangely ambiguous, thought-provoking collection of interconnected mystical short stories. It was one of three books Benson wrote before his complete conversion to Catholicism. The others were *The Light Invisible* and *Oddsfish!* The latter is a historical work that was to be in an almost continual state of revision before it finally saw publication in 1914, the year of Benson's death.

---

[30] Letter from Dom Bede Camm to Rev. C. C. Martindale, S.J., Robert Hugh Benson's biographer, quoted in Martindale, Vol. I, 266.

Interestingly, Benson re-wrote certain portions of *By What Authority?* to tie characters in the original version of *Oddsfish!* — a "Restoration" adventure featuring Charles II and the disgusting Titus Oates — to their "ancestors" in *By What Authority?* These tie-ins became a characteristic of Benson's historical fiction, none of which fails to add something to an immense (if extremely loose) saga, even if only marginally.

Benson's research paid off. *By What Authority?* contains very few historical errors, and none that should really concern even the most particular reader. Does it really matter that Benson has scotch fir trees lining the roads in England a generation before they were believed to have been planted? Or that he has the Brighton Road in existence some time before it was built? Of greater moment is the fact that the hero's eyes change color from blue to brown when he is described during an audience with Queen Elizabeth I. Even that could probably be explained away, in much the same fashion as Baker Street Irregulars reconciling mistakes in "the canon."

These are, of course, trivial matters. Benson achieved something in this novel that approaches the remarkable. In his day, any novel about Elizabethan England, when it mentioned the Catholic Church at all, simply used stereotypes that would have shamed a Dime Novel hack writer. A Jesuit was inevitably the villain, lacking only a tall silk hat and a demand that the rent must be paid to complete the picture of a stock blackguard. The Catholic Church was (of course) intent upon the Conquest of England, usually foiled by Quick Action on the part of True Englishmen (and Women), maintaining themselves with a Stiff Upper Lip.

Benson set out to counter this practice with a different picture of the times, presenting matters from a Catholic point of view. This approach was genuinely revolutionary. Benson, especially given his mild notoriety as a recent convert at the time of publication, could reasonably have expected the book to fail. Instead, it became a best seller — and not just with Catholics. Ironically, Benson was afraid that Catholics wouldn't even care for the book!

The novel's popularity was helped not a little by his insistence on historical accuracy. He captured the flavor of the times with much more fidelity than other writers, who, throwing in a few references to doublets and hose and larding the dialogue with strings of "thees" and "thous" (often used incorrectly) succeeded only in projecting contemporary attitudes onto a former age. Reading the typical historical novel at the turn of the last century sometimes might make a thoughtful reader wonder why, instead of riding in those uncomfortable carriages (which always "wait without" — without *what* is another question), they don't simply take the train or motor down.

Benson *studied* the times, and then verified his studies with independent consultants, such as Dom Bede Camm, noted above. His dialogue has the flavor of the times, even to the sometimes-irritating-to-the-reader use of absolutely accurate terms long fallen into disuse.

By What Authority? was originally titled *Magnus Valde* or "Extremely Great." Might this apply to the novel as an outstanding work of fiction — or simply its length? the quote is from the Gospel reading for Easter Sunday. The work is a vast and sprawling novel suggestive of today's fictional family sagas. Weighing in at nearly a quarter of a million words, some critics (a very few) complained that certain long passages contributed nothing to the plot. They failed to realize, of course, that Benson's plot was not the story line, but "England" —

> . . . the gallant spectacle of England, England awakening, England adolescent, stretching her muscles, flinging wide her independent enterprise, creates a complementary vision — the National Church, august in wealth and dignity and royal favour, England seen as spiritual, "the religious voice of the nation that was beginning to make itself so dominant in the council of the world." In fine rhetoric, only too modern, Anthony will preach that Nationalism to his Catholic friend Buxton. Meanwhile he sees it the closer, and its mechanism, as Gentleman of the Horse at Lambeth, in the Archbishop's household, a post received after a wasted year or two following upon Cambridge. But there, disillusioned gradually

by the underside of all the State religion, the sight of the sordid machinery, the Court intrigue, the cynic sacrifice not of men's lives alone, but of truth and honour and the spirit for the better establishment of the Throne, he realises that England, having hacked herself free from the Continent, has severed too the bands which linked her with the supernatural. The Authority of Elizabeth, the ideal of England, confront those of Christ.[31]

The passages that, from a "purely literary point of view" could have been omitted, e.g., relating to Mary Queen of Scots or the martyrdom of Edmund Campion, are absolutely essential to presenting the picture of England. The "sceptered isle" was seemingly eternally poised between two worlds, the ultra material and the fantastic. England in Elizabethan times was a true forerunner of the modern Nation-State. It deluded itself with pastoral fantasies (until it met with the crudities of pastoral reality in Ireland) as much as the modern age deceives itself with mass entertainment.

The typical Elizabethan production (whether play, poetry or political policy) presented a picture of completely unreal reality — all the while relying on a crass materialism and cynical *realpolitik* to maintain the *status quo*. The secret police were not a nineteenth century invention. The plays of Shakespeare should puzzle today's academics and media moguls far more than they do. They were astonishingly successful and presented an unequaled picture of human nature in all its complexity in an age that practiced willing self-deception and deceit — an age, as Charles Dickens said in another context, so like our own as to be virtually indistinguishable.

Thus, people still worship the State, and still delude themselves with fantasy. Neither results in a true picture of the real state of affairs. Of course, neither does a historical novel, even one as well written and exciting as *By What Authority?* The difference, of course, is that Benson was not trying to relate straight history, but to counter a prejudice and present an accurate "feeling" for the time.

---

[31] *Ibid.*, 354.

In this he succeeded — brilliantly. Not only is the novel exceptionally entertaining, it creates a lasting impression about a different Elizabethan England, one much more realistic and accurate than that depicted in many textbooks.

Benson's biographer favorably compared the "conversion" passages in *By What Authority?* to the presumably "more serious" sections in John Henry Newman's 1848 under-appreciated masterpiece, *Loss and Gain*. Benson's novel has much more action and has the advantage of the "historical veil" to allow an uncomfortable reader to distance himself from the individual conflicts in the story, but the effect on the reader is the same.

What any serious reader cannot distance himself from, however, is the growing realization that, for hundreds of years, humanity's social development has not only been retarded, it has in many ways regressed due to reliance on the outdated Nation-State system. Almost as damaging as the equally debilitating reliance on the wage system in the economic realm, worship of the State undermines the sovereignty of the human person under God as mercilessly as the propertyless worker's utter dependence on his employer.

In *By What Authority?* Benson brilliantly depicted the rise and entrenchment of the Nation-State and the replacement of a supernatural Lord and Savior with an earthly Virgin Goddess. The results were only what might have been expected — and to which we have become sadly accustomed.

The King's Achievement

When men have power to commit and are resolved to commit acts of injustice, they are never at a loss for pretences. We shall presently see what were the pretences under which this devastation of England was begun: but to do the work there required a workman, as to slaughter an ox there requires a butcher. To turn the possessors of so large a part of the estates out of those estates, to destroy establishments venerated by the people from their childhood, to set all law, divine as well as human, at defiance, to violate every principle on which property rested, to rob the poor and helpless of the means of sustenance, to deface the beauty of the country and make it literally a heap of ruins; to do those things there required a suitable agent, and that agent the tyrant found in Thomas Cromwell, whose name, along with that of Cranmer, ought "to stand for aye accursed in the calendar."[32]

That was how William Cobbett, a well-known "radical" in the late eighteenth and early nineteenth century, described the changes that took place in England as a result of the Reformation. Cobbett is renowned as the "Apostle of Distributism." Distributism is a vague economic theory formulated by Gilbert Keith Chesterton and Hilaire Belloc based on widespread direct ownership of the means of production, with a preference for small family farms and artisan manufactures.

Distributism "sabotaged" itself by relying on unrealistic and unworkable ideas of money credit, banking and finance — i.e., the fixed belief in the necessity of using existing accumulations of savings to finance new capital formation. That, however, is not relevant to Robert Hugh Benson's *The King's Achievement*, any more than the fact

---

[32] William Cobbett, *A History of the Protestant Reformation in England and Ireland*, 1826, § 157.

that the process of concentrating ownership in the means of production started with Henry VII Tudor after his usurpation of the Crown from the Plantagenets.

What concerned Cobbett — and, of course, Benson — was the near-total overthrow of the substance of "England," as opposed to the outward forms so carefully preserved. This was so successful that Walter Bagehot would base his theories of political economy on how well England had maintained the outward forms of freedom and democracy, all the while becoming an elitist and absolutist State and economy.[33]

The Reformation, so Cobbett claimed, "was engendered in lust, brought forth in hypocrisy and perfidy, and cherished and fed by plunder, devastation, and by rivers of innocent English and Irish blood."[34] The story was, in truth, sordid from every angle, reflecting little credit on anyone. It comes as no surprise then, that after Benson finished this novel on the dissolution of the monasteries, he wrote in a letter to a friend that,

> The only reason why I am entirely ill at ease about *The King's Achievement* is that it doesn't represent really any part of my being. Not one of the characters is my intimate friend.

Benson apparently communicated this feeling to others, many of whom hastened to reassure him of the book's value. Benson's sister, Margaret, wrote to her brother on her second reading of the novel. After a long critique, she concluded,

> I do think it is a much better book than I had remembered. It's beautifully written, a pleasure to read, and either you have improved it very much in concentration or it was not so invertebrate as I thought. Still, it's not so engaging as the others, though Beatrice is really very fine indeed, and really I do give you credit for understanding the way in which women can be friends. So few people do under-

---

[33] *Vide* Walter Bagehot's *The English Constitution* (1867) and *Lombard Street* (1873).
[34] Cobbett, *op. cit.*, § 450.

stand, and I can't remember any man, a novelist, who does. Beth [Benson's old nurse] wished me to say that she thought some of the people were very unkind and crewel; but sometimes they were very kind and loving, and altogether it ended better than she expected; but she does wish you'd write a book about people who were less disagreeable with one another.

Benson's penchant for honesty had apparently gotten him into trouble with his own relations. His old nurse kept after his sister, who had helped her brother with the research for the book, demanding to know "why were they all so — disagreeable?" The only possible answer is that it was a very "disagreeable" time. Families were turned against one another, and the country was split asunder into that contradictory character so well chronicled in C. S. Lewis' novel, *That Hideous Strength.*

Originally titled *The King's Conscience*, the novel relates the story of the dissolution of the monasteries in response to the king's desperate quest for money to cover his colossal extravagances. In typical Benson fashion, however, the figure whom lesser writers would have put center stage — Henry VIII Tudor — while achieving the status of "monster" (Martindale's description), scarcely appears at all in the book. The principal role is taken by and the whole atmosphere of the book is charged with the character and personality of Thomas Cromwell.

The rest of the cast familiar to us from Robert Bolt's play *A Man for All Seasons* also makes its appearance. Sts. Thomas More and John Fisher of Rochester flit through, but seem more symbols of rectitude than actual human beings. This was a treatment rare for Benson, who was unusually gifted at delineating very human characters.

Henryk Sienkiewicz seems to have had a similar problem dealing with Sts. Peter and Paul in *Quo Vadis*. He was apparently unable to see the two great proto-saints as anything other than patterns of perfection. This is a picture we most certainly do not get from the Bible.

In *The King's Achievement*, Anne Boleyn, herself something of a symbol in Bolt's play, does become more real than she usually appears in works of fiction or history. It is, however, Cromwell who sets the tone, who seems to lurk around every corner and behind every page in the story, achieving a level of reality far above that of anyone else in the book.

Cromwell's presence so pervades everything that when a group of schoolboys undertook to write to "famous authors" as a class project, it was not the tragedy of the dissolution of the monasteries or the pauperization of the great mass of the people that affected them most. Instead, it was the death scene of Ralph Torridon.

> Rev. Sir, — One improvement might be made with regard to the closing sentence of *The King's Achievement*. You say the dying words of Ralph Torridon were: "My Lord." Well, those words are a trifle ambiguous. I presume they refer to Cromwell, and that they mean Ralph, even at his death, was more faithful to Cromwell than to God. Otherwise you would have "My God." But couldn't you alter them a little, and make the meaning plainer? — T. M.

Apparently schoolboys haven't changed much in the past century. Seriously, the young man did highlight what turned out to be possibly the book's greatest weakness — the "hero" was supposed to be the monasteries themselves, but it's a little hard to connect something not human and so distant in time to the reader. In *By What Authority?* in which the "hero" was England, it was much easier, for England was still there, and still England, for all its flaws. The monasteries were, however, to all appearances, gone forever as a significant aspect of English life.

Consequently Cromwell literally haunts the book — to such an extent that Benson realized it himself, an outstanding achievement in humility for any author, who, as a group, are convinced they know their own books better than anyone else. As he responded to the criticism,

> Mr. T. M. has hit upon the very point that was in my own mind as I wrote the last words of *The King's Achievement*. He says they are ambiguous; I intended that they should be. Dying persons who have lived

more than doubtful lives generally are ambiguous. I also intended to suggest that in accordance with Miss Beatrice Atherton's words, on a few pages before, it was possible, considering all things, that loyalty to even such a villain as Cromwell might be a virtue rather than a defect. It is sometimes better to be faithful to a villain, in an indifferent matter, than to be faithful to nobody.

Finally, if I am asked whether I meant the words "My Lord" to refer to Cromwell or to Almighty God, I can only answer that I am as doubtful as Mr. M. R. [another student who wrote]. I wish, however, it was untrue to life to make an evil liver die evilly — though I don't say that Ralph did.

As a side note, Benson apparently couldn't resist giving the young men's adolescent pretentiousness a little jab. His P.S. stated, "I trust all the other authors to whom you have written will answer also." They were Scott, Dickens, and Coleridge — all long dead by 1905.

Ultimately, in *The King's Achievement,* it appears that Benson wrought better than he knew. There was, however, evidently a growing dissatisfaction on his part with historical novels. This seems to have been strengthened by his next project, *The Queen's Tragedy* — a very difficult book to write. This would have been confirmed by the increasingly frustrating rewrites through which he suffered on the novel that was to become *Oddsfish!*

Benson seems to have become disenchanted with the historical genre for a time, only returning after a respite to write what became his personal favorite of all his novels, *Richard Raynal, Solitary,* a work entirely removed from the horrors of the Reformation. He concentrated on science fiction and, especially, his incisive satires of English middle and upper class life. He finally returned to what he considered his particular literary vocation in 1912 with the magnificent *Come Rack! Come Rope!,* soon after which he found the inspiration to complete, at long last, the rewriting of *Oddsfish!,* covering the reign of Charles II Stuart, the "Merry Monarch" and the hideous Titus Oates conspiracy.

The Queen's Tragedy

Now I want to begin on Queen Mary. A great many reviews have taunted me with having avoided that side, and I want much to show that a case can be made. Mary is one of the most pathetic figures in history, I think — snubbed, misunderstood, soured by trouble, with a conscience and convictions such as few have.

* * * * *

I am on the verge of the Mary Book, exactly as on the edge of a pond on a cold day — dawdling over trifles, and meaning to plunge, and then thinking I must do something else first — it is an appalling undertaking.

Martindale, writing in 1916, reported that *The Queen's Tragedy* was a difficult book to like. It would have been more accurate to say that the subject matter — Mary Tudor, one of the most unpopular rulers England has known to date — is something for which few people want to have or admit any feeling at all. Rather than epitomizing great virtue or great evil (both of which exercise a certain fascination for us), Mary at her best merely succeeds in being, as Benson noted, pathetic.

Consequently the reader is almost physically prevented from identifying with the main subject of the novel. Had Mary been susceptible to gross flattery and adulated as England's Great Virgin Queen, Oriana, the Glory of the Western World, *etc.*, *etc.* (and thereby easily manipulated as was her half-sister Elizabeth), it would have been simple, regardless of the reality of the situation. All Benson would have had to do is repeat the lies of the past. Had Mary managed to acquire a reputation for magnificently great evil, it would have been easier still. Books about Hitler and the Third Reich outsell books about Mother Teresa of Calcutta by a substantial margin.

But no, Benson was handicapped from the very beginning, regardless of his desire to do Mary Tudor even a modicum of justice. She was an ordinary woman of ordinary abilities and talents, trapped in a situation that had already destroyed a number of men and women of heroic virtue, and would be the ruin of many more.

Benson could have taken the same route as a growing number of modern authors. Novels about Mary Tudor ranging from historical trilogies to romance have proliferated. There are even a couple of science fiction tomes. The one about cyborgs in "evil Mary's court" seems particularly far-fetched. Mary's personality in these productions is always exaggerated, for good or ill. Altering a few facts here and there would have resulted in an extremely compassionate and misunderstood heroine — but that was not Benson's way. He had to tell the truth as he saw it, and that meant depicting a very unsympathetic central character. A whitewash was not in order.

That Benson foresaw a difficult job of it is indicated by his reluctance to begin where more usually his problem was trying to work too fast on too many projects. He tried to delay matters by finding other things to do, probably unconsciously. He even dragged out the novel that, after being eternally rewritten, was finally to see print as *Oddsfish!* —

> I am dingily rewriting an old book. What weary work that is! . . . This is the fourth time of rewriting . . . . Also I am doing about eleven thousand other things simultaneously . . . . When I write for the first time my characters do their own business and say their own words entirely. Then I have to select them in rewriting, and have an eye on the readers, and it is just exactly this that I HATE.

It apparently didn't occur to Benson that part of his difficulty might have been that he was finding other things to do precisely to avoid doing that which he thought he ought to be doing. "Multi-tasking" had never bothered him before — or would afterwards. Nevertheless, he managed finally to get down to work.

I have begun "Mary" with dreadful fear. If only I can do it right, it will be by far the best thing I have done; but it is difficult beyond belief. I am telling half from my hero's point of view, and half from Mary's — mixing them up. My man's is easy enough; but the Queen's is fearful! I have to know every conceivable detail.

What resulted was a very modern method of story telling, one familiar to readers through F. Scott Fitzgerald's *The Great Gatsby*, considered revolutionary in its time — and imitated so often as to seem very ordinary today. *The Queen's Tragedy* is broken up in an almost "anti-chronological" order, continuity being almost non-existent. As Martindale remarked, "The book is therefore to be a psychological study rather than a romance with an ordered plot, and will involve, in the main, the Queen herself, and Master Guy Manton, a gentleman of her court."

In an ironic twist, this method of construction should resonate well with modern readers, where it acted to alienate Benson's Edwardian audience. As Martindale related,

At a first reading, Benson, who could do, no doubt, without plots, does seem to have, as it were, just chucked down his psychological impressions in slabs, sandwiched between page after page of pageantry. The pageantry of the book is, one may confess, superb.

In *The Queen's Tragedy* we discover, then, a "long lost" gem that, had it achieved a greater popularity during Benson's life, might well have accelerated the trend initiated by *Gatsby* in the succeeding generation. Most readers of historical fiction, however, then as well as now, are more interested in the subject matter than in the artistry with which the story is constructed. (It's another little ironic twist that *Gatsby*, the quintessential "modern novel," is viewed by an increasing number of students as a historical novel, surviving largely as "required reading" in high school and college literature courses.)

It is thus with the subject matter that most readers will have their greatest difficulties. Mary Tudor was a mass of contradictions and, however much people today contradict themselves, they tend to reject it in others. As Benson has his hero describe her,

> She is pious; she is zealous; she has a will of her own; she is cold; she is hot; she is miserly; she is liberal; she has a sad soul and a merry dress; she is silent; she can speak like an orator, for I heard her at the Guildhall in February, and she set my heart afire; then she put it out again next day by her coldness.

No — not an easy task at all. As Martindale stated,

> Could Hugh Benson "make a woman out of that"? Well, somehow, he succeeded, I believe, despite the very many Catholic critics who felt, no doubt, that the Catholic Queen ought to have been pictured as more attractive. And to begin with, observe this artist's honesty. If, indeed, the portraits of the crimson-faced and swollen Henry, and the haggard wanton, his daughter Elizabeth, were propagandist caricatures (and in *The Queen's Tragedy*, Elizabeth in her radiant, seductive youth is no less repulsive) why could not Benson have made Queen Mary charming? Quite simply he refused to tamper with what he thought the truth — he gave full rein to that rather terrible realism which side by side with his mystical sense and creative imagination was so fast developing in him. Mary in this book is tragically impotent to charm, and half the time shocks, offends, and alienates her court, her country, and, as I said, so many moderns who were fain to love her.

> Frankly, the title gives the book its key. The whole motive is failure within; from without, defeat. Mary dies quite sure that her husband scorns her, having left no heir, foreseeing Elizabeth's accession, and the collapse of her one hope, the restoration in England of Catholicism. No death of her own body could compare with the spiritual ruin of one soul, even; and she foresaw that of an entire nation, and she felt that had *she* been other, all still might have been well. She had acted always for the best, and her action had brought ruin. There was her tragedy.

Nevertheless, Benson could never write a completely depressing book, not even the appalling *Lord of the World*. As he described Mary's death —

"*Jesu! Jesu!*" she whispered, "esto mihi *Jesu*! I have failed, dear Jesus, but Thou hast not."

3. The History of Richard Raynal, Solitary (1906)

Saying anything about a book that is not only a favorite of many readers, but is the favorite work of the author who composed it is never easy. This is rendered even more difficult when the critic believes that other books are both more representative of the author's work, and of more universal appeal.

Such is the case with Robert Hugh Benson's *The History of Richard Raynal, Solitary*. The book is quite good, even "gem quality" in the opinion of many people. The "problem" is that "it's not Benson," being extremely atypical of anything else Benson turned out. This is probably why, although this appreciation appears early in the more or less chronologically arranged essays in this book, it was written last. It just seemed more difficult to do the work justice.

It may therefore seem paradoxical that, in my opinion, no fan of Benson can afford to miss *Richard Raynal*. Is it (as the author believed) his best work? That is for the reader to decide. That it was Benson's favorite can perhaps tell us more about Benson than some of his other stories. The fact that it is also entertaining is a bonus.

Richard Raynal is a startling book, both to its readers and to its author. Using a common fictional device — the discovery of a "long lost" manuscript instead of claiming direct authorship in the text (only on the title page) — Benson seems almost to be engaging in a bit of wish-fulfillment. Unlike his other works, there is no great national conflict or personal crisis on which the plot hinges.

The issue of vocation is there, of course, as it is in all of Benson's fiction. There is, however, a difference. It is not seen in the purposelessness of people, like Benson characterized the English upper classes, the members of which drift aimlessly through life apparently not realizing that they have removed the critical issue of vocation from their lives. Neither is it manifested, as I hinted, by individuals or groups — even nations — undergoing a testing in order to bring them to a realization of their vocations and their true selves. Rather, it is a story of someone who, having found his vocation, has now determined to act on what he believes to be God's Will in a manner consistent with God's Intellect or Nature.

There is always, of course, a great deal of danger — to one's self, to others, and to the common good as a whole in such a course of action. More harm has been done in the world than most people can imagine by individuals and groups that have decided they are recipients of a direct message from God and who have an adamantine conviction of their own rectitude.

Very few people (if any) set off on a course of destruction and hate by proclaiming, "Today I will be as evil as I can possibly be." Rather, somebody decides that God has delivered to him or her the truth in a special manner. God has therefore vested the recipient of this revelation (that often exists only in the mind of the self-proclaimed prophet) with the authority to do whatever is necessary to bring matters to a conclusion that someone has decided is desirable or mandatory.

Nor does the truth have to be from God, *per se*, but from any number of false gods that people worship, beginning with their own egos. At the time Benson wrote *Richard Raynal*, 1905-1906, he had just been ordained as a priest into a church beset on every side not so much by external enemies, but by the philosophy of "Modernism." Modernism is a development of the Manichaean controversy that precipitated an intellectual war in the twelfth century between Intellect and Will as the basis of the natural moral law.

Modernism is still with us, and stronger than ever. Nor is the Catholic Church the only institution afflicted with the curse. Described by St. Pius X as "the synthesis of all heresies" and by subsequent pontiffs as "the plague of relativism," Modernism is one of the most insidious and slipperiest sets of errors to try and counter. This is because, unlike most heresies throughout history, both religious and secular, it does not consist of a specific set of beliefs with which one can argue. Instead, Modernism —

cially in its secular manifestation, positivism — redefines truth itself; it is an approach to truth, not a statement or application of something on which humanity has reached a consensus as to its truthfulness.

Getting into a debate or arguing with a Modernist is an almost terminally frustrating task. Words, even thoughts and truth do not have the same meanings to both parties in the debate — nor can they. Changing definitions is the Modernist's stock in trade, with the paradox being that many people who have succumbed to Modernism don't even realize they have done so.

When such a person can even be brought to the table, the most anyone can get out of him or her is either a string of reiterated private interpretations, or a condescending, "Well, that may be how *you* define X, but *I* define X as thus-and-so." Not surprisingly, such redefinitions are usually where they will do the most harm, such as humanity's inalienable and natural rights to life, liberty (freedom of association), the acquisition and development of virtue (the "pursuit of happiness"), and, most especially, private property. A Modernist, firmly believing that retaining outward forms is the same as retaining a thing's substantial nature, will even redefine Modernism if convenient or expedient. As long as the words stay the same, the Modernist believes, the thing itself stays the same, regardless how you define it.

Thus, the Modernist has a strong tendency, verging on necessity, to redefine the exercise of a natural right in terms more acceptable to him or her, and then confuse the redefined exercise of the right with the essence of the right itself. There is no distinction made between a principle, and the application of the principle, a distinction that is at the heart of the Catholic Church's social doctrine, indeed, consistent with its acceptance of the philosophy of St. Thomas Aquinas as its guiding philosophy, the entire body of Catholic teaching.

More often, however, the Modernist is baffled by his or her opponent's insistence on basic principles and definitions — that is, on maintaining a thing's substantial nature or essence. Not understanding or refusing to understand the importance of all parties in a debate speaking the same language, the Modernist has a tendency to stalk off in a huff, or retreat after giving a presumably Parthian shot in the form of a statement to the effect that he or she could easily refute everything you say . . . *but isn't going to*!

Nor is Modernism a new thing. In various forms Modernism has haunted not only the Catholic Church, but civilization itself from the beginning. There are always people who insist that they know better than everyone else how things should be done, and they have God's Word, the people's will, or the revelation of their own "inner light" to prove it. Everything must go down before this new revelation, even if it means the destruction of the whole of the social order.

In the Catholic Church, the conflict came to a head in the twelfth century with the "rediscovery" of Aristotle. Because the texts were sometimes corrupt and passed through the hands of some very unorthodox Islamic philosophers who were recognized as heterodox by their own religious authorities, confusion galloped in regarding the relationship between faith and reason.

The Catholic Church split into warring factions. One party claimed that reason must give way before faith. God Said So, therefore reason must be wrong. No, insisted another group. Reason is paramount, and faith must give way before reason. A third party asserted a bizarre compromise: that faith is wrong in the light of reason, and reason is wrong in the light of faith. As Chesterton described this oddity, propounded by one Siger of Brabant,

> Siger of Brabant said this: the Church must be right theologically, but she can be wrong scientifically. There are two truths; the truth of the supernatural world, and the truth of the natural world, which contradicts the supernatural world. While we are being naturalists, we can suppose that Christianity is true even if it is nonsense. In other words, Siger of Brabant split the human head in two, like the blow in an old legend of battle; and declared that a man has two

minds, with one of which he must entirely believe and with the other may utterly disbelieve.[35]

All of this developed out of misunderstanding the natural moral law, an expression of ultimate truth based on God's Essence (Nature") that is self-evident in His Intellect. Basing the natural law instead on someone's private understanding of something that he or she believes to be God's Will changes everything. Truth itself becomes flexible and subject to change. As Heinrich Rommen explained in his analysis of the natural law and the effect that Modernism had on our understanding of it,

> With Duns Scotus (d. *cir.* 1308), and with the principle of the primacy of the will over the intellect so much emphasized by him, there began inside moral philosophy a train of thought which in later centuries would recur in secularized form in the domain of legal philosophy. The principle that law is will would be referred in legal positivism, as well as in the theory of will in jurisprudence, to the earthly lawmaker (self-obligation).
>
> For Duns Scotus morality depends on the will of God. A thing is good not because it corresponds to the nature of God or, analogically, to the nature of man, but because God so wills. Hence the *lex naturalis* could be other than it is even materially or as to content, because it has no intrinsic connection with God's essence, which is self-conscious in His intellect. For Scotus, therefore, the laws of the second table of the Decalogue were no longer unalterable. The crux of theology, namely, the problem of the apparent dispensations from the natural law mentioned in the Old Testament and thus seemingly granted by God (the command to sacrifice Isaac, Raphael's apparent lie, Osee's alleged adultery, the polygamy of the patriarchs, and so on), was now readily solved. Yet St. Thomas, too, had been able to solve such cases. Now, however, an evolution set in which, in the doctrine of William of Occam (d. *cir.* 1349) on the natural moral

---

[35] Chesterton, *op. cit.*, 92-93.

law, would lead to pure moral positivism, indeed to nihilism.[36]

Modernism thus undermines truth itself by attacking the essence of truth: God.

Not that Benson consciously or unconsciously accepted any of the tenets of Modernism, or (especially) its philosophy of relativism. As a prominent convert and a candidate for ordination to the Catholic priesthood, he would have been examined very closely on an issue that the Church had identified as its greatest danger at the time. St. Pius X, whom Benson greatly admired (to the point of modeling his ideal pope in *Lord of the World* on him[37]) had already gone on the attack against Modernism before Benson converted to Catholicism, and would carry on the effort until his death, passing the torch on to subsequent pontiffs.

Instead, in *Richard Raynal* we find the main character very clearly in tune with the essential natures of both faith and reason. The fictional hermit (unlike real people) has perfectly discerned his vocation and has fitted himself into the real world. This phrase, "the real world," doesn't mean that the character had become *worldly*, but that he had, in effect, returned to the Garden of Eden, to the way man was originally meant to exist in harmony with nature.

Unlike Benson's genuinely historical novels (as opposed to what can only be termed a historical fantasy), the story itself is straightforward. This is a good reason for not linking the story to any particular time and getting bogged down in trying to fit known details of a specific time and place into the plot as Benson was forced to do with his

---

[36] Rommen, *op. cit.*, 51-52.

[37] Benson appears to have considered St. Pius X as the archetype of the "Angelic Pope" described in some "Catholic apocalyptic" literature. He seems to have viewed Benedict XV as a rather ordinary man stepping into some very big shoes. Nevertheless, Benson's respect for the papacy was such that he appears to have modeled his rather "ordinary" pope in *The Dawn of All* on Benedict XV, and then made him heroic as soon as events demanded it — as, ironically, events did as Benedict XV was called on to lead the Church through the virtual Armageddon of the First World War.

historical novels. As Martindale commented, "The story is fragmentary, and portrays the life of a young hermit from the time when the call of God came to him, bidding him visit the King — Henry VI presumably, for Benson affects that his MS. omits all names of places and persons and all dates, a proceeding which certainly saves a deal of trouble."[38]

Thus, while living out the general vocation of humanity — to become more fully human by acquiring and developing virtue — Raynal is inspired to deliver a message to the king. From the very first Benson is careful to distinguish Raynal's inspiration from the absolute certainty that characterized the Modernists: "When I stood up there was a knowledge in my heart — I do not know whether from our Lord or the fiend — that I must leave this place, and go to one whom I thought must be the King with some message; but I do not know the message."

Although a hermit, Raynal has acquired or manufactured a few — a very few — prized possessions, clearly valued for their spiritual significance, not for their market value. Chief among these is a tiny bottle of "Quintessence," significantly distilled from Raynal's own blood, "according to the method of Hermes Trismegistus." Raynal carries this "quintessence" to the king, delivers his message, and (as we might expect) is misunderstood. Raynal undergoes great suffering, but finally gets the king to understand and accept his message.

While carefully not named, Henry VI, one of the most vacillating kings England ever had, would be an appropriate ruler to whom to deliver a message accompanied by the "quintessence" distilled from the blood of a (fictionally) perfect man. There are, of course, many ways to understand this. One is that Raynal is a Christ figure, delivering the essence of what it means to be fully human to the world in the person of the king. Raynal undergoes a "passion," but in the end saves the king by warning him of the trials that are to come.

We might also take the story as a parable on Modernism. Raynal, the embodiment of what it means to be fully

---

[38] Martindale, Vol. I, 394.

human without taint, may be a stand-in for St. Pius X. He delivers the essence of truth to the world, is attacked mercilessly by the forces of untruth, but triumphs in the end.

On a more personal level, Richard Raynal could also be an idealization of what Benson thought might be his vocation: delivering the essence of truth to the world, but what, specifically, and how it is to be done Raynal — as was the case with Benson himself — is left in the dark until he undergoes enlightenment through suffering, a theme that recurs throughout Benson's fiction and nonfiction.

This is why I think that *Richard Raynal* might be a species of wish-fulfillment on Benson's part, as well as the reason he denied that he was himself the model for the book's protagonist. Benson may have been exploring in fictional form what life could be like for someone who had found his vocation, and describes what amounts to an idyllic existence.

No disturbing elements occur in the story — just in the story-telling. Benson invents a rather tedious narrator, Sir John Chadfield, the local pastor, who can't help inserting himself into things with inappropriate comments, shallow observations, and so on. Many of these are allegedly carefully "edited" out by Benson, who presents himself as the translator . . . except for those parts in which Benson seems almost inviting the reader to laugh at him in the person of Chadfield. Sir John seems to be comic relief in a book that doesn't need any.

The whole book, in fact, takes on the air of an act of humility on the part of Benson, almost as if he felt a little ashamed at writing something that didn't address momentous historical events or deeply troubling spiritual issues, and didn't want to put himself forward too much. Instead, he put Chadfield into the story as his stand-in, and then proceeded on a mild course of self-mockery.

What we seem to have is a half-unconscious conceit on Benson's part. He projected his idealization of the hermit's life through the character of Richard Raynal — and his perception of his role as an author through Sir John. Richard Raynal might thus be an idealized Benson as he thought he might want to be, but knew full well he never could. Sir John might be Benson as he thought he appeared to others — a manifestation of his inherent shyness, which seemed to make him regard himself as faintly absurd for daring to create worlds and manipulate characters.

This might even explain the typical vague Benson ending. Having created an entire world, as it were, in a novel or short story, he might have been unwilling to go the whole way and act as final judge of his creations.

What we might have, then, is a book in which Benson managed to hide himself not once, but three times, thereby possibly accounting for the fact that *Richard Raynal* was always his favorite of all his books. Benson hid behind the hermit Richard Raynal as a projection of his idealized self, used Sir John to divert attention away from the ridiculous idea that he, Benson, was so bold as to think himself a creator, and then performed a final self-abnegation by claiming — in the text, at least — to be only the translator.

We might, then, almost believe that Benson viewed *Richard Raynal* as a delightful joke that he shared with his readers. The humor lay in the fact that he was able to overcome his reluctance to reveal too much of himself at the same time that he revealed far more than ever before. It is a very serious joke, to be sure, and one with a very important point: the critical need to act out one's vocation to the fullest and to integrate the essence of truth with how we live our lives and structure society. Ultimately, however, the book is a bit of fun that allowed Benson to do exactly as he wanted without appearing to do it at all.

The story is very skillfully written and steeped in the fifteenth century. Still, no attentive reader would have any trouble realizing that Benson was using the tried-and-true literary device of the rediscovered manuscript, even if he or she had missed the rather clear notification on the title page to which Benson constantly referred anyone who questioned whether *Richard Raynal* was truly fiction:

> But, really, if anyone will take the trouble to read the title-page of *Richard Raynal*, I do not think he could

possibly fall into the mistake again. A "translator" could possibly write *The History of Richard Raynal, Solitary*, BY Robert Hugh Benson.

In any event, there are too many anachronisms in the text for it to be something planned as a deliberate forgery. Benson was far too careful a scholar for that. Instead, to keep the willing suspension of disbelief intact, he was extremely vague about such details as time and place, and the identity of anyone other than Richard Raynal and Sir John. It isn't even entirely clear who "the king" is, an important detail that a real chronicler would never have omitted. Instead, "the king" is used as a symbol of temporal authority and, by extension, the whole of earthly existence.

Do I know any of this for certain? Of course not. It does seem plausible, though. It fits in with Benson's known character, his comments regarding the book, and even Martindale's analysis. Benson's brother Arthur also seemed to think there was something special about *Richard Raynal*, so much so that he considered the work completely apart from the rest of Benson's fiction and nonfiction:

> I believe that the most beautiful book he ever wrote *was Richard Raynal, Solitary*; and I know he thought so himself. Of course it is an archaic book, and written, as musicians say, in a *mode*. It is easier in some ways to write a book in a style which is not authentically one's own, and literary imitation is not the highest art; but *Richard Raynal* has the beauty of a fine tapestry designed on antique lines, yet replenished and enriched by modern emotion, like Tennyson's *Mort d'Arthur*. Yet I am sure there is a deep charm of pure beauty in the book, both of thought and handling, and I believe that he put into it the best essence of his feeling and imagination.[39]

According to Martindale, there are three main motifs in the book. These are, 1) The value of solitude in bringing

---

[39] Arthur Benson, *Hugh: Memoirs of a Brother*. New York: Longmans, Green, and Co., 1916, 178-179.

man closer to God, to the point where, instead of resisting nature in order to find God, man finds God by, in the crude language of today, "becoming 'one' with nature." 2) The value of pain and suffering in discerning one's vocation, for a true vocation cannot be discerned with some form of suffering. 3) The impossibility of coming to a knowledge of one's vocation, even the meaning of life itself, by material or purely scientific means.

Again, unlike Benson's other fiction, there is no gray area. All is stark black and white, or clear, pure colors.

> Extreme simplicity, perfect *cleanness*, much clear colour — yellows, skiey blues, all the tender greens of vegetation — characterise the life Raynal leads in his thatched hut in the forest. Benson deliberately leaves all dark or gloomy elements to one side at the first. This lovely life with God is to be sheer happiness, in which all creation, life of beast and bird and leaf, joins. Richard was a Parsifal, for whom Good Friday did but make the world sweeter and more "childlike pure" with flowers. *Exultavit spiritus meus.*[40]

While a seemingly anomaly in Benson's fiction, then, *Richard Raynal, Solitary*, might just well be the quintessence of what Benson believed Benson to be.

---

[40] Martindale, Vol. I, 395.

4. The Conversion Stories

The Religion of the Plain Man (1906)
Papers of a Pariah (1905/1907)
Confessions of a Convert (1912)

This trio of works by Benson is unusual to begin with. At first glance from the titles there doesn't seem to be any connecting theme. Further, looking closer, we discover that only *Papers of a Pariah*, published as a complete work in 1907, is purely a work of fiction. An early version of *Papers* appeared in 1905 as a series of articles in a magazine called the *Month*. Additions were written in 1906 to fill in gaps in the story. Despite a rumor that persists even to this day, the pieces were clearly acknowledged as fiction by Benson. As he wrote in a letter to the later-infamous Frederick Rolfe ("Baron Corvo"),

> The article on a Requiem is the nucleus of a new book — consisting of essays, written by a Non-Catholic actor, describing emotions. I am enjoying it immensely.... It offers a wide liberty to an ordained priest. I, R.H.B., merely edit the work, priggishly hesitating as to whether I am justified in including this or that paper. Doesn't that promise a very pleasurable set of poses?[41]

Bringing up Frederick Rolfe even in so tangential a fashion requires a little explanation of this odd character for modern readers, who, with another of his circle, "Marie Corelli" (probably not her real name), virtually epitomized Edwardian decadence and the unhealthy fascination with the "flowers of evil." Perhaps we can do no better than to quote Evelyn Waugh in his wonderful and, unfortunately, little-known essay on Benson that ap-

---

[41] Martindale, Vol. II, 89.

peared as the preface to a 1956 edition of Benson's *The History of Richard Raynal, Solitary*.

At the time of writing Hugh Benson was briefly but deeply under the influence of Frederick Rolfe. Fr. Martindale, in his full and admirable biography, said little about this striking character. Since the publication of A. J. Symons's *Quest for Corvo* the need for reticence is past. Frederick Rolfe, though less than Byronic, was certainly "mad, bad and dangerous to know." It took Benson three years to discover this. When he did, he dropped him, promptly and without remorse, and was pursued by vilification as Rolfe became yearly more desperate and abandoned to vice.[42]

From the fictional setting of *Papers of a Pariah*, we move to *The Religion of the Plain Man*, published in book form in 1906. This is a work that can only be described (if the description even makes sense), as a "semi-fictional" treatment from a reasonable and logical perspective of the material covered in *Papers* from a purely emotional point of view.

Now, even though the two books are substantially different in treatment, we begin to see a very strong similarity between them. Both are "conversion stories," but, while they arrive at the same goal (entry into the Catholic Church), they do so by what most of us would assume are mutually exclusive routes. How is it possible, after all, to approach the same thing in such diametrically opposed ways, and still come to the same destination?

Papers relates the story of a convert from an almost purely subjective point of view. There is no construction of syllogism ("If this, then that"), or carefully reasoned argument or response to objections. *The Religion of the Plain Man*, on the other hand, is nothing but syllogism and the application of human reason to the problem that Benson considered the most important issue in life. That is, as we might expect, "the religion of the plain man," who, "after all, has a certain claim on our consideration, since Jesus Christ came to save his soul."

---

[42] Evelyn Waugh, "Preface" to *The History of Richard Raynal, Solitary*. Chicago, Illinois: Henry Regnery Company, 1956, xiv.

The Religion of the Plain Man, given its predominately didactic character, thus doesn't submit too well to fictional treatment. Benson may have had a thought or two about turning the series of lectures that he gave at Cambridge, and from which he drew the material for the book, into a novel. Setting out various dogmas and doctrines in a work of pure fiction as the main plot, however, is a very dangerous thing for an author. It is rarely done well, and (even when it is done well) appeals to a very small class of readers. When done poorly, as in a number of recent works promoting various Gnostic teachings thinly disguised as novels,[43] a best seller may result (particularly if enough salacious and scandalous tidbits are added to the mix), but the end product could only (and with extreme charity) be described as "tripe."

Benson thus wrote *The Religion of the Plain Man* as "non-fiction," but embedded it in a fictional setting, the story of "John Everyman." Even then Benson apologized in the "Preface" for the book's "rhetorical emotionalism." Perhaps — but it is that same "rhetorical emotionalism" that makes the book outlast the very specific age and culture for which it was intended and makes it interesting to the modern reader, even non-Christians. With Benson, as with many other authors, the artist is not always the best judge of his own work.

These two short works, *Papers of a Pariah* and *The Religion of the Plain Man*, thus represent two sides of the same coin — and two sides that you'd never know were related unless you turned the coin over and over to see the actual relationship. Just like any other coin, of course, both sides are necessary, even if many people only see the value of or are interested in one of them.

The only parallel that comes readily to mind from the pen of any other modern writer are Chesterton's short biographical sketches of Saint Francis of Assisi and Saint Thomas Aquinas. The former saint seems to appeal to our emotional side, while the latter is a glowing tribute to the power of the unclouded human intellect. Both, however,

---

[43] Two that come most readily to mind are *The Celestine Prophecies* and *The Da Vinci Code*, but other examples are easily found.

represent valid paths on the broad road to self-knowledge. As Saint Augustine exclaimed, "O Lord, may I know myself; may I know You!"

As a side note, the lectures from which *The Religion of the Plain Man* was drawn appear to be the same series that later caused such consternation among various elements at Cambridge. As Benson's brother Arthur related in *Hugh: Memoirs of a Brother* of a visit that Benson made to the University a few years after his conversion,

> Hugh became known at once as the best preacher in Cambridge, and great congregations flocked to hear him. I do not think he had much pastoral work to do; but now a complication ensued. A good many undergraduates used to go to hear him, ask to see him, discuss religious problems with him. Moreover, before he left the Anglican communion, Hugh had conducted a mission at Cambridge, with the result that several of his hearers became Roman Catholics. A certain amount of orthodox alarm was felt and expressed at the new and attractive religious element which his sermons provided, and eventually representations were made to me that I should use my influence with Hugh that he should leave Cambridge. This I totally declined to do, and suggested that the right way to meet it was to get an Anglican preacher to Cambridge of persuasive eloquence and force. I did eventually speak to Hugh about it, and he was indignant. He said: "I have not attempted, and shall not attempt, any sort of proselytization of undergraduates — I do not think it fair, or even prudent. I have never started the subject of religion on any occasion with any undergraduate. But I must preach what I believe; and, of course, if undergraduates consult me, I shall tell them what I think and why I think it." This rule he strictly adhered to; and I do not know of any converts that he made.[44]

Moving from straight fiction through didactic semifiction, the third and final piece in this set, *Confessions of a Convert*, from 1912, is the closest thing Benson ever

---

[44] Arthur C. Benson, *op. cit.*, 161-162.

came to writing an autobiography. Despite his expressed intention in the opening, this little *Apologia Pro Vita Sua* may be as close as he could have come, even given his untimely death.

An intensely private, even shy individual, Benson shrank from anything even remotely smacking of direct self-revelation. Up to a certain point, Benson might almost have agreed with Lord Marlborough ("Lord Protector" of Queen Victoria after the death of Prince Albert) that a man's soul was his own business. This may account for Benson's growing dislike (and continuing popular approval) of his first published work, *The Light Invisible* (1903), a collection of mystical short stories that, he may have felt, revealed just a little bit too much of their author.

Confessions of a Convert reveals Benson's rational, almost completely cerebral approach to religion, an aspect of his character that he evidently tried very hard and with a significant measure of success to ameliorate, at least in his preaching and personal relations. In the first part of *Initiation*, for example, Benson describes the dirt and squalor of Italian peasant life in the early twentieth century. He does this in terms that, contrary to his assumed attitude of "Northern coldness," would indicate a fascination with, even a fondness almost for what Englishmen of that day and age habitually denigrated and which gave them such disgust.

Given the focus of these three works on conversion — and, even more narrowly, conversion to a specific belief system, why would anyone other than a Catholic want to read these books? The answer to that is actually quite simple, once we think about it. One of the most neglected aspects of "man's search for meaning" in this day and age is the search for truth, or, if it doesn't seem too pretentious, Truth.

Nowhere is this more evident than in academia, the one milieu in which truth should be the overriding concern. Such is the structure of modern academia, however, that special interests — particularly the very special interests of obtaining a job and gaining tenure — rule supreme. Instead of searching for the truth at all costs, what is searched for is a novelty to shock or amaze centers of academic power in order to impress them sufficiently to give a scholar a "name." As A. R. Burn lamented in his "Introduction" to the Penguin edition of Herodotus' *Histories*, commenting on a particularly vapid thesis advanced by some scholars,

> I use the word thesis advisedly; since the excesses of *Quellenkritik* are mainly due to the Ph.D. system, which makes a high salary depend on producing original work. In a field as well-trodden as that of classical literature, to require a young scholar to be original is as inhumane as requiring him to be a humorist, or a poet; a truly original theory has a high probability of being a perverse theory, and a branch of study that has not been well worked over is likely to be one that is not worth much attention. (This does not apply to archaeology, the chief growing-point of modern classical studies, nor, of course, to modern history or the natural sciences; though the danger exists in any study.)[45]

All three of these short works by Benson are more intensely and directly concerned with the search for truth than any of his other books. If we take Socrates' reminder to heart that "the unexamined life is not worth living," we find in *Papers of a Pariah*, *The Religion of the Plain Man* and *Confessions of a Convert* a "road map," as it were, to follow in our own quest of self.

A non-Catholic, even a non-Christian reader might find the specific topics covered a little too removed from his own area of interest. In the method and the depiction of dogged perseverance in seeking out and obtaining truth, however, any reader from any faith tradition or belief system should be able to find inspiration.

Even the secular humanist, satirized by Benson in *Lord of the World*, should be able to find an interesting and entertaining guide in his own search for meaning. Nor should this surprise us. Benson had a genuine admiration for the sincere believer in any creed — whatever he might

---

[45] A. R. Burn, "Introduction" to *Herodotus, the Histories*. London: Penguin Books, 1972, 23, n.

think of the specific beliefs. The most attractive character in *The Dawn of All* is an unrepentant heretic who wins everyone's respect and sympathy for knowing exactly where he stands — and who understands precisely why everyone else considers him a heretic! Rather than whine that he is "misunderstood," he willingly sacrifices his own life in the service of what he believes to be true. This is a far cry from today's academics who willingly sacrifice what they believe to be true in the service of a high paying job or to gain popular approval.

Thus, as we might expect, these three books contain a great deal of "what." Nothing, after all, is more boring (at least as entertainment) than a couple hundred pages of "how." Few people read computer manuals for fun, but to find out exactly how to tell their computers what they want them to do. Nevertheless, Benson succeeded admirably in conveying a great deal of "how" while telling us "what" — and that "how" applies universally to all belief systems.

Nevertheless, while all three works are ostensibly addressed to Anglicans, I believe that the real point of all of them for Benson was, ultimately, to get Catholics to think seriously about what they believe. Thus, by extension, all believers in any system can be inspired to examine what they believe to be true — particularly if they have always believed it. It doesn't matter whether the area of concern is religion, philosophy, politics or economics — whatever it may be — the important thing is for all believers (regardless of what they believe) not only to know where they stand, but *why* that is where they have taken a stand.

To do that, we must, each of us, leave behind our social, cultural, political, economic — yes, even religious — preconceptions and work to see things as they *are*, to see behind whatever applications and rituals we have grown up with and discern the truth behind them. Applications and rituals are not meaningless encrustations covering up some hidden truth, but very necessary means for conveying truths in a way that they should become obvious to us through participation in our institutions.

The Philistine who ridicules all ritual as meaningless and every application of principles of natural law or eternal truth as forcing an alien morality on him is as mistaken and unthinking as the Pharisee who accepts such things without question. "Meaningless ritual" is not redundant, but an oxymoron. The act of social justice itself is dedicated to examining rituals and applications of principles and empowering us to reform our institutions — our rituals and applications of principles. That is so that we as individuals working with others can ensure that our institutions continue to meet our individual and social needs, and, above all, to respect the dignity of the human person.

To understand our dignity as human persons, of course, requires that we know who we are. That is what these three works were designed to do, and why I grouped them together in one essay. Not only that, they are entertaining — as is all of Benson's writing, whether fiction, semifiction, or non-fiction. *Tolle lege*[46] — it's well worth the small effort.

---

[46] "Take and read."

5. The "Sensational" Novels

The Sentimentalists (1906)

Lord of the World (1907)

The Conventionalists (1908)

The Necromancers (1909)

The Dawn of All (1911)

The Sentimentalists

In one of his early short plays for the German-Reeds, an acting family that took as its self-appointed mission the moral improvement of the theater, W. S. Gilbert lampooned in his inimitable fashion the late Victorian taste for "sensational" literature. The sketch, *A Sensation Novel (In Three Volumes)*, was probably suggested by Captain Marryat's hilarious "How to Write a Romance" in *Olla Podrida*. Gilbert's sketch is superbly clever, extremely witty and, unfortunately, dated. No one today would really understand the Gilbertian satire of spirits of the departed sentenced to expiate their sins (such as frequenting music halls and singing comic songs) by playing roles embodying the direct antithesis of their actual crimes and characters in a hack writer's "sensational three-volume novel."

The modern reader would be much more appreciative of the popular urge to read sensational trash with no point to it. One merely has to look at the flood of "reality television" to gain a very low opinion of the human race's taste in entertainment. Of course, the degree to which this is due to the general refusal on the part of the media to present moral entertainment of a reasonable quality can never be known.

Or can it? Mel Gibson's *The Passion of the Christ*, contrary to the predictions of the media pundits and despite Gibson's later fall(s) from grace, was an outstanding popular success. Nearly a generation ago Alan Bloom's *The Closing of the American Mind*, a somewhat dry academic study, became an overnight best seller, stunning the author and the publisher. A century ago, Robert Hugh Benson took the bull of popular culture by the horns by publishing *The Sentimentalists*.

Much to the surprise of just about everyone (himself included), Benson achieved a popular triumph with a "sensational novel" that went against the current by having a definite point. This was even more surprising in that the novel was written by what had to be one of the most unlikely authors the public at the time could imagine — a Catholic priest! (The spectacle of clergymen of whatever faith using their status to achieve additional sensationalism was decades in the future.)

Despite its grounding in sound philosophy and morality, *The Sentimentalists* verges on the lurid in parts, at least by Victorian standards. There is nothing to "bring the blush of shame to the cheek of modesty," to quote that quintessential Victorian Gilbert again. The quote is from *Patience, or, Bunthorne's Bride (An Æsthetic Opera)* — a production (as we might expect) about a couple of *poseurs* using the æsthetic movement to get girls. (Most authorities believe the "Bunthorne" character to have been modeled on Oscar Wilde.)

Still, the raw emotionalism of a number of the scenes in *The Sentimentalists* — absolutely necessary to drive home the point — made some readers decidedly nervous. The theme, while similar to *Patience*, is much more serious in treatment. Even Benson was a little embarrassed by the scenes he created in which a human being's pretensions are stripped away and affectations come home to roost. All that happens to Bunthorne when he is revealed as a phony is that all the women — even the ugly ones — lose interest in him. Chris Dell attempts suicide.

The public didn't stop reading *The Sentimentalists*, though. For all the "sensationalism" (rather tame by today's standards as there is nothing gross or gory) that Benson built into the story, it is that very sensationalism that provokes thought in the reader. Benson set out to show the logical conclusion of the effect of a supremely selfish egotism — and, in the process, created one of the most thought-provoking novels of the early twentieth century.

> Did I tell you about my yet more new one? to be called, probably, *The Sentimentalists* — modern times — relating the reformation of a *poseur* by brutality. Sometimes I think it Extremely Good, and sometimes Extremely Bad. It's certainly one of the two, and I don't know which.

Odd words from any author! Still, Benson was very worried about the book:

I have begun *The Waster* [Benson changed the title when he began writing, and then back again when it was published], but I am seriously concerned as to whether it will be possible to publish it. It is the grossest caricature of X. I can say honestly that it is not him, but a violent parody of him. . . . HONESTLY, it has already ceased to be him. It is his dramatic element, caricatured to absurdity, and practically none of his virtues, which are many.

Finally, though, Benson was able to complete the work:

Half an hour ago I finished my book. It will probably not be called *The Waster*. Perhaps *The Conventionalists*. I am not sure. I really am all right. It is perfectly true; though I dare say reviews will say that I make a deal of fuss about nothing, but I don't think that they will deny its truth. I have employed a device of Henry Kingsley's at the end — suddenly telling the story from my point of view, and relating what I saw happen at a garden party, with which the thing ends. It makes it startlingly real — as if a statue suddenly moved.

The critics, apparently confused by the appearance of a sensational novel with a point, reacted ambiguously. The public reacted with enthusiasm — even those who claimed to hate the book. Discussion was endless over the real identity of the model for "Chris Dell," who was never explicitly revealed except to a select few individuals. (Everyone, of course, "knew" who it was . . . or at least thought they knew.)

Far from being insulted, the original was, by his own account, absolutely delighted with the novel and the effect it had. He even undertook to write his own novel (apparently never published) in which he caricatured Benson, a sort of friendly "tit for tat."

When it became known that the "real" Chris Dell approved of the book, the critics had to take other tacks. First (of course), "Chris Dell" wasn't "true to life." He wasn't supposed to be, as Benson had pointed out even before publication. "Chris" was a composite of several individuals, although inspired chiefly by one.

Second, the critics asserted that the author, being completely sane, couldn't really understand or depict the insanity of egomania. That, however, wasn't the point. Benson was concerned with the redemption of the *poseur* soaked in self-pity, not the details or causes of his disease. There's very little as to *why* "Chris" is the way he is — Benson's priority was to get him to stop being that way.

And so on. None of this, of course, detracts from the value of *The Sentimentalists*. The novel, along with its sequel, *The Conventionalists*, has had something of a small "cult" following since its first publication — handicapped, as we might expect, by the scarcity of copies. Once Benson's work becomes better known, however, perhaps more people will be able to appreciate the whole point of what Benson hoped to accomplish with his "sensation novel":

> I did not ask myself if it would make converts, but rather whether it would make things any more hopeful for the thousands of souls who are going straight to hell because no one understands them or makes the best of them . . . . I don't know what the good of being in union with our Lord is, unless we try to do what He did — i.e., make *the best of sinners, and not the worst* — and, above all, never expect gratitude, and never allow the faintest self-love or bitterness or resentment to remain in one's heart.

Lord of the World

> I have an idea for a book so vast and tremendous that I daren't think about it. Have you ever heard of Saint Simon? Well, mix up Saint Simon, Russia breaking loose, Napoleon, Evan Roberts, the Pope, and Antichrist; and see if any idea suggests itself. But I'm afraid it is too big. I should like to form a syndicate on it, but that it is an idea, I have no doubt at all.[47]

So was born the germ of the idea that grew into *Lord of the World*, Robert Hugh Benson's brilliant satire on the secularism of Edwardian England, and his most popular — and most misunderstood — novel. *Lord of the World* takes all the secular assumptions of the science-obsessed masses of the early twentieth century and carries them to their logical conclusion. All that the so-called "secular humanist" considers as good and desirable for human society inevitably engenders an inhuman nightmare.

A great literary tragedy that occurs much too often is the ease with which heavy-handed satires have been interpreted as straightforward opinion or even prophecy. Saint Thomas More's *Utopia*, for example, satirizes the evils of Tudor England (especially the virtual abolition of small holdings of private property) — yet many otherwise intelligent people mistake the tale for the blueprint of an ideal society.

Unfortunately, Benson's satires, often gentle yet always pointed, have either been ignored by our modern age in search of literary pabulum and blood-spattered thrills, or taken as something far different from what they were intended. A case in point is this "apocalyptic" masterpiece, *Lord of the World*, first published in 1907 and reprinted frequently since. It is credited as the prototype of apocalyptic novels that have proliferated in the late twentieth and early twenty-first centuries.

---

[47] Robert Hugh Benson, letter to his mother, December 16, 1905.

Many commentaries on *Lord of the World* have focused on the presumed originality of the work, and how Benson "predicted" such events as World War I, the creation of the atomic bomb, the overthrow of the European monarchies, and the triumph of secular humanism. Unfortunately, these analyses start with a series of faulty assumptions, beginning with the idea that the author's "predictions" somehow originated with him.

Benson was an avid reader, and was familiar with a sub-genre of science fiction that was extremely popular in the last quarter of the nineteenth century and the first decade of the twentieth. This was the "future war" novel, launched in 1871 with the publication of *The Battle of Dorking* by Sir George Chesny. *Dorking* is actually an extended short story, a "novella," not a novel proper.

The "future war" stories had a number of common elements. A super-explosive of some kind was almost inevitable, as was a flying machine. With few exceptions, most writers put the war as taking place between 1910 and 1920, with most, ironically, putting the start of the war in 1914.

Benson loved science fiction, especially the "scientific romances" of H. G. Wells — although he was adamant that he had no sympathy for Wells's philosophical or theological thought. He just liked the adventure and the sense of wonder such stories generated. Clearly he was strongly influenced by the flood of "future war" fiction available during his youth and that apparently had a profound effect on his entire generation. When Benson set out to write science fiction, he chose a popular form, and one with which he and countless others were already familiar.

Benson thereby employed classic storytelling technique. The author draws in his readers by using a familiar premise or form. A fairy tale inevitably begins, "Once upon a time," and the setting — an ordinary peasant's hut or the castle of the local king — is one familiar to the intended audience. (It's only the passage of time and space that makes such things unfamiliar or exotic to us.) Every episode of *The Twilight Zone,* for example, opened with Rod Serling's voiceover assuring the viewer that the scene is perfectly normal.

Thus it was with Benson. A reader in Edwardian England might purchase Benson's latest work on the assumption that it was nothing more than a very popular author's entry into an equally popular sub-genre of science fiction. Benson was already known for his satire. This had usually appeared as little asides or comments in his historical romances, all the more startling for their casual presentation. Describing the aftermath of the Spanish Armada in his immense (almost a quarter of a million words) *By What Authority?*, Benson laconically stated that "everywhere half drowned or half starved Spaniards, piteously entreating, were stripped and put to the sword either by the Irish savages or the English gentlemen."

Lord of the World, however, marked a turning point in Benson's literary career. After its publication his satire was much stronger and often the thinly veiled thrust of the work. The smugness and self-satisfied snobbery of the English upper classes were hammered flat — albeit more gently than the world has grown accustomed to since. Benson could not have written his masterpiece, *An Average Man* or his damning indictment of upper class ideology, *The Coward*, before *Lord of the World*.

The elements Benson used in *Lord of the World* to construct the world of the year 2000 were familiar to his readers before he put pen to paper. His contribution, as with all his fiction, was to add an explicitly religious theme to the work. This was, not surprisingly, Benson's chief accomplishment as a popular writer. It appeared from the very first, in one of his earliest written (but almost last published) novels, *Oddsfish!*, a Restoration adventure, and was present in each of his works of fiction.

Other writers were beginning to experiment with frank discussions of human sexuality, a trend continually ridiculed by P. G. Wodehouse. Benson brought into the light of day (or at least the glare of popular culture) the *other* "forbidden" subject: the Catholic Church. His Elizabethan swashbucklers took the usual presentation of the Catholic Church (and, of course, the Jesuit Order) as the stock villain, complete with black cape and twirling mustachios, and turned it on its head. It strikes modern readers simply as giving equal time to an unpopular group, but a century ago this was considered revolutionary.

Also revolutionary was Benson's refusal to deify technology. Science was not a villain for Benson, but neither was it a savior. Father Franklin in *Lord of the World* is startled to find a typewriter (still rare in 1907) in the Vatican — but why not? Technology is simply a thing, potentially beneficial or potentially harmful, particularly when worshipped as a false god.

Benson thought highly of Americans, but he made the antagonist in *Lord of the World* an American. Most "future war" novels, although written largely by English authors, made Americans the heroes, sometimes virtual demigods. Americans, however, are not demigods, but as fallible and as subject to great evil as any other people. The Germans would prove this in the next generation with the rise of Hitler among a nation presumed to be one of the most civilized on earth.

The book is deliberately sensational, as Benson admitted, and just as deliberately exaggerated. "I am perfectly aware that this is a terribly sensational book . . . . But I did not know how else to express the principles I desired (and which I passionately believe to be true) except by producing their lines to a sensational point. I have tried, however, not to scream unduly loud."

The satire thereby comes across as a club rather than his usual rapier. The characters, the plot, the futuristic machines, the very incidents were simply props to the idea he wanted to convey. His point was that failure to conform the world to the truth of religion and universal moral values would lead to disaster. Given the general attitude toward religion among the typical member of the English upper classes of his day, this struggle could only go one way — and that is the way Benson took it.

> Where faith goes out, superstition comes in. Man is a worshipping animal, and Humanity-worship, even in Comte's day, demanded an organized cult.[48]

The task of conforming one's self to truth is a theme that pervades all of Benson's fiction in one form or anoth-

---

[48] Martindale, Vol. II, 72.

er. Typically, in *Lord of the World* Benson used a science fantasy to highlight this theme, prevalent in all of his work. Obsessed with the meaning of life, and his own specific vocation, Benson was wont to agonize whether he was truly answering God's Call, or simply following his own inclinations. Like the question as to whether one has a soul, perhaps that question is best answered by the fact that one can ask it.

Most people did not understand that Benson was juxtaposing a sound exercise of the virtue of religion with a deluded self-sufficient secularism. His public in England reacted to the novel very negatively at first. In other places, such as Ireland and France, the book proved to be extraordinarily popular, but still misunderstood.

After the near apocalypse of World War I, the book acquired the popularity it enjoys today, and probably for the same misguided reason. To many readers, *Lord of the World* took on a prophetic character, something that Benson explicitly denied. He intended the novel as a parable, not a future history at all. He was fully aware that the science he posited was impossible and the plot line outrageous. It was, however, the most graphic way possible to present the idea of man vs. God, of human self-delusion confronting ultimate truth. As Martindale observed,

> This, then, is what Benson pictures: humanity consciously refusing the higher kind of life which the Church proclaims to it, and insisting on reaching merely that incredibly lofty goal to which its intrinsic efforts can carry it.[49]

---

[49] *Ibid.*, 82-83.

The Conventionalists

The *Conventionalists*, first published in 1908, is the third in a group that Robert Hugh Benson vaguely grouped as his "sensational" novels. It's not immediately clear why he regarded it in this light, for the novel is hardly shocking to modern readers. Nevertheless, the *Conventionalists* delves very deeply into a subject that "nice" people didn't discuss: conversion to Catholicism. With the exception of the pseudo-biographical *Papers of a Pariah*, all of his previous novels had dealt with conversion as a *fait accompli* before the story began, and did not address it as a plot element. The novel is also unique in that it is the only explicit sequel that Benson wrote, a follow-up to the *Sentimentalists* from 1906.

The *Conventionalists* also stands alone in that it provides a sort of *via media* between Benson's sensational novels and his later "mainstream" fiction. The *Necromancers*, a much more obviously sensational piece (and almost completely misunderstood by many of today's readers), was to follow the *Conventionalists* in 1909, but the earlier work provides a promise of things to come — a promise that Benson more than kept. Good as his earlier work is, and justifiably famous, his later works are actually much superior, making it extremely puzzling why they have tended to languish in semi-obscurity.

Finally, the Conventionalists is one of only two novels (the other being the *Dawn of All*) that Benson wrote in direct response to critics of an earlier work. Where he would turn out the *Dawn of All* to demonstrate to unheeding readers and critics the satiric nature of *Lord of the World*, the *Conventionalists* made its appearance due to the apparently widespread belief that he had treated the real-life original of "Chris Dell" very badly in the *Sentimentalists*. As Martindale commented, ". . . in the relations of these two men had been much which was, beyond all that is ordinary, fine and inspiring. It may be guessed, then, how appalled Hugh was when, to his amazement, he heard what consequences were arising from his book."[50]

Consequently, "'Chris Dell' himself was alternately inclined to treat the whole affair with that breezy good nature which is so noticeably his, or, in his moments of fatigue, with anger, not against Hugh, but against his critics."[51] Nor did "Chris" spare the equines in responding to critics of his friend's novel: "Let asses say or think what they will."[52] "My dear Hugh, if I have related the circumstances once to unkind critics, I have related them a thousand times. If people will be such blazing fools as utterly to misunderstand after all the lengthy explanations I have given, I cannot help it. I had no idea people were so malicious or so unreasonable. Let them go."[53]

Other than some minor criticisms of the book by its "hero's" model,[54] Benson quickly got over his frustration based on how easily and readily people misunderstood his work. Oddly enough, a number of the critics — almost all of them ladies! — would have preferred that the author spell out certain common expletives which then-current propriety demanded be left to the readers' imagination. At least one extremely astute commentator pleased Benson by noting that a large number of readers were "shocked" by "Chris Dell's" sojourn in Paris . . . and missed completely the far-from-veiled references to much more real and far more serious sins.

Pressure for a sequel to the *Sentimentalists* came from many quarters and for many reasons. Benson's sister loved the book, and wrote that it "hasn't only the interest of making you want to go on, but also of making you want to stop and think through again what you have read. It hadn't quite the *aroma* of some of your books; and there are one or two sentences which seem to me as clever as

---

[50] *Ibid.*, 56.
[51] *Ibid.*
[52] *Ibid.*
[53] *Ibid.*
[54] In commenting on a proposed dramatization of the *Sentimentalists* for the stage, "Chris Dell" wrote, "I feel I shall hate your man. He is bound to have all my hateful qualities. Do hang him in the end. I am sure he deserves it." *Ibid.*, 57.

you please, but a little less fine than your own style. I think now that it would not only admit but *need* a sequel. You can't live happily ever afterwards just yet."[55]

Almost from the first Benson recognized the pivotal nature of the *Conventionalists*. When the book was still in the outline stage in early April of 1906 he wrote that, "The spiritual world is going to come up like a thunderstorm, appallingly real; it is going to carry Algy away . . . and leave everybody staring at one another like fools. It will really make a book."[56]

Here we have the key to understanding the *Conventionalists*. Benson was still hard at work on *Lord of the World*, but (what with the obvious misunderstandings that sprang up around the *Sentimentalists*) may have had a sneaking suspicion that his most spectacularly sensational novel would be misinterpreted even more egregiously — which has proved to be the case for a full century. Benson thus set out to make the spiritual — the ultimate truth — as real as possible, juxtaposing it against the extreme artificiality of the English upper classes and their twisted ideas of what constituted truth.

Benson had already tried this with his historical novels, but (in a certain sense) there is nothing so unreal as facts. Interpreting them — which is what both straight historians and historical novelists necessarily do (there is no such thing as "objective history") — is quickly asserted as merely the historian's or author's opinion. In his previous sensational novels, the *Sentimentalists* and the then-as-yet unpublished *Lord of the World*, he went after institutions, and by extension, the individuals enmeshed in them.

In the *Conventionalists* he changed his tactic and went after individuals, from whom we are, as Aristotle dictates, to generalize the underlying principle. Benson was to perfect this technique in his later six "mainstream" novels with such success that he created, possibly without intending to do so, literary works that might well be classified as great. This change in technique also meant that

---

[55] *Ibid.*, 59-60.
[56] *Ibid.*, 61.

his work would become much more personal and, being personal, much more visceral.

Perhaps with an eye on the *Sentimentalists*, Algy in the *Conventionalists* was also, according to Martindale, drawn from life, although not as closely as in the case of "Chris Dell."[57] Benson, however, changed the circumstances to such a degree that there was no backlash from that quarter. The worst that could be said of the fictional Algy was that, from one point of view, he is "railroaded" into a vocation. From another point of view, of course, Algy simply receives a great deal of assistance in discerning his vocation, assistance that Benson felt he would have liked to have — an author's prerogative of using his characters to engage in wish fulfillment.

Nevertheless, the *Conventionalists* is an extremely cruel book, perhaps the reason why Benson considered it sensational. The Protestant minister, the Reverend Mr. Mortimer, is flayed alive. Benson was to demonstrate impatience with the Catholic clergy at times and disapprobation of certain personal traits exhibited by less-admirable members of the priesthood, but nothing like that accorded Mr. Mortimer. The minister's entire belief system is examined as if under a microscope and its utter futility in the face of the appalling tragedy that strikes the hero's family is nakedly exposed.

If the Protestant Mr. Mortimer is delineated in terms that call to mind P. G. Wodehouse's description of a character as having the appearance of "an earnest sheep," the Catholic Lady Brasted, virtually the quintessential religious poseur, comes in for some very rough treatment. Through her, Benson almost manages to make superficial religious practice tantamount to a sin. No one — with the possible exception of "Chris Dell" — comes off well . . . in consequence of which you can almost hear Benson say, "Take that!" to the critics. Even Algy is put through the meat grinder.

Benson's treatment of his characters was so harsh — for him — that it may have seemed a bit overdone to him. The later mainstream novels reflect an honest admiration

---

[57] *Ibid.*, 64.

of the Protestant clergy, even (or, especially, in *Loneliness?*, his last novel), those who come across as somewhat superficial — but (it is extremely important to note) *never* insincere or hypocritical. Even Mr. Mortimer, for all his demonstrated inadequacy (which presages the self-doubt of Mr. Main in *An Average Man*) is absolutely convinced of the truth of what he teaches.

Paradoxically then, Benson actually succeeds in treating Mr. Mortimer and the rest of his targets with gentleness, even sympathy. The fault is not entirely in them, although personal choice is always the determining factor when such important acts as life and its direction are under consideration. They are trapped by their institutions — by "convention" — and lack either the incentive or the perspicuity to break free of it. Only Algy manages, and then only after a spiritual awakening that he stubbornly resists until almost the very end.

Thus, the question of vocation — always present in Benson's fiction — begins to achieve the dominance it was to assume in his later works, to the advantage of the author and the benefit of the reader. As Evelyn Waugh was to note, this question consumed Benson all his life. Perhaps it was one reason (apart from the desire to educate the public through popular entertainment) why Benson felt driven to explore the question again and again, in novel after novel, finally working himself to death in 1914.

As we might expect from Benson, his "sequel" starts to overshadow the original — not that the original is in any denigrated. Still, if a reader felt himself forced to read either the *Sentimentalists* or the *Conventionalists* (the sort of artificial choice modern pollsters and economists love to present us with) . . . pick the *Conventionalists* — wondering why it is necessary to choose. On the other hand, you could act in a perfectly reasonable manner and read them both with a great deal of enjoyment.

The Necromancers

By the late nineteenth and early twentieth century interest in the occult — "Spiritism" or "Spiritualism" — had become virtually an epidemic. People were clearly losing more and more control over their lives as ownership of the means of production became increasingly concentrated in fewer and fewer hands, and traditional religion seemed to have failed them. Consequently the concrete manifestations of "spirits" created by the Spiritualists and Mediums seemed to offer something tangible on which to focus our natural human need to practice the virtue of religion and, in addition, achieve some kind of temporal security as materialism took over as the predominate philosophy of life.

It made no difference that in virtually every case the "manifestations" were shown to have been caused by very tangible human beings rather than intangible spirits, or sometimes even by simple coincidence. Harry Houdini (Ehrich Weiss, 1874-1926), for example, made discrediting the claims of Mediums and Spiritualists his chief avocation. He contributed an article to *Weird Stories* relating one of his adventures along those lines that, had it come from a less reputable source, would have seemed too incredible to believe, being the result of an almost preternatural coincidence ("The Hoax of the Spirit Lover," 1924). The story is too fantastic not to relate.

A man in Chicago left his fiancée and committed insurance fraud by taking his dead twin brother's identity. Believing him dead, the girl moved to Montana. The man ran through the money he received for his own presumed death and took a job as a Medium's hidden assistant, dousing himself with phosphorescent paint to fool the marks. Leading citizens of the town in which the Medium set up shop, and in which the girl had taken up residence (being one of the Medium's "clients" to contact her dead lover), hired Houdini to expose the Medium, and he arranged to attend one of the séances.

In the course of the evening, Houdini began his usual investigation, but before he could act decisively to expose the swindle, the girl recognized the "apparition" as the presumed ghost of he whom they were gathered to summon. She hurled herself at him, and wouldn't let go until it was revealed that, far from being an unsubstantial spirit, it was a living man — and the one she had believed dead! (The girl recovered from the shock and, outraged, ended up marrying somebody else, her mourning ended by the exposure of the fraud.)

Nevertheless, people are apparently so gullible (or, at least, Hollywood believes them to be) that when Houdini's life was made into a movie starring the late Tony Curtis, Houdini's phenomenal achievements as a stage magician — which Houdini himself claimed were due solely to purely human skills — were credited to some "mystic" power. (This writer strongly suspects that Mr. Curtis, a fine actor, was under contract and had no real choice in the matter.)

In spite of all this, Robert Hugh Benson seems to have had a certain level of credulity in such matters, which almost equaled his suspicion of them. Martindale suggested that this might have been due to a rather unusual circumstance:

> All his life Hugh Benson was followed continuously, in his mind, by the awareness of a Fear.. . . but how to explain Fear — Fear, that is, *as such*, and not fear of this or that; Fear which is essentially the "denying of the succors of thought" — it is hard to see.. . . I would suggest that Benson, probably quite unconsciously, provided himself with all sorts of strange opportunities for fear, that his *fearing faculty*, so to say, might have sufficient exercise, and leave him in regard to all that really mattered more at peace. If we can agree to this, we shall see him, even at his most frivolous and almost vexing, engaged in laying one ghost by the evocation of another, and, all his life, a haunted man. Here not least, I mean in this spectacle of a really brave man exorcising the phantoms of his soul by spells that half were jests, is to be

found one element of that pathos which always, to my feeling, softens the contours of his portrait.

As a result of this semi-interest in the occult, Benson cultivated the acquaintance of some rather unsavory characters, notably the sinister Frederick Rolfe ("Baron Corvo") and the bizarre "Marie Corelli," whose real name and identity have never been adequately established. Mark Twain visited Miss Corelli during a trip to England and thought her deluded, insane or, at the very least, a fraud. She was, nevertheless, an extremely popular novelist with a significant cult following even today. Several of her books were made into movies, notably *The Sorrows of Satan*, by D. W. Griffith, whose taste in literature didn't seem to have improved since choosing Dixon's *The Klansman* to film as *Birth of a Nation*.

Benson's family and friends apparently warned him against having too much to do with such people, but with indifferent success. It was his own growing conviction that there was something not quite right about the whole thing that led to a deeper investigation and, finally, his own fictional "exposé" of the movement with *The Necromancers*.

The plot is fairly straightforward and, coincidentally, has a number of similarities to the story related by Houdini. A young man's fiancée has recently died and, in an excess of emotion, he becomes involved with a group of Spiritualists gathered around "James Vincent," a figure obviously modeled on Frederick Rolfe. It turns out that Lawrence Baxter, "Laurie," the young man, has a deadly talent for going into spiritualist trances, which "Mr. Vincent" is delighted to discover — and exploit. Maggie, a young lady of typical Bensonian sound female mind (who has a romantic interest in Laurie, obvious to everyone except Laurie) succeeds in separating the young man from the group, but apparently (in one of Benson's more ambiguous endings) at a very high cost to herself. The ending may reflect Benson's own discomfort with Spiritualism, or possibly his growing awareness that something might not be completely "right" with his friends.

The Necromancers treats Spiritualism as a very real and very dangerous thing. With the modern appearance of various "New Age" cults and belief systems, the danger is still with us, regardless whether or not we accept the claims of proponents. Nevertheless, adherents of Spiritualism are treated very kindly in the book, relatively speaking, even the extremely sinister Mr. Vincent. Benson, after all, still considered Frederick Rolfe, the model, a friend, although mislead by his increasingly unhealthy interest in the occult. Mr. Vincent is depicted as both sincere and charming, if ultimately sliding into evil — well-intentioned evil, but still evil.

Unfortunately for Benson's feelings and fortunately for his eventual peace of mind, Rolfe and Corelli took the whole thing very badly. Rolfe in particular considered himself insulted. The duo attacked Benson viciously in speech and in print. Rolfe put an obvious (and extremely unflattering) caricature of Benson in one of his own novels.

It turned out that neither Rolfe nor Corelli was ever really interested in Benson as a person. They seem to have cultivated the acquaintance solely so they could keep him on a string as their "pet Romish priest," giving them, as it were, the *imprimatur* of the Catholic Church, a theologically if not socially respectable institution.

This was an orientation completely alien to Benson, who tended to accept people for themselves, however much he might reject their beliefs. He was deeply hurt. After all, the principal model for "Chris Dell" in *The Sentimentalists* had been treated with much less consideration and, in fact, almost cruelly at times. He, however, had been absolutely delighted, even flattered at being the object of Benson's solicitude, even as a caricature, crediting his appearance in the novel as helping to "save" him.

Sadly cutting the connection, Benson seems to have resolved to remain firm in his renewed opposition to all forms of Spiritualism. As he informed a lady who made inquiries concerning the power of the occult,

> You belong to God, which is the point. The Church will follow. (1) Spiritualism could not conceivably cure you. (2) If it could, it could only be by diabolical power. The Devil gives nothing for nothing.

Here's an interesting note for Savoyards, as fans of the Gilbert and Sullivan operas are called. George Grossmith, the famed comic baritone who created many of the most popular roles in the operas (Sir Joseph Porter from *H.M.S. Pinafore*, Major General Stanley from *The Pirates of Penzance*, Koko the Lord High Executioner from *The Mikado*, and the tragic Jack Point from *The Yeomen of the Guard*, among others), was also an author in his own right (*Diary of a Nobody*) — and a good friend of Benson. It was due to his influence that *The Necromancers* was the first of Benson's novels to be dramatized.

The Dawn of All

The trouble with writing a book on a controversial subject is that the book itself tends to become controversial. So it was with *Lord of the World*, Robert Hugh Benson's initial foray into the science fiction genre. It became clear almost from the start that, whether people thought well or ill of the novel, the vast majority failed to understand the point the author was trying to make.

Simply put, *Lord of the World* was, as Benson stated in the very beginning, a satire on social trends and tendencies he observed in Edwardian England. He used the venerable satiric technique of carrying these social factors to their *reductio ad absurdum*. By adding a Catholic orientation, he produced a work that showed, in his opinion, what would happen in the unlikely event that "secular humanism" managed to gain complete control of the world.

Although *Lord of the World* is the only novel Benson wrote completely lacking in his wry sense of humor, there is a basic underlying humor in the situation — or so he thought. Benson believed the whole situation fantastic and sensational, and therefore comedic — if tragic — in its own way. He was genuinely appalled at the dead seriousness with which the book was received, both by its supporters and its critics.

This appears to have moved him, before beginning the draft of *The Dawn of All*, to write, "[Systems other than the Catholic faith seem] to be built up to a large extent on a lack of the sense of humor. I wonder whether the sense of humor will ever be exalted in the Church to the dignity of a virtue! . . . it saves people from so much foolishness and heresy."[58] Coincidentally, the founder of "solidarism," the great Father Heinrich Pesch, S.J., working about the same time in Germany, remarked to some of his students, "Boys, never lose your sense of humor; lack of humor almost always suggests that something is wrong with a per-

---

[58] Martindale, Vol. II, 83.

son's religious life."⁵⁹ With that in mind, Benson prepared to begin writing a response to the criticisms of *Lord of the World*. As we might expect, this took the form of another novel.

> After some considerable time Benson published a kind of counterblast to *The Lord of the World*. He took some exactly opposite tendencies, and produced their line indefinitely, and stated the results. The book was called *The Dawn of All*, and in it the Catholic Church was seen triumphant.⁶⁰

Properly speaking, *The Dawn of All* is not one of the "sensational novels," except, perhaps, to a rabid anti-Catholic who would be incensed at the description of an admittedly fantastic (in the sense of fantasy) Catholic England in the enlightened twentieth century. Rather, the novel is something of an addendum to *Lord of the World*, an effort to correct the general misimpression the public had gained of the earlier work.

Using a technique suggestive of Billy Pilgrim's unsettling affliction in Kurt Vonnegut, Jr.'s *Slaughterhouse Five*, an apostate priest dying in or about 1910 suddenly finds himself with no memory — and a promotion to the Monsignori — sitting on a platform during an ecclesiastical ceremony in London in the year 1973.

This time travel device seems to have fascinated Evelyn Waugh, who highly valued Benson's work. Waugh used it to good effect in his short story, "Out of Depth." Waugh's version, which may have inspired Vonnegut's use of the plot device, centers on a "modern" Americanized Englishman of 1933. The protagonist is appropriately named "Rip" Van Winkle. This might have been Waugh's way of emphasizing that the man was already "dead" in a social or spiritual sense — "R.I.P." — in addition to recalling Washington Irving's character. Paralleling Benson's apostate priest, Van Winkle is a lapsed Catholic completely unaware of reality. He drifts (or sleeps?) through life in a haze of trivial social engagements. Where Benson's apos-

---

⁵⁹ Franz H. Müller, "I Knew Heinrich Pesch" *Social Order*, April, 1951, 150.
⁶⁰ Martindale, Vol. II, 84.

tate was dying, Waugh's layman was already dead — spiritually and intellectually, anyway.

At a party Rip becomes involved with an obvious clone of the notorious Aleister Crowley, the Satanist who attempted to revive paganism and "magick" in the twentieth century, ending up insane. Rip is duped into being a guinea pig for an occult investigation. As a result, he finds himself 500 years in the future. The English are savages. London ("Lunnon") is a single row of fifty or so wattle and daub huts on stilts over a Thames mudflat. The Londoners' chief occupation is digging in the ruins and collecting trinkets to exchange for the cloth, axes and glass beads of the civilized African traders. African missionaries valiantly attempt to civilize the English barbarians and convert them to Catholicism.

One of Waugh's satiric twists is to make the African missionaries Dominicans. Thus, instead of white men dressed in black preaching to black men, he has black men dressed in white preaching to white men. When Rip wakes to the present of the 1930s, returned as a result of assisting at Mass, he abjures his esoteric adventures and returns to the sacraments.

Waugh's story was clearly inspired by Benson's novel. The themes are identical, except that Waugh was dealing on the individual level, while Benson was exploring the social effect of a return to the sacraments or conversion to Catholicism by an entire society. Both "Out of Depth" and *The Dawn of All* end with the protagonists asking to go to confession — and neither of them quite sure whether the whole thing has been a dream.

In *The Dawn of All*, the Catholic Church is virtually the only religious body on earth. The only holdouts are a few Lutheran pockets in Germany, and the socialists. During the course of the novel, the German Kaiser "comes over" and converts, bringing the rest of the Reich (the *Second Reich*, of course), with him. Unfortunately, the socialists — portrayed as extreme reactionaries — see this as a capitulation to the tyranny of Rome, and begin murdering emissaries sent by the Vatican. To stop the bloodshed, the pope confronts the socialists in person, even though the socialists have threatened to kill him on sight.

The most striking thing about *The Dawn of All* is the almost appalling ordinariness of the characters. We have become accustomed in our science fiction and fantasy to men and women of super-heroic stature doing incredible deeds against impossible odds. This violates one of the basic tenets of storytelling, which is to have either heroic individuals in ordinary situations (very effective for satire and comedy), or ordinary individuals in extraordinary circumstances.

Much of today's science fiction and fantasy suffers from a lack of identification with the story by the average reader. As a result, science fiction and fantasy (despite periodic announcements to the contrary) have moved from the mainstream to the purview of a relatively small and self-consciously select reading public. The stereotype of the geeky science fiction fan who secretly views himself as Conan the Barbarian may not be far off the mark.

This was not always the case. Jules Verne, H. G. Wells, George Griffith, R. W. Chambers, Louis Tracy . . . these were not "science fiction writers," but writers who happened to write science fiction. The first two were popular — extremely popular — with the general public, a status virtually unheard-of for even the best of today's science fiction writers. The last two in particular wrote novels of adventure, romance, science fiction, fantasy — you name it, anything to keep the pot boiling.

Chambers wrote the horror classic, *The King in Yellow*, but was most famous during his lifetime as the author of "shop girl romances." Tracy wrote the stunning "future war" novel, *The Final War* ("military science fiction" is not a new sub-genre), but made his name (and a very good living) writing adventure, "Graustarkian" romances, and mysteries. By and large, the pioneers of modern science fiction and fantasy refused to be categorized or labeled. They were fearless about exploring new ideas, but also, by and large, maintained a sound traditional philosophical and moral orientation in their work.

Returning to Benson, the characters in *The Dawn of All* seem at first glance to be both uninteresting and dull. They don't have the usual problems that beset the customary science fiction or fantasy hero. There is no heroic nerd (usually the author, thinly disguised) or sniveling hulk wandering about constantly lamenting his self-doubt or promoting some politically correct anti-morality.

No, except for a genius or two who seem at first to be thrown in for local color, the people inhabiting *The Dawn of All* are plain and ordinary. People are virtuous, and, face it — virtue is "boring." *Il Paradiso* is the least popular section of the *Divine Comedy*. No wonder the jaded quip that "virtue is its own punishment." The extremes of virtue simply do not appeal to an age in which the "extreme," in sports and everything else, has become a "virtue" itself — whatever it takes to hold adrenaline addicts in thrall. The subtle horror of *The King in Yellow* is lost on readers of Stephen King.

The dullness of the people portrayed in *The Dawn of All* is almost too much. In some measure it may actually detract from the point Benson was making. The most fascinating character in *The Dawn of All* is an unrepentant heretic who is eventually executed for the civil crime of heresy. In my opinion, Benson deliberately set out to make him the most interesting and sympathetic character, and succeeded. It is only when the situation with the socialists heats up that the pope, whom Benson painted as the most ordinary of men, becomes heroic — as did the "ordinary" Benedict XV who followed St. Pius X in Benson's lifetime and was then confronted with World War I. Even then, it's clear that it is not the *individual* who is the hero —

> This then was the new type of man who had at last conquered the world. It was not superman that had been waited for so long, not a demigod armed with powers of light; not man raising himself above his stature, building towers on earthly foundations that should reach to heaven; but just man, utterly true to himself and his instincts, walking humbly before his God; looking for a city that has no foundations coming down to him out of heaven. It was supernature, not superman; grace and truth transfiguring nature; not nature wrenching itself vainly towards the stature of grace. It was man who could suffer, who could

reign; since he only who knows his weakness, dares to be strong. . . . *Vicisti Galilaee.*

That is the basic message of *The Dawn of All*. It is not that the world will be perfect when the Catholic Church is triumphant, nor even that restructuring the social order will automatically result in the creation of good men within a good society. Benson reiterates the ancient dictum that "all will be well" when man becomes most truly himself. From a Catholic perspective, of course, this will be when he conforms himself and the structures of society to the Law of the Gospels. Ordinary human beings become extraordinary while remaining themselves in the fullest sense.

To carry this message, Benson again used the satiric technique he had perfected in *Lord of the World*. The earlier novel took everything that the materialists and secular humanists considered best in the world and carried it out to its logical conclusion. The result was the end of the world. In *The Dawn of All*, Benson took everything that Edwardian England professed to hate or despise most in Catholicism and, by carrying out an extremely exaggerated *reductio ad absurdum*, showed that it could result in the foundation of a new age of peace and prosperity — the dawn of all.

Not that Benson viewed his fantasy as the blueprint for an ideal society — far from it. As Martindale made clear, "Benson wrote often and emphatically that he did not for a moment expect the pictured solution to realize itself, and that he even hoped it would not. Neither Science, nor the State, nor Religion would ever, he was convinced, find themselves in such mutual relations as he had invented."

One favorite if brief passage in the novel is the toss-off line by one of the characters to the effect that a now-independent Ireland had granted "Home Rule" to all its colonies rapidly, with very little trouble and, apparently, to the benefit of the entire British Empire. This is a rather trenchant comment on the "Irish Question" that consumed Imperial politicians for nearly the whole of the nineteenth and the early twentieth centuries until the frustration finally exploded in the "Easter Rising" of 1916, two years after Benson's death.

One topical allusion that may send a chill down the spine of more sensitive readers is the mention of *"Titanic*-class liners" — a reference that helps date the novel as well. (Benson also remarked on a very old nobleman who had been present as a boy at the coronation of George V — which took place in 1910, another topical reference that puts the writing of the book squarely in 1911.) The *Titanic* was under construction at the time Benson wrote *The Dawn of All*, and was the largest human artifact built up to that time, with the exception of the pyramids. Ironically, Benson was returning from a lecture tour in the United States in April 1912 when the liner on which he was traveling suddenly changed course. The captain was responding to the distress call sent out by the *Titanic*, but went back to his original course when it became obvious he could not reach the doomed ship in time.

The novel itself incorporates some minor faults. More concerned with demonstrating the extraordinary nature of the ordinary, Benson tended to become somewhat too much immersed in some of his background material. He gave his fascination with technology full rein, and spent just a little too much page space describing his fantastic inventions in detail — even though he was fully aware that the science was seriously flawed.

Benson also presented a distorted idea of Catholic political concepts. In common with many English Catholics, Benson was concerned with demonstrating his political loyalty to the British crown while maintaining his religious independence. He appears to have believed that the so-called "Divine Right of Kings" — the idea that God directly endows civil rulers with the right to rule — was somehow consistent with Catholic teachings. In any event, Pius XI's pointed repudiation of the "Divine Right of Kings" (preceded by the writings of Sts. Augustine, Thomas Aquinas and Robert Cardinal Bellarmine), was fifteen years in the future when Benson wrote.

Unusually for a man who wrote a short biography of St. Thomas à Becket, who died resisting Henry II's attempts to take over the Church in England, Benson also seemed to support the idea of an "established church." This concept was anathema in the Middle Ages, and only gained a foothold in England with the Tudors, who also abolished popular sovereignty and the elective kingship. (It comes as a surprise to many people that Richard III Plantagenet was elected king of England by the parliament. Henry VII Tudor, however, claimed the throne by virtue of an ephemeral "right of conquest," and was "confirmed" — not elected — by the parliament after judicious threats.)

Unfortunately, some readers of *The Dawn of All* have taken it not as satire, but as the blueprint of an ideal society. Lest we look on these individuals with condescension, however, recall that St. Thomas More's *Utopia* has been understood by many academics in the same way — and in spite of St. Thomas's clear statements to the contrary.

The modern commentator tends to forget or ignores the fact that More was a lawyer and knew exactly what he was talking about. More put the tale of *Utopia* in the mouth of a man whose name loosely translates as "Lying Traveler Who Tells Fantastic Tales" — "Raphael Hythloday." Nevertheless, not a few of today's experts continue to insist that the book is actually a plea for communism and a condemnation of private property — ideas specifically refuted by More. Similarly, Benson stated in the very beginning of *The Dawn of All* that it is not to be taken seriously as a detailed factual or literal account. In the preface he calls it, in fact, a "parable."

For that reason, when reading *The Dawn of All*, we should keep in mind what Benson was writing, and not, necessarily, what we hope or would like to find in the novel. Remember we're reading a satire, not a blueprint for social order. Above all, of course, bring your sense of humor — and prepare to be entertained.

6. The Holy Blissful Martyr, Thomas à Becket

Depending on your point of view, it is either singularly appropriate or strikingly ironic that Robert Hugh Benson should write a biography of Saint Thomas à Becket (or "Beckett"), the man around whose martyrdom at the instigation (conscious or not) of Henry II Plantagenet, grew the famous pilgrimage to Canterbury. Benson was the son of the Anglican Archbishop of Canterbury. Henry VIII Tudor created the Anglican Church when he succeeded where Henry II had failed in asserting the dominance of the State over the Church, managing to make another martyr named Thomas in the process.

This book was conceived as a joint project between Benson and Frederick Rolfe, a one-time friend of Benson with whom he had a parting of the ways once Rolfe's real character became evident. Rolfe's views and beliefs on a number of subjects, once they began to surface, proved anathema to a man as concerned about orthodoxy and truth as Benson. After a relatively short period of friendly interaction, Benson cut himself loose from "Baron Corvo" (a title that Rolfe claimed) and Rolfe's compatriot "Marie Corelli" (real name unknown), and was pursued with increasing vituperation and vilification for the rest of his life.[61]

Still, that left Benson with the work that he had done on a project originally conceived as a fictionalized biography of Saint Thomas. Rolfe did do a significant amount of background work for his portion of the project, but virtually none of this was incorporated into the final product.[62] This makes the co-attribution to Benson and Rolfe that we see in some editions somewhat problematical; Rolfe's contribution could reasonably call for an "acknowledgement" of assistance, but certainly not co-authorship.

---

[61] Evelyn Waugh, "Introduction" *The History of Richard Raynal, Solitary*. Chicago, IL: Henry Regnery Company, 1956.
[62] Martindale, Vol. II, 99-106.

After years of back and forth and vicissitudes of fortune, the book changed character completely and became straight biography. The final product is almost completely — and quintessentially — Benson. We are tempted to think that Benson's production may have inspired Evelyn Waugh to write a biography of a man they both admired as well — Saint Edmund Campion,[63] another champion of religious rights against the tyranny of the State.

Fresh from writing his early series of historical novels, the parallels between the story of Saint Thomas à Becket and Henry II Plantagenet on the one hand, and Saint Thomas More and Henry VIII Tudor on the other would almost have forced themselves on Benson. Writing of Becket so soon after completing *By What Authority?*, *The King's Achievement*, and *The Queen's Tragedy*, it would have been obvious that Henry VIII succeeded where Henry II failed. The only question that remained was, why?

In the case of Becket's murder, the public outcry was so great that there was no support for Henry II. He had been attempting to erode the rights of the nobility and the freemen of England for some time. They saw in Henry's instigation of Thomas' murder not only an attack on God and the Church, but one more attack on their own rights and liberties. The English upper classes and the lower classes were, for once, united.

The situation was different by the time the sixteenth century rolled around. For one thing, the Reformation was in full swing. Martin Luther had shown it was possible to defy the pope and get away with it — God would not strike you down (nor would He strike down *your* enemies, however much you might demand it). Further, the interests of the English upper classes and those of the lower ranks of society were directly at variance. Henry VII Tudor had started a trend toward centralization of political power and concentration of economic power. By the time his son Henry VIII inherited the throne (as opposed to being elected and confirmed as rulers prior to the Tudors had been), the "New Men" were already immensely rich

---

[63] Evelyn Waugh, *Edmund Campion, Priest and Martyr*. London: Longmans, Green & Co., 1935.

and powerful ... and the king was firmly under their control.

The Tudor Reformation succeeded where that of the Plantagenets had failed because the English upper classes in the sixteenth century — in common with the upper classes of much of northern Europe — desired money and power above all else. Henry VIII could get what he wanted — a divorce from his lawful wife — and the upper classes could fatten themselves further on the property of the Church, and all at the small cost of cutting themselves off from everything that, in the analysis of William Cobbett, the astute early nineteenth "radical" commentator, had made England great, as well as from their true spiritual home in the Catholic Church:

> "The liberties of England" is a phrase in every mouth, but what are those liberties? The laws which regulate the descent and possession of property; the safety from arrest, unless by due and settled process; the absence of all punishment without trial before duly authorized and well-known judges and magistrates; the trial by jury; the precautions taken by the divers writs and summonses; the open trial; the impartiality in the proceedings. These are the "liberties of England." And had our Catholic forefathers less of these than we have? Do we not owe them all to them? Have we one single law that gives security to property or to life which we do not inherit from them? The treadmill, the law to shut men up in their houses from sunset to sunrise, the law to banish us for life if we utter anything having a tendency to bring our "representatives" into contempt; these indeed we do not inherit, but may boast of them, and of many others of much about the same character, as being unquestionably of pure Protestant origin.[64]

So — did Benson write this book out of a sense of duty, of reparation? Probably not. The introduction that he wrote indicates that his main object was to highlight the problem of worship of the State instead of God — a deification that meant virtual godhood for the ruling classes.

---

[64] Cobbett, *op. cit.*, § 456.

This was an ancient pagan idea that surfaced again with the Reformation. It spawned a resurgence of the creaking "Divine Right of Kings" so beloved of a significant number of Catholics disappointed with the presumed failure of democratic government and the steady march of modern civilization away from religious belief of any kind.

Unfortunately, while the faith of such individuals is undoubtedly great, they fail to realize or understand that they are espousing a position directly at odds with the ancient teaching of the Catholic Church. They insist, even in the face of explicit papal and magisterial statements regarding individual sovereignty, democracy, and the proper roles of Church and State — which have never changed, despite the changing forms in which the roles manifest themselves — that democracy, individual sovereignty, free will . . . even the venerable doctrine of the separation of Church and State, the very issue that both Saint Thomas à Becket and Saint Thomas More died supporting, is anti- or non-Catholic.

There is, of course, a deeper problem in all this, but one that we will only touch on here. That is, a great many people today of all religious beliefs insist that faith must rule over reason. Most likely rooted in a reaction against the rapid growth of secularism, the *fides solo* — "faith alone" — stance is itself a Protestant doctrine, deriving from the great debate of the Middle Ages over whether God's Will or God's Nature ("Intellect") was preeminent. Yet another Saint Thomas — Thomas Aquinas, the "Angelic Doctor" — won the debate for the Catholic Church in favor of God's Nature. That is, we are to understand Revelation and Tradition in light of what little we can know of God's Holy Nature, which we see reflected analogously in human nature.[65]

That is, if we interpret a passage in the Bible or an encyclical as meaning that we may take property from the rich to redistribute to the poor, we must "measure" that interpretation against the standard of the natural law. When we see that the human race has always and everywhere condemned theft — a violation of private property

---

[65] *Vide* Chesterton, *op. cit.*

— we must conclude that private property is proper matter of the natural law. Theft cannot be justified, any more than the killing of an innocent human being — whether or not the State recognizes that human being as a "person." As Doctor Heinrich Rommen explained,

> It follows from the fact of *natura vulnerata* as well as from the ethical character and goal of community life, and of the state in particular, that positive human laws are absolutely necessary for determining the further inferences from the first principles in the interest of a more exact and readily discernible establishment of order and for the setting up of institutions needed for community life. The natural-law prohibition of adultery implies at the same time an affirmation of marriage and of the general norms that are most needed for its functioning as an institution. "Thou shalt not steal" presupposes the institution of private property as pertaining to the natural law; but not, for example, the feudal property arrangements of the Middle Ages or the modern capitalist system. Since the natural law lays down general norms only, it is the function of the positive law to undertake the concrete, detailed regulation of real and personal property and to prescribe the formalities for conveyance of ownership.[66]

There is, of course, a strictly determined set of circumstances — much more rare than many people today like to believe — when, due to immanent danger of death or permanent disability, it becomes licit to take what you *need* (not want) for yourself or your immediate dependents from the superabundance of another. "Superabundance" means that which the nominal owner clearly does not need, will ever need or, even, in some instances, want in order to maintain himself and his dependents in a manner befitting his station in life. In that case, the absolute minimum that is *needed* (again, not simply *desired* for an improvement in the "quality" of life) becomes "common property." The needy individual may take only

---

[66] Rommen, *op. cit.*, 59.

what he or his dependents need . . . after exhausting all other recourse.

Naturally, there is a "Catch-22" in this "permission to steal." The needy individual incurs no moral guilt, but the social order is such a great good that certain bad things are permitted to maintain order, while certain good things are forbidden for the same reason. Usury, for example — the taking of a profit when no profit has been generated — is a great evil. Profit-taking is in and of itself a very great good, only becoming "evil" (despite the insistence of the socialists) when no profit has been made.

Modern corporate finance and (more especially) the consumer credit industry are, however, based firmly on the presumed need to take a profit whether or not profit has been made. This extends even to the presumably "just" demands of workers for fixed wage and benefits packages sufficient to meet the needs of them and their dependents . . . whether or not they produce goods and services of equivalent value to the wages and benefits they receive.

Thus, even though it is a great evil, usury — a form of theft, and thus a violation of private property — must be allowed to continue, even though the usurer incurs grave moral guilt when he has another viable choice. This is because simply abolishing usury in all its forms unilaterally and without changing the basic structures of the modern financial system would destroy civilization.

Paradoxically, stealing from the superabundance of another — for which the taker does *not* incur moral guilt — must *not* be allowed! That is because if simply taking what one needed from another became the accepted and ordinary way of obtaining the necessities of life, society would collapse. Private property is one of the pillars of the social order, along with life and liberty. If anyone could take what he wanted from the goods of another, the productive would be punished by not being allowed to profit by their industry, while the lazy and shiftless would be rewarded. People would soon only produce at the point of a gun, as became obvious in the former Soviet Union. Does this mean that there is no recourse, that mankind is locked into unjust social structures for all eternity?

Of course not. As Pius XI made clear throughout his pontificate, each human person has the power (meaning the right) and the duty to organize with others when the institutions of the social order are flawed to an intolerable degree. We do not simply abolish an evil and prevent it with the coercive power of the State. On the contrary, we first convince others that a more rationally structured social order is desirable, then work to bring it about. The unjust institution — such as usury or widespread poverty — is either reformed or falls of its own dead weight, replaced by a better institution.[67]

Many people, however, find this "act of social justice" — organizing for the common good in order to effect beneficial change in our institutions — too slow or presume it to be ineffective. They demand that the State take charge of as much as possible in order to implement instant social change — enforced, as we might expect, at the point of a gun: the police power of the State. This ultimately results in the deification of the State, and inevitably a joining of Church and State in some fashion, whether through the establishment of an official State church (and thus under the control of State bureaucrats, and manipulated for political purposes) or the elimination of competing faiths, leaving the State the only "religious" body.

This, then, was the whole issue between Archbishop Thomas and King Henry. In the Middle Ages the Catholic Church had "from time immemorial" certain rights and privileges on which the civil power — the State — could not encroach. Often, of course, the State *had* interfered in these matters, with consequent repercussions, both serious and, in some instances, almost ludicrous. There were not a few worldly ecclesiastics who sought to curry favor with the civil authorities by asserting that the princes of this world ruled by "divine right," thereby muddying the waters even more.

The whole Guelph and Ghibbeline struggle in Italy and Germany, which spilled over on occasion into France and England, was a struggle between civil authorities who

---

[67] *Vide* Rev. William J. Ferrree, S.M., Ph.D., *The Act of Social Justice*. Washington, DC: The Catholic University of America Press, 1943.

wanted to take over the Church and use it for their own ends, and ecclesiastical authorities who wanted to use the spiritual power of the Church to set things right in the civil sphere, backed by the coercive power of the State. Once that struggle was decided, the Guelphs and Ghibbelines (and their spiritual descendents) continued fighting amongst themselves to decide *how* Church and State were to relate to each other once the separation was effected.

The ancient doctrine of separation of Church and State was rooted firmly in the Roman civilization that was Christian Europe. The Romans — at times to modern eyes seeming to drift between being the quintessential individualists and the perfect collectivists — carefully divided human society into three discrete forms.

To most people today, the only "society" that exists is the civil order: the State. As far as the Romans were concerned, this was only one form of society and, in a sense, the least important of the three. Civil society was concerned with the body politic, the *Res Publica* (the "Public Thing"), and was supposed to stay out of the other two forms of society, the family and the temple.

Then there was, first and foremost in Roman eyes, domestic society, ruled over by the *Pater Familias*, the "Father of the Family." Domestic society — the family — in Roman society was the basis for everything. The family was both a civil and a religious body distinct from the State and the temple. A family had its own "household gods" — its domestic religion (making the "domestic church" more than a catch phrase) — and its own legal code, almost inevitably unwritten, but very real and supported by an immense weight of tradition.

The *Pater Familias* was thus, within the confines of the family, both head of a mini-State and the chief priest. In theory the power of the *Pater Familias* was so great that he could assemble a "domestic court" and try members of his *familia* (the nuclear family, ancillary relations, and slaves) for crimes against the family, whether domestic or religious (there frequently being no real difference between the two). Until the influence of Christianity and, to some degree, Stoicism, became pervasive, the *Pater Fa-*

milias could act as accuser, judge, jury — and executioner. Some of the most famous stories in Rome's admittedly somewhat mythical history involved the *Pater Familias* executing a disobedient son or daughter, while the punishments meted out to "bad" slaves were often ferocious in their savagery. The only check on the power of the *Pater Familias* was social pressure.

Nor could the State or temple authorities interfere. Once while attending a banquet, Augustus Caesar — head of both Church and State — was only able to stop the execution of a slave who had accidentally broken a valuable goblet by instantly doing the same thing himself. The owner had the domestic right to do anything he liked to his clumsy slave — but Augustus' action made it clear that the owner would no longer be a "friend of Caesar" if he did so.

Next was "religious society," that which over the gods ruled directly, which we understand today as "Church." As far as the Romans were concerned, anything that came directly under some god or other was the purview of the priests, the heads of each discrete religious society or "temple." The games, for example, had to be opened by a priest, because they were ostensibly in honor of the gods. Foreign relations, because they involved relations between the people of one god to the people of another god, were handled by a special class of priests, as were a host of other things that we today simply assume should come under the State.

Crimes within religious society in the Roman view properly came under the jurisdiction of the temples. If someone committed what would ordinarily be considered a civil crime within the precincts of a temple, he was tried in a temple court. Similarly, if a priest committed a crime, he was either tried in a temple court, or stripped of his priesthood and tried in civil court.

Because certain functions of the head of State were thus construed as "religious," the head of State had to be a priest. Since he was civil head of the Roman people, it made sense (to the Romans) that he should also be religious head of the Roman people. Hence Caesar was usually named Chief Priest of the Republic, or *Pontifex Maximus* — "Great Bridge Builder" between the gods and man, and primary intercessor for the common good and the needs of the "Public Thing," the *Res Publica*. Oddly enough to modern understanding, most of the Caesars tried to keep religious and civil affairs separate — civil society and religious society were considered two distinct things, and the orderly Roman mind refused to mix them.

It was with the coming of Christianity that things changed. Formerly Caesar — the emperor — had been head of both Church and State. Christianity, however, shares a distinction with Judaism in that its God is a "jealous god." That is, there is no question that a Christian or a Jew (or, later, a Muslim) could accept the head of another religion as head of his religion — which meant that Caesar as *Pontifex Maximus* had no authority to act as religious head of the Jewish people or, later, of any Christians.

That, as we know, caused problems. The Romans granted the Jews the special privilege of not having to recognize the Roman *Pontifex Maximus* as head of Judaism. This was, at first, extended to include Christians, considered initially to be nothing more than another type of Jew. When it became clear, however, that Judaism and Christianity had parted ways, Christians were considered traitors. Most Romans, even the emperors themselves, didn't really believe that Caesar was a god[68] — but they believed that the social order could only be properly maintained by enforcing the cult of the emperor and worship of the Roman State, personified by the goddess Roma.

Refusing to burn a little incense to the emperor (whether or not you believed that the old fool on the throne really was a god) meant that you were an enemy of the social order, and thus an enemy of the human race. When we consider today that we are forced to accept widespread abortion or, formerly, slavery due to the effect that its unilateral abolition would have on the social order, we can

---

[68] As the cynical Vespasian was dying, Suetonius (*The Twelve Caesars*) relates that he said, *"Puto dues fio"* — "I believe I am turning into a god." *De Vita Caesarum, Divus Vespasianus*, XXIII, 3.

understand why the early Christians were persecuted with such cruelty.

Understand, yes — but not accept. Again, when faced with a condition of society in which intolerable wrongs are made possible by our institutions, the proper response is not to attack or destroy those institutions and, consequently, the social order that relies on those institutions for its maintenance. Instead, what we must do is precisely what Pius XI told us to do: organize for the common good, and reform (restructure) our institutions so that they once again function within acceptable parameters.

If that were not enough, Christianity claims to have its own chief priest, the successor of Saint Peter, the personally named Vicar of Christ on Earth. The pope is thus in Christian belief divinely appointed — that is, holding the office of *Pontifex Maximus* by divine right, not because the Legions had elected him and the Senate and the People of Rome had confirmed him.

That meant that Caesar, whatever his claims with respect to other religions, could not be head of the Christian religion. Not being head of the Christian religion, Caesar had no authority whatsoever in purely Church affairs. As far as Christianity was concerned, however many titles and earthly honors a man might have, it meant nothing for either Church doctrine or discipline.

Naturally this did not sit well with the Caesars. Constantine the Great evidently couldn't help interfering in Church affairs. He did this to such effect that when the center of Roman power shifted to Byzantium and was further infected with eastern civil and religious despotism, so-called Caesaro-papism became a serious problem.

In the west, with its claim to be the legitimate heirs of the Roman *regnum* (especially from the days of Charlemagne) the problem was not quite as serious, but still bad enough. The only check on the drift to Caesaro-papism in the west was the fact that the western emperors (the "Holy Roman Emperors") usually needed the support of the pope against the active hostility of the Byzantine Emperor — whose claim to the Roman *regnum* was at least as valid as theirs.[69]

When the power of the Byzantine Empire began its rapid decline after the Dreadful Day of Manzikert in 1071, the Holy Roman Emperors no longer needed the support of the papacy quite as much — and not at all after 1453, when the "Queen City" of Constantinople fell to the Turks. As we might expect, civil rulers in the west began asserting the supremacy of the temporal order over the Church. This, as we already hinted, reached its immediate climax with the Guelph and Ghibbeline struggle. The other princes of the earth were quick to follow the lead of the emperor, considered the temporal head of Christendom, as the pope was the spiritual head.

The ultimate climax, of course, was the Reformation. Because of his authority in matters of faith and morals, the primary target of all the reformers was the pope, regardless of the specific point of disagreement. Unfortunately for the cause of human liberty, the pope (who at times might be a very bad man indeed) also happened to be the only effective counter to the claims of civil rulers over the whole of society, whether civil, domestic, or religious. All the polemics about the presumed tyranny of the popes begin to sound a little hollow once we realize that the princes of men — the rulers of civil society — desperately wanted absolute power, and (in classic form) had to make the only thing standing between them and the realization of their goal sound more evil than the goal.

Ranking close after the pope, of course, were the rights, privileges, and immunities of the Church herself. Naturally the most obvious manifestation of this was the property of the Church. Without property, the Church would have had no power to protect itself against the inroads of the civil authority. "Power" as Daniel Webster observed, "naturally and necessarily follows property," and nowhere was this more evident than in Medieval Europe. In order for the princes of men to reign supreme on earth, the Church must be stripped of its power — and that meant

---

[69] The Venetian Republic attained the status of world power by playing the claims of the Holy Roman Emperor off against the Byzantine *Basilius* — and *vice versa*.

stripping it of its property. The fact that this meant that the civil rulers got a delightful little dividend in the form of an immense influx of wealth (usually squandered within the space of a few short years) simply moved things along more rapidly.

It was against this background and with this history in mind that the drama related in Benson's short book was acted out. An attack on any right, privilege, or immunity of the Church was not only an attack on the social order, but could (and did) lead to the virtual overthrow of a sanely ordered society — or so a man like Archbishop Thomas of Canterbury would have believed as firmly as it is possible to believe anything. The actual right was unimportant; what mattered was the fact that it was a *right* — and the civil authority had no power whatsoever to interfere in that right.

Silly persons like to point out that every right Saint Thomas died to defend was eventually recognized as being properly the purview of the civil order, so that his death was — in their eyes — totally useless and meaningless. Some even end up agreeing with Henry VIII Tudor, who put Saint Thomas on trial for high treason *post mortem*, that the Archbishop was a consummate villain who was trying to assert the supremacy of the Church over the State . . . rather than the supremacy of the State over the Church, as Henry Tudor did.

Again, that was never the point. What mattered was that Henry II Plantagenet was claiming — by right — certain privileges and immunities that the Church in England had always had, regardless how well or ill it managed to defend them over the centuries. Henry did not make an argument or present a case to support his contention. Like many people today, he simply asserted it as self-evident. He wanted it, therefore it was his.

Archbishop Becket, however, knew that whether the rights over which they struggled properly belonged to the Church or to the State, they were — at present — recognized as belonging to the Church. Further, Thomas knew Henry well enough to know that had the king managed to get his way in this instance, he would soon begin encroaching in other areas as well — areas that were not as gray as whether clergy accused of civil crimes should be judged in a civil or Church court, the latter being the custom of centuries.

Thomas was well aware that surrendering in a minor matter would mean surrendering as well such things as the power of clerical appointments, and even the determination of doctrine. Truth would become a political football, and sacrificed to expedience whenever it became uncomfortable. Ultimately (as indeed proved to be the case under the Tudors), the Church would become the State's lackey, enforcing politically motivated religious doctrine with the coercive power of the State.

What happened is well known. King Henry, a man with the notoriously short Plantagenet temper, became so enraged at the stubbornness of Archbishop Thomas and his refusal to act reasonably (*i.e.*, to give Henry what he wanted) that he spoke words at a banquet, probably without thinking of the power that the words of a powerful or influential man often have over subordinates: "What sluggish knaves are these of my kingdom! Is there not one that will rid me of this troublesome priest?" Four knights took this as a royal command, and that very night crossed the Channel to England, eventually murdering the Archbishop.

The outcry was enormous and immediate throughout the whole of Europe. Whether or not he consciously intended that anyone should act on his intemperate utterance, Henry was held responsible for Thomas' death — as, indeed, he was. A public figure or journalist who openly and publicly advocates anything — even in jest — is responsible for what happens when someone acts on it. The newspaper reporter who published a map to the house of Medgar Evers and hinted that he should be killed was as responsible for the murder as the man who pulled the trigger. It is the equivalent of yelling, "Fire!" in a crowded theater.

Henry's words — regardless whether or not the death of Thomas was his intent — made the king guilty of murder. Only public penance saved him from excommunication and loss of his throne. Even so, the sins of the fathers are visited on the sons. When the Barons of England rose against King John, Henry's son, they were able to count on the help of Stephen Langton, Archbishop of Canterbury, and successor to Saint Thomas à Becket.

Nor could King John do very much about it. John certainly made Archbishop Langton's life miserable, but John had nowhere near the popularity of his father or his brother, Richard the Lionheart. John could not risk actually harming Stephen and creating another martyr. Consequently the king was forced to accede to the Great Charter — *Magna Charta* — reaffirming the rights and privileges recognized by his ancestor, Henry I Plantagenet, a century before. First and foremost among these rights were, of course:

> Have in the first place granted to God, and confirmed by this our present charter, for us and for our heirs forever,
>
> That the churches of England shall be free, and shall enjoy their rights and franchises entirely and fully: and this our purpose is, that it be observed, as may appear by our having granted, of our mere and free will, that elections should be free (which is reputed to be a very great and very necessary privilege of the churches of England) before the difference arose betwixt us and our barons, and by our having confirmed the same by our charter, and by our having procured it moreover to be confirmed by our lord the apostle Innocent the third. Which privilege we will maintain: and our will is, that the same be faithfully maintained by our heirs forever.

The Founding Fathers of the United States of America, based on this noble tradition, also promised to protect the rights of Church against the encroachment of the State, particularly the evil of any religion established as a State bureaucracy or branch of the government. The reader may judge for himself how well the United States has adhered to the clear intent of its Founding Fathers in this and other matters.

7. The Contemporary Novels

A Winnowing (1910)

None Other Gods (1911)

The Coward (1912)

An Average Man (1913)

Initiation (1914)

Loneliness? (1915)

A Winnowing

With the possible exception of *Lord of the World* and *The Dawn of All* — and that only because of extreme familiarity with those two works — I cannot read any fiction by Robert Hugh Benson without finding some previously unsuspected treasure, another level, in the text. *A Winnowing*, from 1910, is a good example of this.

The novel struck me as particularly entertaining the first time I read it. There seemed to be something that outdid P. G. Wodehouse at his most sublimely ridiculous. Take, for example, a passage of which I quickly became enamored:

> I refuse to describe the flower show held at Sir Samuel Cohen's beyond saying that it was exactly like all other flower shows; and I forget whether it was in support of any charitable institution. I think it must have been; otherwise I do not think that even Lady Carberry would have made a speech. There were all the usual things — hot tents, moderately cold ices, awnings over the windows, grass trampled till it bled a dark green, a nerve-shattering noise of talking and brass-band playing, an enormous crowd that ebbed and flowed continually, motorcars, carriages, dust turnstiles, a good deal of crossness, small girls with black legs and white frocks, men in straw hats, women with Zulu headdresses: and there were some flowers, I think.

". . . and there were some flowers, I think." If a reader doesn't fall in love with Benson's writing on the strength of that line alone, then we must contradict Sir Walter Scott and declare that there *does* breathe a man with soul so dead. We can see why Evelyn Waugh was so fond of Benson's work.

But, of course, the glories of *A Winnowing* do not rest on that passage. Take the description of a character who drifts between being a major player and part of the scenery:

I love contemplating people of this kind, because the subject is so endless and evasive. I have no certainty of what Mr. Fakenham thinks about, but I am stimulated by him to form unverifiable conjectures forever. Thoughts undoubtedly pass through his mind beyond those to which he gives expression, but I have no idea as to what they are; words proceed out of his mouth — often, so long as the subject is on his own plane, shrewd and suggestive; and actions are done by him. He lives, and he will die; and as to what he will do then not even I dare to form conjectures of any kind. He is the strongest argument for the annihilation of the soul that I have ever met. . . .

I wish now to describe his appearance this morning — not that anything depends upon it. (He is not, later on, to be convicted by its means of some nameless crime.) I wish only to gaze upon him for a minute or two.

Such a character seems to be thrown into the story for comic relief. Despite his pretensions to gentility and his assessment of virtually the whole of the rest of mankind as cultural philistines, he is a boring nonentity, very nearly a boob. He isn't even amusing enough to challenge Bertie Wooster's preeminence as the quintessential member of the incredible Drones Club, serving to entertain the lower classes.

This is where Benson's superlative talent comes into play. At first reading we're tempted to think that the author throws these light, yet barbed comments in to lighten the mood. *A Winnowing* is, after all, seemingly drenched in an obsession with death. The novel opens with one of the protagonists at death's door. Every couple of chapters it seems as if somebody either dies, or is waiting for somebody to die. The French Carmelites who take up residence in the convent built for them by Jack and Mary Weston seem to be buried in death while still living behind their walls and grills. To add an even more macabre note, they bring with them from France the incorrupt body of their "saint," a sister who died some years previously, incongruously carted about in a cheap wooden packing crate.

Benson, however, wrote nothing without a definite purpose. Even *By What Authority?*, his first published novel, although it weighs in at nearly a quarter of a million words, doesn't waste a single one. Well-meaning editors who have abridged a number of Benson's works have not succeeded in improving the works, but in robbing them of much of their meaning.

Take *A Winnowing*, for example. As I hinted, at first reading it seemed to have a definite taste of being a potboiler. Despite the continual references to death, there is a flippancy, even breeziness in the writing that takes you off guard, especially if you've read any of Benson's earlier works, particularly the relentlessly grim *Lord of the World*. Reading *A Winnowing*, however, is so effortless that the reader is tempted to conclude that the author threw it together to meet a contractual obligation or make some extra money, and for a change didn't really give a damn about being "serious."

That judgment, however, would be a mistake. Benson did not write to make a living. He had independent means. He wrote because that was one of the ways he used to say the things he needed to say, not to churn out something to meet the monthly rent.

The problem becomes, What is Benson saying? *A Winnowing* is ranked among Benson's most obscure works. This is undeserved, even for Benson, whose novels as a body require a bit more effort to appreciate than a significant number of modern readers might be willing to put forth. Perhaps a better question would be, What was Benson *doing*?

Although these divisions are far from hard and fast, I see *A Winnowing* as marking the beginning of the third major phase or grouping of Benson's literary career. He had begun by setting out on a tremendous journey that he was unable to finish — creating an alternative to the (very) bad historical novels that afflicted the reading public of his day. The often-conscious (but usually not) assumptions in these productions color much of what many people to this day still believe is the absolute literal truth about the Catholic Church — and bears about as much resemblance to that institution as the shuffling, comic darky in bad films does to someone of African birth or descent.

The historical novels of this first period, *By What Authority?*, *The King's Achievement*, and *The Queen's Tragedy* are a splendid — and successful — attempt to present the "Catholic side" of the Reformation in England. Eschewing the bigoted and tedious "facts" cut out of whole cloth by other English historical novelists, Benson's concern for historical accuracy was so great that (had it not been for his native charm and the obvious importance of his self-imposed task), he was in serious danger of becoming a pest to a number of scholars as he checked and rechecked his work.

Oddsfish! properly belongs in this phase, for the first drafts were written (and endlessly rewritten) at this time before being set aside. *Come Rack! Come Rope!* however, would throw my neat categorization into a cocked hat were it not abundantly clear that the book is (as a number of authorities have pointed out) "in a class by itself." It defies an easy categorization — so we can safely let the novel rest on its own stunning merits.

Nevertheless, despite his obvious success as a historical novelist, it became apparent to Benson that he was not getting his point across. I could be wrong (and very likely am), but a growing conviction that historical fiction might not be the best medium for him could have been the reason why *The Queen's Tragedy* was such a difficult book to write, and why he was unable to complete *Oddsfish!* at this time — unconsciously he may have known that "it wouldn't do."

Benson seems to have caught on to the fact that, bad as the portrayals of the Catholic Church were in historical fiction, the view of the institution in early twentieth century contemporary opinion was worse — for it was current. This may account for the fact that the second phase of his career consisted of a "screaming" (Benson's own word) wake-up call in the form of his four "sensational" novels, *The Sentimentalists*, *Lord of the World*, *The Conventionalists*, and *The Necromancers*. Perhaps not coincidentally, these were also the years of his fortunately brief acquaintance with the weird "Baron Corvo" and "Marie Corelli" (both pseudonyms).

Yet these novels, too, failed in the sense that people still missed the point. The four "sensational" novels are possibly the most intelligent, clever, and biting satires of Edwardian England ever written. They are also Benson's most popular works — and for all the wrong reasons. *Lord of the World* in particular flays the assumptions and cherished beliefs of secular humanism (the real religion of upper class English Edwardian society) until there isn't a whole piece of skin left on the carcass.

Unfortunately, while he turned out what many regard as a classic of early twentieth century science fiction, many people even to this day take the novel — admittedly fantastic science and all — as a work of "prophecy." To counter that opinion, Benson took the time in 1911 to turn out *The Dawn of All* as a "counterblast" to *Lord of the World*, and to beat the horse from the other side. Naturally people took Benson's exaggerations in *The Dawn of All* as the blueprint of an ideal society, an interpretation that the author himself (tearing out his hair in frustration) explicitly rejected.

In 1910, however, Benson seems to have come to the realization that enlightens all good writers eventually. If you want to get your point across most effectively, write what you know. And what Benson knew better than any man alive was upper-class English society, both from the inside as a son of the most powerful Anglican clergyman in the British Empire — the Archbishop of Canterbury — and from the outside as a convert to the Catholic Church. This unique perspective supplied the raw material from which Benson forged half a dozen novels that, astonishingly, are little known today.

Thus began a run of satirical contemporary novels that delighted Evelyn Waugh and seems to have completely baffled generations of readers. Benson quickly found his "voice." He then turned out works that, read with a basic understanding of the author's goal — to discover the deepest meaning of life and discern one's vocation — are superficially easy to read and entertaining and yet at the same time contain such profound depths that they demand several re-readings.

The series began with *A Winnowing* and continued with *None Other Gods*. Then in rapid succession came *The Coward*, *An Average Man*, *Initiation*, and the posthumous *Loneliness?* This achievement is even more astonishing when we discover that it was during this time Benson also completed or composed entirely a number of essays, two historical novels, three dramas, and a science fiction epic — in addition to a full schedule of lecturing, preaching, and missionary work. At the time of his death in 1914, Benson had already outlined yet another novel, set in war-torn France during the German invasion.

So — what do we have with Benson's first foray into "mainstream" fiction? Despite the seeming obsession with death, it turns out that the subject of *A Winnowing* is not death, but life — and the question, "What is life for?" Anyone familiar with the least of Benson's writings is aware that, if anything, he was obsessed (if that is even the right word) about his vocation, his calling in life. Why had God made him and put him here on earth?

Good writers write about what they're familiar with. Naturally, Benson being concerned with the question of vocation, he wrote about the question of vocation in virtually every one of his novels. The subject is so vast, however, that we are not treated to a dismal parade of the same plot, endlessly rewritten. No, the question of vocation is so important and broad in scope that, except in his historical novels (written with another purpose in mind, yet the issue is there, too), it, like life itself, provides endless permutations for study.

Reading Benson's different treatments of the question of vocation reminds me of the story told of Picasso, in which a friend criticized the artist for painting a picture of the same vase over and over again. Picasso responded by pointing out that he kept painting the same vase because it appeared continually different to him, and he wanted to paint the essence of the vase, not a fleeting impression of the vase. Yes, Benson kept going over the question of vocation, but it is a different question for each member of the human race, and each one has a different story to tell.

That brings us to the story in *A Winnowing*. At the most superficial, yet still meaningful level, the novel is a study in contrasts. Apart from the evident death-obsession, we find the utterly pointless lives of the local English gentry juxtaposed with those of the *nouveaux riches* Jack and Mary Weston and their newly discovered devotion to Catholicism. On a smaller scale, we see a continual rejection and misunderstanding on the part of the gentry of any life with purpose.

We see this later almost perfectly developed in *The Coward*, but in *A Winnowing* the picture is much starker. Life without death or even a purpose other than the trivial pursuits of upper class society as ends in themselves is, ultimately, devoid of meaning. Mary Weston, the central character of *A Winnowing*, seems to grasp this at some visceral level, yet is repelled by every shred of evidence or suggestion that pain and suffering — things she regards as obscene and something to be avoided at all cost (a theme visited again in much deeper terms in *Initiation*) — give meaning to life and are paths to something much greater than the mere world.

Mary's interview with a Carmelite appears to confirm her worst fears about being buried alive, of the sisters being dead in the midst of life. The fact that the sisters pay such veneration to the corpse of a sister — a nobody in life — who had died some years before and whose remains had been shipped to England in an ordinary wooden packing crate simply confirms this. The long memories of the sisters in regard to their "saint" offer a sharp contrast to the funeral of the local social queen, Lady Carberry, complete with silver-plated coffin and elaborate ceremonies . . . that are forgotten along with Lady Carberry a week after she's in the ground.

The description of Lady Carberry's funeral and its juxtaposition with the situation of the Carmelite "little saint" suggests that Benson may have had in mind the funeral of Sir Philip Sidney (1554-1586), which would have been familiar to him from his research for his historical novels. Sir Philip was considered the quintessential Elizabethan courtier, being (in Tudor terms) what every woman wanted, and what every man wanted to be.

After his death in the Netherlands Sir Philip was given a State funeral unequaled in England until that of Sir Winston Churchill in 1965. Sir Francis Walsingham (the founder of the secret police and Sir Philip's father-in-law) staged and paid for the production, a description of which in sufficient detail to give the reader a good idea of the proceedings would be much too lengthy to relate here. Suffice it to say that "opulent" and "extravagant" are very weak words in some circumstances.

What would have struck Benson most of all was the near-total focus on the loss of Sir Philip and the orgiastic mourning instead of the solemn rejoicing that should accompany a Christian's "birthday into heaven" as the reward of a life (however short) well-spent. Yes, death is sad for those of us left behind, but should always be tempered with the knowledge that God is never unjust or wasteful. If we focus too much on our loss rather than on the deceased's gain, we risk falling into despair, a point that Benson was to make a significant subplot in *Initiation* a few years later — *Initiation* being a novel that, in a certain sense, may have been Benson's literary effort to prepare his readers for his own approaching death.

Benson saw one of the effects of the Reformation as turning people away from the spiritual and focusing on the material. Funerals such as that of Sir Philip Sidney and the fictional Lady Carberry exemplify this tendency by putting on an extravagant show that takes attention away from the reason and the purpose of death. Evelyn Waugh, who greatly admired Benson, made this same point even more graphically in his grotesquely funny novel *The Loved One: An Anglo-American Tragedy*. Waugh's story shredded the southern Californian manifestation of this tendency to "materialize" rather than spiritualize death — which specifically exempts Catholics and Jews (two groups that, in Waugh's opinion, viewed death properly) by noting that they "had their own cemeteries," and thus weren't good markets for elaborate funerals.

Benson would also have noted (probably with repugnance) the combination of genuine sorrow connected with Sir Philip's death and Walsingham's cynical exploitation of the staged production to take people's minds off the recent execution of Mary Queen of Scots and the planned upcoming war with Spain. This, too, finds its echo in Lady Carberry's funeral, in which Benson does not call into question the mourners' sincerity, but at the same time makes it clear that the real importance of the funeral for them is as a social event and a promise of wealth that will allow the heirs to do absolutely nothing of any real importance for the rest of their lives. This, again, is in sharp contrast to the Carmelites, who spend their earthly lives making certain that the next one fills its purpose.

Thus, is it not only the attitude toward death that sets the Carmelites apart from the gentry. Benson describes the life of Lady Carberry, James Fakenham, even the Westons in terms that suggest they are merely taking up space before dying and celebrating the happy event (for the heirs) with elaborate funerals. He uses up virtually no space at all on the lives of the Carmelites — their lives are, in terms of this world, utterly repulsive, directed as they are toward the next . . . thereby paradoxically making this one meaningful. The English upper class has everything except a purpose at the same time that the Carmelites have nothing — except a purpose.

All of the major characters in the story start out with this utter purposelessness. The closest any one of them comes to anything outside himself is Jack Weston with his devotion to cricket. Playing for one's county or country is a step in the direction of selflessness. It at least takes the sportsman out of himself, doing something for the greater good of the team instead of just himself. Ironically, when Jack "gets religion," he burns his cricket bats, warning the reader (and Mary, his wife) that something is wrong from the first. A genuine conversion would not cause someone to reject anything that draws him out of himself, at least not without long and profound reflection and with the concurrence of a sound spiritual advisor.

Unlike the opinion that some readers have of Benson's endings, the titles of his contemporary novels are unambiguous. *A Winnowing* is no exception. The "winnowing" is that of the wheat from the chaff, of those with a vocation from those without one. James Fakenham as a stereotypical member of the upper class even succeeds in "rescuing"

Sarah from meaning. She returns the favor by persuading him to resign from his government post after their marriage so that neither one is distracted by having a purpose in life.

The question that *A Winnowing* forces the reader to ask — and answer — is, Who, ultimately, is dead, and who is alive? Not just Catholics and Jews, but any sincere believer in any religion will be led inevitably to the answer that Benson forces the reader to confront in all its paradoxical glory.

None Other Gods

At first glance, *None Other Gods* seems to be nothing more than a talented author's none-too-subtle satire on the infamous British tendency to take nonsense just a trifle too seriously. "By Gad, sir," you can almost hear the Colonel bluster down at the club (stiff upper lip and all, late of 'Is/'Er Majesty's Service in Inja, don't-cher-know), "this fellow Benson is being most impertinent. Fun and foolery is a serious business, what? I say, Gilbert, what? Sullivan! Even that Papist Chesterton, what? Egad, I say! Bad form!"

This first impression has evidently turned many readers away from either enjoying or, worse, understanding the novel. One otherwise very astute critic stated that, aside from *Lord of the World* and *Come Rack! Come Rope!*, the only other work by Benson with which she was familiar was *None Other Gods*. She had read the book in high school — and hated it.

By gad, sir . . . er, ma'am! Bad form!

The key to understanding *None Other Gods* is that, unlike most of Benson's other "contemporary" novels and his science fiction, the work is not a satire within the usual meaning of the word at all. Oh, there are a few gentle jabs here and there, of course. Benson could no more get away from pointing out some of our human foibles and frailties than he could avoid succumbing to them himself. A good writer writes what he knows, and, if there was one thing Benson knew aside from the inhumanity of England's upper classes, it was human frailty. The final passage in the story, as well, is virtually the epitome of the infamous Benson ambiguous ending. It requires an almost Herculean act of will, if the reader has not grasped the point of the book, to understand it.

There are other significant differences between *None Other Gods* and the rest of Benson's novels. (I specify novels, for the short stories are in a class by themselves.) The most important of these differences is that almost every other one of Benson's novels ends with some kind of conversion. *None Other Gods*, unique among all his works, begins with a conversion, and then follows the seemingly confused path of a seeker after God's Will after he has accepted it on blind faith — possibly even on a whim. Neither a whim nor blind faith, of course, is the soundest foundation on which to build a relationship with God.

To understand the end result of the process described in the novel, we need to understand the process itself. In the most graphic terms possible — sometimes even shocking for a late Victorian or Edwardian audience, Benson delineated the trials through which God puts a soul in order to bend it utterly to His Will — ironically a soul that has, apparently, already done so, at least in intent. Every step of the way it is made clear that, as far as Frank Guiseley, the subject of the process, is concerned, he could step away from it at any time. Frank — any time he wished, and with the assistance, even rapturous encouragement of his friends and family — could simply have walked away from the process of surrendering himself to the Will of God.

Instead, Frank wanders about, seemingly frustrated at every turn in discerning God's Will for him — possibly a reflection of the process that, for Benson personally, was never resolved. The most frustrating aspect of all, of course, is that Frank labors under the impression that he has already surrendered to God's Will and is simply waiting for specific instructions, so to speak. Frank is continually presented with more or less obvious opportunities to forsake God by accepting one of the many substitutes available, none of them evil, and many of them objectively good: the respect of friends and family, fame, fortune, a marriage with a virtuous girl, and so on. They are not, however, *the* Good. They are "other gods," although not the most important and deceptive false god of all, the tendency in each human being to declare, "my will, not Thine."

Routes that many believe to be the only way to God — stripping one's self of material possessions, even martyrdom of a sort — prove to be false gods. Not even (or should I say *especially*) his co-religionists show much sympathy for Frank's self-immolation. Virtually the first words out of every priest's mouth in the novel is to wonder in some fashion why an educated and healthy man doesn't just get a job — and stop asking for money that he could easily obtain by his own efforts. Frank's martyrdom (which consists of taking another man's place in prison) comes off as exceptionally foolish, even stupid instead of noble, and for a very silly cause. The man he saved, of course, shows no real gratitude . . . but then, inexplicably, neither does God.

Brief interludes with a hermit (a doctor who studies toxins) and a short stay in a monastery seem to tempt Frank with leaving the world to find his vocation in it, but these pass quickly. Somewhere inside he knows that this is not the path he seeks. These episodes are a particularly clever twist on the part of Benson, for he was fully aware that in late classical times, the ideal life seemed to be that of a hermit in the desert. In the Middle Ages, it was to be a professed religious in a monastery. After the Reformation, the ideal was domestic life, just as in our modern age the ideal is temporal self-actualization above all else. Frank is clearly following a path that many moderns would envy as the ultimate in self-actualization — and it is failing him.

At his lowest point, Frank is even stripped of his implied secret belief that, should everything else fail, God will take care of him for being such a good and faithful believer and make everything turn out all right. This is revealed as yet another false god and an especially deadly temptation to sincere believers in all faiths. Fact and fiction are replete with tales of believers who surrender their belief instead of their own wills because they cannot forgive God for what He let happen. More accurately, they cannot forgive themselves for being such fools as to believe in a God who doesn't return favors, except with vague promises of a Pie-In-The-Sky afterlife. We might almost be tempted to say that for such folks, religion is truly the PITS.

The shallowness of the PITS approach is made evident by one argument often put forth by atheists and agnostics. Non-believers continually accuse religious believers of being gullible dupes as the result of a promised reward in the afterlife. The revelation of an afterlife in a heaven is, however, relatively speaking, a latecomer to the religious scene. The pagan religions almost without exception promised only a shadowy existence (and a rather grim one at that), or oblivion.

Even the Jews two thousand years ago were split on the question. As accounts in the New Testament relate, the two main parties of Judaism, the Sadducees and the Pharisees, frequently debated this point, often with words. The Sadducees believed very strongly that there was no afterlife. God should be served because that was the right thing to do. A "bribe" in the form of a reward in the hereafter cheapened a person's belief, besides being only weakly attested to in Scripture. Their approach to the Law was that it was contained solely in the Torah. Anything that added to this, such as the popular traditions espoused by the Pharisees, and which represented an exposition and an adaptation of the Torah for altered conditions of life, undermined the political and spiritual welfare of the people.

The Pharisees on the other hand believed that an afterlife and the resurrection from the dead gave an answer to the problem of evil. It was apparent to most people that a certain widespread belief (to surface again centuries later in the theological simplifications that came in with the Reformation) could not be true. That is, God rewards and punishes people in this life for their acts and beliefs. If someone is insufficiently punished, his sins are assigned to his children, a literal understanding of the sins of the father being visited on his son.

To the Pharisees, there was something wrong there. True, God had been known to mete out retribution for sin and reward virtue in certain outstanding cases, but what about everyone else? Meting out justice in the here and now might even be construed as interfering with free will. An afterlife, with a day of judgment and reward or punishment, gave a solution to this problem.

With respect to Frank Guiseley, however, the belief that God would reward him for becoming a Catholic and be his sole temporal and spiritual recourse in time of trouble forms one of the secondary themes of *None Other Gods*.

The novel chronicles first the sort of euphoria that ordinarily accompanies a conversion. The novel seems to open some time after the spiritual euphoria has worn itself out, but now Frank has undergone a second, more shallow conversion, and a sort of temporal euphoria has made its entrance. All of Frank's actions indicate that not only is he placing all his spiritual reliance on God, but he is now throwing himself utterly on God's mercy for his temporal needs as well.

This rash action — for it can be described in no other way — sets Frank on the road to a third and final conversion, but it is hardly the counterpart of the Road to Emmaus that Frank seems to expect. No friendly mentor in the shape of a generous employer, nature, or a boon traveling companion manifests itself. Instead (as would be the case with any other feckless adventurer), Frank finds it difficult to obtain employment at all, nature seems singularly indifferent to him, and the companions he can't seem to shake expect Frank to take care of them, rather than the other way around.

Even his own Church seems to forsake him. Applying at different times to a rather stodgy parish priest and at a monastery for assistance, Frank is pretty much accused of "faking" being a Catholic in order to get a handout. The Catholic clergy and professed religious in *None Other Gods* are portrayed as being somewhat cynical when presented with protestations of membership in the Catholic Church from persons who clearly have something material to gain by it. Benson knew full well that most people will say anything when they're truly hungry just to get a decent meal, and that professional beggars usually know exactly what strings to pull to loosen those tied firmly around a purse. Converts for a meal would as quickly join in an anti-Catholic demonstration if it meant an invitation to the traditional picnic on July 12, or a shilling or two on November 5.

Spiritual consolations also withdraw from Frank. God almost seems to be testing Frank to see if He can get him to accept someone or something else in place of God. Ultimately, however, it comes out that it is Frank, not God, who is doing the testing by challenging God. Frank seems to expect God to make some profound personal revelation to him to grant him an infallible guide to his vocation. When God does not do this, Frank steps up his efforts by becoming more and more convinced that he must continue doing what he is doing until God is forced to reveal Himself.

None Other Gods thus takes on something of a personal warning to the author himself not to tempt God in the face of adversity. Benson struggled for most of his adult life with the question of vocation. In this novel he singles out a very common and very dangerous habit that all converts to any religion or ethical system have. That is, to assume that God or some spiritual leader will take an intense, personal and, above all, an immediate interest in the convert's spiritual and material welfare. Cult leaders take advantage of this habit, making it very difficult for new converts to gain an objective view of what is going on, rather than submit a candidate to a lengthy and arduous catechesis before admitting him to communion with full believers.

Benson was fully aware that God's interest in each of us is both intense and personal — but that our immediate welfare, both spiritual and temporal, is largely up to each of us and to our fellow man in solidarity with us. God would otherwise be violating free will, and He wants friends and children, not slaves. We must be allowed, even forced, to take care of ourselves and our own temporal needs, either through our own actions or by joining with others within our milieux to restructure the social order. With respect to religion, the Catholic Church or any religion has the duty of making the sacraments and various other avenues to God available, but cannot force them on anyone.

In short, everyone must grow up. No one is permitted (absent extraordinary circumstances) to remain a child. Frank Guiseley, unconsciously accepting the English upper class idea that God and everything in the universe was created to serve him and take care of him, is through the course of the novel forced into becoming an adult, and to undergo a final and deep conversion. At one point his fiancée even remarks that Frank seems to be a perpetual twelve-year-old. Paralleling the plot in the Medieval morality play *Everyman*, Benson carefully strips Frank of all recourse other than mere faith. Even Frank's last name echoes the play, as it seems to be something of a pun — *Guise*-ley indicating that Frank must go forward in faith with nothing but himself, and not in dis-*guise* — he abandons his surname in favor of "Gregory."

Thus, in contrast to all Benson's other novels, *None Other Gods* takes the more difficult task of exploring what happens after a convert has submitted to the Will of God. All of Benson's other novels are concerned, to a greater or lesser degree, with what brings a soul to the point of conversion. *None Other Gods* examines the infinitely more subtle process of absolute surrender after conversion.

This novel is also unique in that it is the only one of Benson's in which the action can be pinpointed with absolute accuracy with respect to the time in which it takes place — spring through early winter of 1908. Paradoxically, this renders the novel both irretrievably locked into a specific time and place (many of the circumstances, even types of people who appear in the story could have existed at no other time or place in history), and utterly timeless.

Topical references abound, so much so that, for the edition we've been preparing, we found it necessary to add footnotes in order to make certain aspects of the story intelligible to the modern reader. Oddly, however, while the references, the time and the place serve to fix the action, they also serve (in common with the after-death action in *Everyman*) to cut it loose from time altogether. The average reader, having no real experience of the various milieux described, is forced to extrapolate and interpret matters in a more universal context. This would not have been the case of readers of even a generation ago. This possibly accounts for the fact that the difficult subject matter, combined with a host of unfamiliar details, served to obscure both the point of the story and Benson's very real genius in putting it across to the reader.

The subject itself, not just the difficulty of it, may also have contributed in some degree to the fact that *None Other Gods* is not ranked with Benson's more popular works. Perhaps the fact that many of us are so much like

Frank Guiseley, or he is so like many of us in trying to manipulate God in some fashion, has caused the story to strike too close to home.

Frank Guiseley is, without a doubt, one of the most attractive characters Benson ever invented. He is the virtual embodiment of a dream that so many of us have of just chucking all the minutiae of daily life and going in search of what is truly important. Even his obvious goodness and virtues don't detract from the fact that most readers feel that Frank would be a very good fellow to know and have as a friend, to share a drink with or accompany to a social event.

The reader, then, finds himself in an uncomfortable position that Benson, perhaps, entirely intended he should be in. The reader finds himself sympathizing with Frank to the point that (were this not clearly a work of fiction), he would be tempted to start demanding to know why God just doesn't cut poor Frank some slack. It is only when we realize that it is poor Frank who should be cutting God some slack and accepting his chosen role as God's servant first, but his own second, that we can understand the point of the story. Yes, the final sentence of the book tells us that the Failure was complete . . . but was it God's failure, or Frank's — and by failing to impose his will on God, are we not to assume that Frank's failure was, in fact, the greatest of all Triumphs?

The Coward

Titling a book, "The Coward" when the subject is the upper class of Edwardian England — which practically invented the "stiff upper lip" — might seem either like picking on an obvious target, or being deliberately provocative by attacking what seemed to most people as the very basis of the social order. The latter was the case with Robert Hugh Benson.

Nevertheless, Benson was not the first to essay this difficult undertaking. A. E. W. Mason's epic *The Four Feathers* (1902) embarked on the task of attempting to show a late Victorian reading public that true heroism was not a matter of convention. Mason, however (being more concerned with turning out an exciting "ripping story" — at which task he succeeded admirably) — failed to explore the true nature of courage and the debilitating effects that society's preconceptions can have on the human soul. No reader is ever in doubt about the real courage of Mason's hero. He overcomes the ridicule and scorn of his detractors on their own terms, and in a manner with which not even the most rigid Colonel Blimp or exacting Mrs. Grundy could find fault.

Benson took on a much more difficult task. It's not a matter simply of *doubting* someone's courage. Along with almost everyone else in the story, Valentine Medd "of Medhurst" — the "coward" of the title — *knows* he is a sniveling craven. Only two people believe that Val is not what he and the rest of the world believe him to be, at least when they bother to think about Val at all. The first is his old nurse, "Benty," who gives Val (as she gives every other member of the family) absolute and unconditional love. She does not believe what even Val's father says of him for the simple reason that he is "her boy." The second is a local Catholic priest, Father Maple, who makes almost the briefest appearance of a major clerical character, Catholic or Protestant, in any Benson novel.

Ironically, both these characters in a sense weaken the force of the story. I have a suspicion that Benty was included as a tribute to Benson's own nurse, Beth. Judging from Martindale's biography and the memoir by Benson's brother Arthur, Beth appears to have shared many of Benty's characteristics, even to the wholehearted if bewildered acceptance of Benson's conversion to Catholicism. In Benty this was translated to a conviction that Master Val couldn't possibly be the coward everyone believes him to be. With the goal of lambasting the English upper class, it would have been better, in a sense, if everyone without exception regarded Val as a "coward." (Of course, from another perspective, the fact that Benty is clearly not "upper class" serves as a stark contrast between a normal "lower class" individual, and the unthinking obedience of the upper classes to a mindless and meaningless set of artificial principles.)

Fortunately for the enjoyment of the reader, removing either Benty or Father Maple would have involved lengthening the novel far beyond what was strictly necessary to get the point across. While it might seem odd to modern critics in view of the length of his novels, Benson wrote no more than he needed to. Taking away the Father Maple character (an unusually perceptive cleric, even for an intelligent Benson priest), would have meant adding several chapters either delaying the horrifying climax or extending the story long after the point was graphically made and the reader lost interest. Benson's subtle satire would not have worked well in page after page of introspection; he needed somebody to explain the real situation at the end as briefly as possible in terms that the reader could understand, and (to highlight the satire) that Val's family could have understood if they had not been brassbound by their own prejudices and preconceptions.

The *Coward*, which first saw publication in 1912, was the third of Benson's six "mainstream" novels. He had not yet achieved the height of his powers that he would demonstrate in *An Average Man, Initiation*, and the posthumous and sublime *Loneliness?*, but that is a quibble that should not trouble even the severest of critics. The distinction between "great" and "greater" is often in the eye of the beholder.

It is in *The Coward* that Benson gave vent to a number of subtle hints of something that had been bothering him for some time. As he wrote in August 1907,

> There's no doubt a great sense of disaster coming in England. It is all rather vague and indefinable; but it seems to me that evil is coming closer and closer — I don't mean to me, that would be hysteria — but to other people; it's in the air. It's like a coming thunderstorm. Well, I'm thankful I'm safe indoors.[70]

Noting that the date — 1907 — is the same year in which the apocalyptic masterpiece *Lord of the World* was published, any fan of Benson's is sure to nod sagely here and say to himself that he knows exactly that to which his favorite author referred. As with so many things we "know," however (such as Val Medd's presumed cowardice), we would be exactly wrong.

Benson was not speaking of a coming showdown between the forces of Satan, personified as secular humanism and freemasonry, and the forces of God, embodied in the Catholic Church. Very much the contrary. He wrote *Lord of the World* and its companion piece, *The Dawn of All* as satires on an extremely decadent society. He even "apologized" for "screaming" his message in an uncharacteristically unsubtle way.[71] Had he foreseen the disaster as a direct attack on the Catholic Church (as forms the basic plot of *Lord of the World*), he would hardly have breathed an obvious sigh of relief that he was "safe indoors," or hoped (as he did) that the "utopia" that some people see in *The Dawn of All* would never come to pass,

---

[70] Martindale, Vol. II, 218-219.
[71] "I am perfectly aware that this is a terribly sensational book, and open to innumerable criticisms on that account, as well as on many others. But I did not know how else to express the principles I desired (and which I passionately believe to be true) except by producing their lines to a sensational point. I have tried, however, not to scream unduly loud, and to retain, so far as possible, reverence and consideration for the opinions of other people. Whether I have succeeded in that attempt is quite another matter." — Robert Hugh Benson, "Preface" to *Lord of the World* (1907).

viewing any union of Church and State as a ghastly mistake.

So what was the nature of the disaster that filled Benson with such foreboding? Martindale probably analyzed it better than anyone else, understandable, given his intense study of his subject's life and works:

> . . . he was almost passionately indignant with the ordinary life of the English rich, as I have often had to indicate. Country-house existence was to him one long killing of time, that earthly reflection of eternity; it was a bleeding of the soul white. And he had not the slightest doubt that the whole of the old system was crumbling into collapse. He does not preach or applaud this so much as half-anxiously surmise it; Lady Beatrice and the Vicar, in *The Coward*, give occasion for a number of little hints, if you will look for them, that the reign of Squire and Lady Bountiful is finished. He has no doubt of the impending revolution, though he will not define its character.[72]

In common with many people, then, Benson saw that the existing system was very bad. The only thing worse than the current system of his day, was its decay and subsequent replacement by a much worse system. Only in the life of man in the Catholic Church — paradoxically whether explicitly by Catholics or implicitly by non-Catholics — did Benson see any hope at all. In more comprehensible terms, Benson seemed to have an instinctive "feel" that only by restructuring the social order so that it rested solidly on a basis of a restored and reinvigorated Thomist interpretation of the natural law — as had already been explicated by Leo XIII and Saint Pius X and would be further developed by Pius XI and subsequent pontiffs — would the world be saved.

Neither was Benson in danger of assuming that a purely individualistic or collectivist understanding of the applications of natural law found in the social encyclicals would serve. Pius XI's astounding breakthrough in moral philosophy in the area of a specifically social virtue was still more than a decade in the future when Benson had

---

[72] Martindale, Vol. II, 218.

his forebodings, but Benson was intelligent enough to know that if the individual virtues, even if applied on a vast scale to the whole of society and enforced with the coercive power of the State, were somehow not the right answer.

In a letter sent to the *Westminster Gazette* (a Catholic newspaper) on July 15, 1913 but never published, Benson tried to make this clear. After referring to a letter by a lady that pointed out that before the Reformation there had been no widespread problem with "tramps," Benson agreed — but then pointed out that the ancient charities of the Catholic Church were still in force, and doing their utmost to relieve the dire situation of the poor. Without actually saying so, however, Benson hinted that social and economic conditions were somehow substantially different than half a millennium ago. This, as we know from the analysis in Louis Kelso and Mortimer Adler's Binary Economics, is due to advances in technology in a social context in which our institutions — especially that of corporate finance — have not kept pace.

Benson was not, however, concerned with what would solve the problem, or how it had happened. It was difficult, even in an English newspaper, to go deeply into a subject in a couple of paragraphs. His concern was to correct the mistaken belief that a more intense application of the individual virtue of charity (specifically almsgiving) would do little more than raise false hopes. As he wrote,

> It is probably impracticable, however, that Religious should do all that is necessary in this regard, especially in our own country. Is it quite inconceivable, then, that your correspondent's suggestion should be widely taken up, and that persons who have sufficient leisure and means should, working on the motive of pure charity which inspires her own efforts, do something at any rate to relieve, in a manner that does not injure the self-respect of the poor, the enormous sum of misery that streams along our roads today.[73]

---

[73] *Ibid.*, 219-220.

Benson was fully aware of the impracticability of asking that private individuals try to relieve systemic problems through the application of private almsgiving. Martindale reported a subsequent conversation that Benson had with the lady who had written the letter to which he was replying, who today would probably be very active in the Catholic Worker Movement. She had asked Benson's advice on whether she should continue to supply articles gratis to Catholic periodicals. As she explained,

> "Do you think it is best just to do exactly as I am asked? — to give what I am asked to give, and to accept what comes? That is how I try to live, believing that God rules the world, and that He will arrange everything for us, if we never think of ourselves."
>
> "Oh! If you are on *those* terms with Almighty God," he [Benson] exclaimed, "you will be all right."
>
> "It seems to answer. We have no income, but we love 'the Lady Poverty,' and out work brings in just enough for our charities and our own needs."
>
> And then Hugh Benson added quickly, "But you must make no reservation: you mustn't say 'Yes, I'll give God everything He asks for, if I can keep my home,' or 'if I can keep my position.' You must be willing to sacrifice *everything* — willing to go to the workhouse, willing to be a tramp on the road. Have you thought of that?"
>
> "Yes. My husband and I often talk of the possibility, and he says he wouldn't mind in the least. He is an angel."
>
> "*He must be.*"[74]

Evidently Benson did not reserve all his satire for his novels.

Part of the "everything" that God demands in such a program is, first and foremost, a sacrifice of pride. As Director of Research for the Center for Economic and Social Justice ("CESJ"), I have probably seen every excuse for

---

[74] *Ibid.*, 220-221.

not implementing a sound program of social restructuring along the lines suggested by CESJ's "Capital Homesteading" proposal. Far too many people have built reputations and careers on protesting the current system . . . and have very carefully refrained from taking any effective action to change that same system. This is understandable, for if widespread poverty were no longer to be a problem, their careers and reputations as saviors of the poor would be meaningless in human terms.

In a smaller sense, this is what Benson saw as the chief flaw in the Edwardian social system, and to which he struggled so mightily to draw his readers' attention. The system was bad, and at some level everyone knew it — but they were unwilling to sacrifice even an iota of their colossal pride, distorted, twisted, even perverse as it was, in the cause of building something better or even staving off the disaster that one of their own saw coming.

The apocalypse of World War One may even have been made marginally bearable in a sense by the unwarranted belief that the upper classes were finally being called upon to pay for generations of privilege with their blood. This possibly created the even more unnecessary delusion that the sacrifice of "the Great Fallen" paid the debt in full — and that nothing further was needed.

Yes, the sacrifice was made, but it was the wrong sacrifice. It increased rather than decreased the pride that lay at the root of the problem. The message in *The Coward* is that false pride not only stands in the way of discerning one's vocation in life, it stands as a barrier to life itself. *The Coward*, shocking as it may seem to the prideful at all levels of society, is more necessary today than it was a century ago.

An Average Man

"Hugh Benson can never describe a house where there is not a second footman." Possibly intended as a snide comment on Benson's presumed snobbery and social pretensions, that snippet from a letter to Martindale is proven wrong by *An Average Man*, perhaps the finest and most incisive commentary on social pretension and snobbery ever written. This is all the more surprising when we realize that Benson was himself a member of the highest echelons of British society, a son of the Archbishop of Canterbury, a personage who, in religious terms, is second only to the reigning monarch with a social position to match. There was no question about Benson being in any way socially "pretentious."

Not surprisingly, Benson stripped bare the altar of the false god of social pretension and caste with such dexterity, sensitivity, and even kindness that some readers might miss the biting satire. In *An Average Man*, however, Benson came as close as he ever did to treating his characters badly, even exceeding the near-cruelty evident in an earlier novel, *The Conventionalists*. Percy Brandreth-Smith, the presumed hero and example of an "average man," in contrast to the ubiquitous sincerity of Benson's villains and most other characters, is portrayed as a self-deluding narcissist who, had he stopped to think for even a moment could have halted his downward plunge into meaninglessness at any time.

It was this utter meaninglessness and lack of purpose that (if anything could be said to do so) outraged Benson. A firm believer in "breeding" and the British caste system, he had, nevertheless, internalized the idea of the servant leader as a basic principle of private and public life. In Benson's eyes the aristocracy of England, no less than its clergy and public servants, were there to serve those "lower" than themselves as well as the whole of the common good. This was, in fact, their sole reason for existence.

Benson saw Edwardian country house life as the culmination of a process that began with the Reformation. The process had actually begun much earlier, with Henry VII Tudor's introduction of the idea of divine right into a formerly democratic England.[75] The English Reformation was, in fact, virtually unique in that it was brought about largely because of the personal desires of Henry VIII, not because there was any popular demand for such an overreaching change.

Most objective authorities acknowledge that the vast majority of the people of England were perfectly happy in the Catholic Church, despite the need for some genuine reforms, and that the Reformation was forced on them against their wishes. Having largely been stripped of property by the policies of Henry VII, the "stingiest man in Europe," the English — to say nothing of the Irish — were ill-equipped to resist the "stripping of the altars" and the confiscation of what remained of widely distributed property under Henry VIII. As the astute Protestant commentator William Cobbett noted,

> ... the "Reformation" has impoverished and degraded the main body of the people of England and Ireland. I have shown that this change of religion was brought about by some of worst, if not the very worst people that ever breathed; I have shown that the means were such as human nature revolts at. . . . It now remains for me to show from the same sources the impoverishing and degrading consequences of this change of religion; and that, too, with regard to the nation as a whole, as well as with regard to the main body of the people. . . . we have now seen the Protestant religion established, completely established, by the gibbets, the racks and the ripping-knives . . .[76]

The direct results of the Reformation were not, then, religious indifference or heterodoxy (despite the break with Rome), although these were certainly indirect and inevi-

---

[75] *Vide* John N. Figgis, *The Divine Right of Kings*. Bristol, UK: Thoemmes Press, 1994.
[76] Cobbett, *op. cit.*, 1826, §§ 350-351.

table fruits of the change. The most debilitating effect of the Reformation was, on the contrary, the creation of a class of purposeless drones, a relatively small class that owned the vast bulk of the productive capacity of the British Empire, an empire that, in Benson's day, encircled the globe. It was, in terms of territory, wealth, and sheer power, the greatest empire the world has ever seen.

It was also an empire in which incredible wealth existed side-by-side with unbelievable poverty. The astounding wealth gap of today, while dwarfing that of a century ago, is less obvious, if only because stopgap social welfare programs have somewhat ameliorated the condition of the poor in developed countries.

At the same time, however, the lot of the poorest of the poor in the undeveloped or developing countries of the twenty-first century has become worse than could ever be imagined in Benson's day, or even that of Charles Dickens or Karl Marx. Advancing technology has so diminished the value of human labor as an input to the productive process that the wealthy and super-wealthy can satisfy their wants and needs easier and cheaper with technology instead of the human labor of a vast army of servants or non-owning employees.

Benson evidently believed (erroneously) that returning the upper classes to a purpose in life would prevent the disaster that he saw looming over the world. A return to the solid practice of Catholicism would, he seems to have felt, reintroduce the philosophy that drives the concept of the servant-leader. Of course, this would also be true of a return to any religious or ethical system based firmly on a sound understanding of natural law, but Benson saw this philosophy most clearly taught — and supported philosophically and spiritually — by the Catholic Church.

Not that a personal conversion to proper principles is not a necessary first step in the restructuring of the social order that, as popes Leo XIII and Pius XI made clear, is the only hope for civilization. A sincere dedication of one's self to something larger than the mere self is also necessary to maintain the personal conversion and provide the incentive to restructure the social order. By itself, however, all it does is inculcate a spirit of religious priggishness and pharisaical superiority over the presumably less-enlightened, a danger of which Benson was constantly aware, and against which he continually guarded himself.

The dangers of spiritual pride were all the more apparent to Benson as the result of his unfortunate and quickly ended relationship with Marie Corelli and Frederick Rolfe. These were two literary and social *poseurs* who were convinced that they had private revelations superior to those taught by traditional religions. Once Benson realized this, he cut the connection immediately. He was pursued ever after by the sneers and attacks of this proto-"New Age" pair of charlatans, the mildest of which included accusations of hypocrisy and even homosexuality, for neither of which there exists any evidence other than the accusations.

In *An Average Man*, Percy Brandreth-Smith is presented with opportunity after opportunity to give his life meaning. Rejecting each opportunity in turn, he succumbs to the lure of an utterly purposeless existence. While he manages to convince himself that he is acting "like a gentleman" at every turn, it is clear even to the most casual reader that he is only acting like a complete cad. He replaces purpose and meaning with social and material pride, which leads to complete spiritual indifference. In one stunning display of near-absolute depravity and intellectual dishonesty, Percy uses his stated intention to enter the Catholic Church to terminate an inconvenient relationship, and (at the same time) makes it clear that he has no intention of going through with his conversion in order to terminate another inconvenient relationship — a classic case of having your cake and eating it, too.

Even Percy's one kindness to Mr. Main — a man who sacrifices everything to accept all that which Percy has rejected — costs him nothing and is ultimately completely ineffectual. Percy sees the favor he does for Mr. Main as an example of *noblesse oblige* . . . on which (characteristically) he fails to follow through, leaving Mr. Main worse off than before.

Mr. Main — we never discover his first name (at least, I am completely unable to recall it) — is, perhaps, Benson's greatest creation. He is, among other things, the surest answer to anyone laboring under the delusion that Benson did not understand ordinary people.

Mr. Main is appallingly ordinary, so much so that he seems at times a repellent creature. Even the descriptions that Benson gives of him seem intended, at first reading, calculated to turn the reader against him. He is, in today's terminology, a "Loser" with a capital "L." He has never succeeded at anything, and it is painfully clear to everyone except Mr. Main himself that he never will. He is so pathetic that situations that would send most of us into paroxysms of fury against the gods, fate, "the system," — whatever — leave him thanking God for his good fortune. He considers his colossally selfish and shrewish wife a blessing, and bears with her unbearable criticisms of him with more than the patience of Job.

Adding more insult to injury (if possible), it becomes very clear that a great deal of Mr. Main's lack of success up to the opening of the novel has been due in large measure to the fact that his wife is clearly "unsuitable" — a *suitable* wife being absolutely necessary to the advancement of a clergyman in the Church of England. Marion Main (she is given the dignity of a first name) has alienated everyone in their little suburb of London, especially her husband's religious superior, the extraordinarily kind Reverend Mr. Bennett, Vicar of the local Anglican parish. After Mr. Main's conversion to Catholicism (at the worst possible time, of course), Mrs. Main immediately begins taking steps to alienate her husband's new co-religionists.

With all that (and much more), Mr. Main is magnificently, if quietly, heroic. He holds up under adversities that would have crushed a less "average" man. Benson brilliantly juxtaposes the heart-wrenching case of Mr. Main, who rises to every challenge with a stubborn perseverance although he lacks the material, intellectual, and social resources — though not the spiritual — to maintain himself, with that of Percy Brandreth-Smith, who either begins with or gains every possible advantage — and who quickly gives way under the least pressure. Adversity makes no inroads on Mr. Main's faith, while worldly success and advancement destroy Percy's.

This is only to be expected, for two equally important reasons. The first is (as I noted above) Benson seems to have been convinced that only a sincere and honest return to the practice of the Catholic faith by the upper classes of England would save them from what he saw as a doom hanging over them. *An Average Man* contains Benson's harshest satire on English upper class society by showing Percy's almost immediate loss of faith as soon as he gains worldly advancement, and the growth of Mr. Main's faith the worse his life becomes. Only the Catholic Church (so Benson seemed to believe) could give purpose to people who appeared absolutely convinced that the height of individual and social development was to do absolutely nothing.

The second reason is that Jesus did not come to save the upper classes alone, however much they might construe the Holy Trinity as a very elite group of English aristocrats. As Benson reminded people in the opening passages of *The Religion of the Plain Man*,

> The book is intended for the "man in the street," who, after all, has a certain claim on our consideration, since Jesus Christ came to save his soul. This man in the street, like myself, is entirely unable to discourse profoundly upon the Fathers, or to decide where scholars disagree in matters of simple scholarship. . . . Now this kind of intellectual attainment seems a poor equipment for the pursuit of salvation; but it is undoubtedly the only equipment that many of us have, and it is God that has made us and not we ourselves. Therefore if we believe in God at all — at least in a God of mercy or even justice — we are bound to acknowledge that this equipment is all that we actually require. To tell me that because I cannot infallibly pronounce upon an obscure sentence of St. Cyprian's, I am thereby debarred from making up my mind about the necessary truths of the Christian religion, is to represent my Maker as unjust and capricious. I am only capable of that of which I am capable.

Thus Mr. Main, for all his lack of material success, his dullness, his unintelligence — is the obvious victor in a struggle that ends up destroying Percy, for all his newfound wealth, social position, and advantageous marriage.

Benson seems to have intended Mr. Main as a horrifying mirror to his own career, a sort of "might have been," a bullet dodged. This was not, however, because Benson thought of himself as specially favored by God. Mr. Main represents the opposite of everything that Benson was, while everything that happens to Mr. Main could, under less favorable circumstances, have happened to Benson himself. Mr. Main's conversion to Catholicism is, speaking in worldly terms, a complete disaster. Benson got off lightly, and knew it. As he had a priest tell a potential convert in *The Religion of the Plain Man*,

> Three hundred years ago we could have offered you great things: the hatred of all who heard your name; the contempt of those who were loudest in their love for England. We could have offered you the Tower as your prison, chains, stinking dungeons, the rack, the whip, the gallows, the hangman's cauldron. Now we have no more than the chips of Christ's cross to tempt you with; a little sneering and lifting of eyebrows; a little good-humored laughter; a few remarks about 'intellectual servitude'; a little smiling pity over your medievalism, your materialism, your lack of the sturdy British spirit, your superstition and your fear of the priest.

Benson escaped even that. As he related in the story of his own conversion, *Confessions of a Convert*, "I must acknowledge with the greatest gratitude that the charity with which I was treated by members of the Anglican communion in general simply astonished me. I did not know that there was so much generosity in the world."

Nevertheless, Benson was fully aware of the pressures to which he could have been subjected. *An Average Man* marked the first of two appearances of Mr. Railton, an apostate Catholic priest, a man whose history included leaving the Catholic Church as well as his ministry, and marrying within the week. He appears again by intimation in Benson's posthumous novel, *Loneliness?*, as an exemplar of intellectual dishonesty and religious hypocrisy.

He has made a career of attacking the Catholic Church in books and lectures, making a very good living at it.

Railton is a bully, both physically and intellectually, and (like most bullies) obviously a coward, as demonstrated by the fact that he spews forth in great detail about the presumed "sins" of the "Romish" Church — "sins" that he, as a priest, knows full well are either extremely twisted half-truths or outright lies — in venues where no defense of the Catholic Church is possible. The lies are so blatant that Benson's numerous Protestant readers would have had no problem seeing their utter falsity.

Percy, flushed with his newfound religious enthusiasm, quite properly refuses to listen to such trash. He has no responses to what Railton declaims with such an appearance of authority, but he instantly divines the man's interested motives. Percy later meets a less rational and much more easily refuted attack, and fails to discern his own interested motive in his failure to defend the Catholic Church. Ironically this is after he has been through the greater part of a course of instruction in what the Catholic Church actually teaches and is presumably well-equipped to respond to such attacks on their own ground. Instead, he weakly acquiesces in emotional condemnations of that institution asserted by a girl who has heard Mr. Railton lecture. Not even the much-vaunted English upper class worship of "fair play" inspires him to give the devil of the Catholic Church its due.

It is thus in *An Average Man* that Benson created — for him — a new kind of character: the religious hypocrite. This signaled a new direction in his satire. He still seemed to be convinced of the sincerity of the great mass of men, even those who came across as the most arrant villains, such as Topcliffe in *Come Rack! Come Rope!*, published the previous year. Still, he began inserting religious hypocrisy into his stories, both (oddly enough) in the person of Mr. Railton, who may have been based on someone of whom Benson had personal knowledge. It forms a minor theme in both *An Average Man* and *Loneliness?*, while (had he lived longer), it might have been the major theme of a novel.

Interestingly, all the religious hypocrisy, while admittedly rare in Benson's characters, is on the part of Catholics, former Catholics, or those seeking instruction in the Catholic faith. No Protestant minister or devout member of the Protestant laity is ever depicted as anything other than absolutely sincere — however shallow or erroneous Benson might think the sincerely held beliefs to be. Even his *poseur* characters (such as the incredible "Chris Dell" in *The Sentimentalists*) are absolutely sincere in their ridiculous posturings and poses — which is the chief danger in them, as Dell's attempted suicide makes clear.

One satiric jab that the reader might miss due to its extreme subtlety is that, after his conversion, Mr. Main is described as dressing in a way that could be a caricature of Mr. Railton's clothing, possibly a private way Benson had of indicating a change of religion — and of highlighting the difference between the two cases. Mr. Railton's apostasy — due to completely self-interested motives — brings him wealth and fame, while Mr. Main's conversion out of conviction results in nothing but disaster.

One more piece of subtle satire is that the church where Percy goes to take instruction in the Catholic faith is "St. Francis'," and is staffed — naturally — by Franciscan friars. Percy's own failure to persevere in his intention to become a Catholic is emphasized by the fact that by the end of the novel he has accepted everything that St. Francis rejected, and lost all that St. Francis gained.

An Average Man thus ranks as one of Benson's best novels, which (in a bit of appropriate irony that might have called forth a wry smile of appreciation from the author) has been almost completely overshadowed by his more "sensational" works. It is an "ordinary" novel about "ordinary" people that is, on the contrary, far from "ordinary."

Initiation

That the Christian can, precisely by his pain, be in Christ, and in a sense, *be* Christ, and effect Christ's own work, is the ascetical secret beyond which, in reality, none other lies.[77]

Like many sensitive people with vivid imaginations, Robert Hugh Benson could not contemplate the idea of physical suffering with anything other than fear, as he admitted on a number of occasions. Even writing of it in his novels caused similar sensations in his own body — a phenomenon that psychologists call "sympathetic pain." In the process of composing his historical novels he deliberately tried to imagine himself undergoing the same tortures as the martyrs to such effect that "he was 'conscious of very distinct, even slightly painful, sensations in his (own) wrists and ankles.'"[78]

It surprised him more than anyone else, then, when after a serious and painful operation on January 2, 1913, he was able to exclaim to a visitor, "*Have* you ever had a severe operation? No? *Do*! It's such an experience!"[79] Evidently his expressed enthusiasm led to the legend that he underwent the operation without anesthesia. This is untrue, but he did refuse morphia after the operation when he found that the narcotic made him sicker. As he related to another friend, "I was not *in* Pain; Pain and I were looking at each other, and he came nearer and nearer till he was upon me with a blue flash of agony."[80]

His experience with real pain seems to have been something of a release for him, for he was able immediately to say, "Do you know what I said under the anesthetic? Nothing but 'Oh, God.' The nurses thought it was so pi-

---

[77] Martindale, Vol. II, 357.
[78] *Ibid.*, 355.
[79] *Ibid.*
[80] *Ibid.*, 356.

ous! But *it wasn't pious*. It was a swear!"[81] It was also a revelation. As Martindale related,

> He loved to discuss its details. "The most annoying part of it to me," a friend, who had also been operated upon, said to him soon after it, "is that you'll write a book about yours, and pay all your expenses out of it." "Much more than pay them!" he gleefully retorted; "and *the book's nearly finished*."[82]

That book, of course, is *Initiation*, the last of Benson's "mainstream" novels to see publication in his lifetime.

Initiation is, first and foremost, an examination of the paradox of the healing effects of pain. Not that this was in any way morbid. All his life Benson was fascinated with pain and the fear he felt for it. As Martindale explained, however, Benson seems to have been able to sublimate this fear and direct it into useful channels:

> . . . his singularly practical tendency always forced him at once to register and *use* it for some outside end, nor suffered him to hug it and live with it interiorly. And his extreme sanity of natural life kept him outside even the dangerous tendencies of religious asceticism. All cruelty he hated, and saw its wrongness, even when he, in some sense, was its victim.
>
> "I hate cruelty more than anything in the whole world," he wrote to Mr. Rolfe,[83] "and find injustice or offensiveness to myself or anyone else the hardest of all things to forgive."[84]

What, however, of the case of a victim of pain who refuses to use it properly, who in fact rejects it utterly? That is the plot of *Initiation*.

The hero — or, rather, victim — of *Initiation* is Sir Neville Fanning. He is a baronet, the lowest rank of English

---

[81] *Ibid.*
[82] *Ibid.*, 185.
[83] Evidently from a note written some time before Benson wrote *Initiation*, for he had broken with the notorious Frederick Rolfe ("Baron Corvo") five years previously.
[84] Martindale, Vol. II, 356.

nobility, and a "cradle Catholic," taking both his station in life and his religion very much for granted. He is, as we might expect, a sufferer from the malaise that Benson saw afflicting virtually all upper class English, whether Catholic or Protestant: purposelessness.

Sir Neville does not even do very much with regard to managing his estates, leaving much of it to his aunt, Anna Fanning (his father's sister-in-law), a widow whose young son, Jim, is Sir Neville's "heir apparent." As the result of a distaste for the obviously plebian origins and behavior of his admittedly cloddish parish priest, Sir Neville does not even set a good example for those of his tenants who are Catholic, holding Father Richardson in open contempt.

While on vacation in Italy, Sir Neville meets a young girl, Enid Bessington, who is accompanying her mother on their annual Grand Tour of the Continent. He is amused — to a degree — by Mrs. Bessington, a woman who never seems to stop talking and yet who never seems to say anything. On a daytrip to Frascati, near Rome, he and Enid exchange confidences, discovering that they seem to have the same attitude towards pain and cruelty.

It seems that Sir Neville has recently become increasingly afflicted with extremely severe headaches. His aunt and his physician have urged him to submit to examination by a specialist. There has, however, been a slight diminution in their frequency and severity. Sir Neville decided that a jaunt to Italy (where he could ignore the headaches) would be much better for his mental and physical health. He declares, "I can't fit that kind of thing into my philosophy. I try to bear them decently, of course; but I don't submit in the slightest. I resent that kind of thing furiously, exactly as I resent cruelty to animals." During a walk they come across a small shrine in the woods.

> It was a particularly realistic *Pietà*.

> Behind the wire netting that was stretched across its face there was the group of the Mother and Son, painted in crude colors, lately renovated. The Mother, in an indigo cloak, sitting with upraised face, supported the ghastly Body across her knees. The

hands and feet ran with crimson; the mouth appeared to grin in a horrible contortion; the limbs were grotesquely elongated and emaciated. Stuck into the meshes of the wiring in front was a small bunch of wilted dandelions. The whole picture was painted in fresco on plaster that had peeled in places; and was half-sheltered by a broken pent-roof of stone.

The two looked at it in silence. They moved on, still in silence. Then the boy broke out.

"There!" he said. "That was exactly what I meant! I think such things are perfectly horrible! What possible good can that do to anyone? It's completely out of harmony too. The very colors are wrong. And, besides, why put it in the woods where things are fresh and clean? And that's exactly why I don't like talking about my headaches."

Ultimately they decide, as Enid declares, that "Pain's a kind of physical sin, don't you think?" As "Part I" of *Initiation* ends, Sir Neville's headaches have become much less severe and have decreased in frequency. He and Enid have returned to England, become engaged to be married, and are facing a very bright future.

There is, however, something of a dark cloud lowering over Sir Neville that (in keeping with his resolute rejection of pain and other unpleasantness) he steadfastly refuses to see. It seems that the almost cruelly honest Jim, with the perspicuity of some children, doesn't like Miss Bessington, of whom he receives a full dose when Enid and her mother pay a visit to Sir Neville's estate. Although she tries to cover it up, Miss Bessington is mean to Jim's collies, Jack and Jill, getting them banished to the stable. She is also artificially "nice" to him, in the way that adults who don't like children often are, and which children are usually quick to detect.

Neither does Aunt Anna, Jim's mother, care very much for her nephew's intended, although she tries very hard to like her. Enid has, however, exhibited a casual cruelty to her own mother, which Neville (although he observed the same thing in Italy) has managed to explain away.

In Part II, as we might expect, Sir Neville's headaches suddenly begin to get worse and (in a move that surprised even Benson, whose original outline for the novel went in a different direction) he is jilted by Enid. It turns out that where Sir Neville's religious indifference is the result of a refusal to acquiesce in God's having given him everything but physical health, Enid's is due to a psychotic selfishness, a condition approaching actual insanity, and which has been responsible for her having destroyed the lives of everyone around her and now, for the second time, of her sabotaging her own chance at happiness by terminating an engagement in a violent temper tantrum over a trivial incident. Sir Neville tries to ignore pain because he refuses to accept the fact of what it is doing to him. Enid ignores pain because she refuses to accept what she is doing to others.

Mrs. Bessington (Enid's mother) is transformed from the ridiculous and rather annoying chatterbox of Part I into one of the most tragic figures in any of Benson's novels. Clearly lacking the mental equipment or spiritual training either to accept or rise above the pain inflicted by her daughter's insane cruelty, she simply bears it and hides behind a constant barrage of nonsensical talk.

Initiation also contains one of Benson's most puzzling creations, Mr. Morpeth, a recent convert from Protestantism who is renting the Dower House on Sir Neville's estate. While obviously of common birth, and a retired businessman with absolutely no pretensions to nobility, Mr. Morpeth is, at the same time, one of Benson's noblest characters. He is quiet, humble, and calm, and has the expressed intent (confided in Anna Fanning) of spending the rest of his life deepening his relationship to God and making up for neglecting his daughter when she was growing up.

Part of Mr. Morpeth's function in the novel, of course, is to offer a contrast to the equally plebian Father Richardson. Father Richardson has an extremely exaggerated opinion of his own importance, far beyond what a good priest should have, and a shocking lack of humility. While chastising Sir Neville for his bad example (which, as Sir Neville's parish priest, is his duty), Father Richardson handles the whole thing very badly, and merely succeeds in increasing Sir Neville's contempt for him:

> "You are very seldom at Benediction," said the priest desperately. (He began to see that he was in a tight corner; but it would never do to acknowledge it, he thought. His dignity might suffer. His motto, as he had confided to his fellow priests more than once, was "Never apologize.")

Things come to such a pass that Sir Neville instructs his servants that he is "not home" when the priest calls, even though the Rectory is on the very edge of the estate, within sight of the manor.

Mr. Morpeth, however, remains something of a puzzle. As chief confidant and informal advisor to Aunt Anna, he assists her in overcoming a very slight tendency to blame God for her nephew's sufferings. That, however, could have been handled by another character, such as her son Jim with the unconscious wisdom of childhood, or even by Aunt Anna herself with a little un-Bensonlike introspection.

There is a possibility that Benson intended Mr. Morpeth to be a model for his readers, an example of how to deal with his own death. As a result of his operation, Benson seems to have had an intimation of his own mortality, and a sense that his own life was drawing to a close — as it did, less than two years later. Just as Sir Neville's sufferings reflected his own, Benson may have had the idea that Mr. Morpeth's acceptance of his own daughter's sudden death and his calm reassurances to Aunt Anna as that of Sir Neville seemed imminent would serve as an example as to how he wanted his readers to behave.

Mr. Morpeth, however, sets an impossible example. He is a "full initiate" and is able to accept his daughter's death with a calm sorrow for the opportunities he will now not have to make up for his earlier neglect, but also a certain solemn joy that he was able to do what little he could. He exhibits no change in demeanor or behavior after his daughter's death, but takes everything with perfect resignation to God's Will.

Naturally there is much more than this in the novel. Benson did not omit his usual satirical jabs at the English upper classes. Another one of Benson's delightful characters appears in *Initiation*, Lord Maresfield, who — because he finds English country house life stupefyingly dull and pointless — sets out to find a purpose in life and finds it in art (and polo, what? "But I'm giving up polo.").

Lord Maresfield knows he's not a very good artist ("I splash about a bit"), but that's not the idea. The fact is that he likes it, finds it fulfilling . . . and it has enraged his father to the point where his father and family have apparently cast him off completely. Lord Maresfield is also, in a small way, a much more genial version of Mr. Morpeth, offering unexpected comfort and just the right amount of concern at exactly the right times. The reader quickly comes to the conclusion that Lord Maresfield, for all his self-proclaimed "idleness," lives the sort of purpose-driven life that leisure should bestow.

Then there are the Americans, a nation and people for whom it was fashionable to affect a certain disdain . . . unless your daughter happened to snag a rich one. The Heckers, a couple of extremely rich Americans, exhibit this laudable trait of having purpose in life. Being rich (there doesn't appear to be any other kind of American in the English fiction of this period, unless you count the uncouth but good-hearted frontiersman, usually the sidekick of the rich young American) they have come to Europe in search of "culture." Charles Dana Gibson made a career satirizing this phenomenon in his art (the "Gibson Girl" is nearly always caught in the act of spending father's money on some expensive bauble, gown, or social event), but Benson saw in it "American get-up-and-go" applied to the problem of what to do with your life once you had the wealth (gained through honest work instead of inheritance) to enjoy it.

The Heckers clearly do not view participation in social activities as a duty, although Mr. Hecker puts on the expected show of the poor husband being dragged around to plays and museums by "the wife" — and at the same time is obviously enjoying himself. While they would not have characterized it in this fashion, the Heckers are engaged in what Abraham Maslow called "self-realization," that is, getting to work on developing as persons.

In contrast, the English upper classes (in this and other Benson novels) are just as obviously pursuing social and cultural activities as ends in themselves, because they believe it is expected of them; it is their purpose in life. The Heckers put on a good show, but it's clear that it's not because it's expected of them (they are, after all, uncouth *Americans*) — they do it because they want to. Their crudely ostentatious party (which Lord Maresfield enjoys immensely and Enid despises) is a means to an end, not an end in itself.

Ultimately, of course, *Initiation* is not about pain, or death, or even the purposelessness of the English upper classes. It is, again, about *vocation* — about discerning the path God wants us to take to Him. As Martindale observed,

> In this book, then, Benson stated his doctrine that it may be Pain which awakens a man's soul when nothing else can, though of course he did not prove it. Easily it can be argued that Pain may contract, numb, cripple, or embitter a soul, and drive it into disbelief, cynicism, or despair. He would not deny this; but simply showed you a case in which Pain had proved successful. That is the artist's privilege. Grant me, he demands, the elements I ask; I will mix them, and add another, and I defy you to quarrel with the results. . . . He will agree that not every soul is worthy of Pain. Not indiscriminately will God grant His privilege of suffering. God permit no winds to blow which might quench a flickering wick, and refuses the shock which breaks the enfeebled reed. But, granting a soul of royal quality, Pain, he teaches, all but infallibly must perfect it. The Crucified is there for proof; to Him the true Christian asks but to be assimilated. Convinced of this, he wrote the book at ease and flowingly. And I think he could have pointed to its verification in his own experience. I have felt, and his more intimate friends have largely corroborated this, that his operation marks in him a real stage of spiritual development. At last boyhood was over. Maturity seemed to have arrived or to be

swift upon the road. . . . "Pain," I have already quoted from him, "is a vocation like another."

Loneliness?

Loneliness? was Robert Hugh Benson's last novel, published posthumously, and quite possibly his least known. This is unfortunate, because it is a bravura performance. Perhaps because the specific subject is more subtle than those with which Benson previously dealt, there is less grimness. At the same time his satiric yet gentle wit found suitable targets. Take for example the brief exchange between Max Merival and his sister Norah, just after Max has become infatuated with Marion Tenterden, an opera singer with previously deep religious convictions who has recently made her *début* on the London stage in a Wagner opera:

"Here we are. What's this? Oh! 'The delirious ravings of the dying Tristan'."

He played four wrong notes, firmly.

"No, it isn't," he said. "This is the . . . the 'saddest melody ever written'."

"I thought it must be," said Norah gravely.

Benson even managed to poke a little fun at "Royals," despite a predilection for the monarchic form of government displayed in his historical and science fiction novels. Miss Tenterden is introduced to an unnamed German relative of the British royal house at a reception. Benson has the princess display an appreciation of opera that is strikingly plebian, the "common touch" with a vengeance. The "Royal" might almost be the weekly help discussing last night's show on the telly during elevenses with another charwoman:

"But they are both such sad parts," proceeded the Princess. "I always think *Tristan und Isolde* such a sad story. And I have often wondered why Wagner could not make it end happily. And *Lohengrin* too. Why could he not have made Lohengrin stop with her?"

"But that would rather spoil the story, would it not, ma'am?" asked Marion desperately.

Nevertheless, these satiric touches are not thrown in simply to lighten the mood or provide a slight diversion from an extremely serious subject — Benson's usual question of vocation. The author displayed his absolute mastery of his medium in having every sentence, possibly every word in some manner draw the reader closer to the point.

Loneliness? explores the conflict between man's final end (in Catholic belief union with God in heaven) and the allurements of materialism, which can lead to religious indifferentism. Benson had covered the same ground in *An Average Man*, but from the perspective of an "average man" (obviously) who has fame and fortune handed to him on a silver salver (literally) with absolutely no effort or talent on his part. Marion Tenterden is a completely different character, thus making for a completely different situation. She has genuine talent, and works her way up from complete obscurity with enormous effort to a position in which she is recognized as having the potential to become the greatest opera singer of her day.

As readers of *An Average Man* know, Percy Brandreth-Smith, Benson's equivocal candidate for a typical middle-class Englishman, has his rather stodgy religious instincts enflamed by hearing a Franciscan friar preach. He begins instruction in the Catholic faith, but then gradually drifts away in the process of succumbing to the blandishments of instant and completely unearned worldly success in the form of the proverbial rich uncle having the decency to die. He also manages to act like a complete cad toward everyone associated with his former life as a clerk in a cocoa factor's firm.

Marion Tenterden, on the other hand, has her ardent religiosity damped down when an impresario discovers her while singing at a church function and she enters the glittering world of Grand Opera. Percy's singing in his local Anglican church choir appears to symbolize the rather superficial nature of his belief, and, incidentally, his character before his awakening. This is emphasized by the choice of music, focusing on an obscure composer and the sort of trite and saccharine composition at which minor English liturgical composers excel. Marion's church singing, on the other hand, seems to symbolize her childlike acceptance of her religious upbringing. Benson presented two almost identical situations that mean opposite things.

Where Percy simply ignores or cuts off everyone associated with his former middle-class life and makes a successful transition to the "Upper Ten Thousand," Marion is never regarded by any member of the "upper class" as anything other than an entertainer — and accepted only for her voice. They make it crystal clear that she can never be "accepted," only tolerated for her immense talent. When that appears to be gone forever, her presumed aristocratic friends disappear along with it.

Benson was himself by birth and upbringing a member of the highest level of British society. As a son of the Anglican Archbishop of Canterbury, he ranked socially in the "royal" stratum. In consequence, no one knew better than he the shallow snobbery, even bigoted ignorance that characterized so many members of the British upper class of Edwardian England — and which he satirized so eloquently. He knew the allure of wealth, birth, and fame firsthand — as well as the slow debilitating effect that all three can have on someone's soul. Appearance becomes everything, with the existence of the religious emotion (the most fleeting and superficial of all religious experiences) being the standard both of one's religious conviction and the utility of religion.

Religion is not, however, emotional feelings, although we should never disparage sentiment. Aristotle and Aquinas classified "religion" as a virtue under "justice," and defined it as "rendering to God (or the gods if you're pagan) His due." Coming under justice, it doesn't matter if you don't particularly "feel" like fulfilling whatever religious duties accompany your belief system. Theologians of many faiths, in fact, insist that fulfilling your religious duties when you "don't feel like it" gains greater merit than when you find great emotional satisfaction in doing so. Marion is brought face to face with this when she, in search of a little creative casuistry that will allow her to do exactly as she wishes, consults a Jesuit.

> "Yes; well —" (she shifted her position a little, so that rather less light fell on her face) — "I am not a very good Catholic, I am afraid. I don't mean that I don't go to Mass, because I do; and I go to the sacraments fairly often, too. I live with a friend who is very devout. Perhaps I shouldn't be as good a Catholic as I am, even, if it wasn't for that; religion doesn't mean much to me personally, I am afraid."
>
> "I don't think that matters much," said the priest.
>
> "How do you mean, Father?"
>
> "Well; feelings are not always under our control. Therefore they cannot matter very much. Obedience is what matters. We can always obey."

Marion eventually tries the same sort of line with a sympathetic Protestant minister, Mr. Chomondeley. Even so, when Marion goes to him hoping that he will support her rejection of the laws regulating Catholic marriage, he (evidently, being sincere and honest "but not very deep," without realizing who "the friend" is of whom she speaks) unintentionally supports not the Catholic position *per se*, but simple intellectual honesty. As Marion puts the case to him,

> "I have heard of another case like it, though not of a priest. Imagine that all consolation in religion absolutely went, so that the whole thing became unreal. Well, I suppose that for a time he would think it his duty to go on and persevere. And then there would suddenly come this — this emotion; and that would wake him up, and he'd begin to ask himself whether he really believed anything at all. Well, suppose he found he didn't; or at any rate that he didn't believe everything that, as a Catholic, he was bound to. What is he to do? Is he to say goodbye to all hopes of happiness, just for fear of what people will say?"
>
> "No, not just for fear of that," said the Rector

"Well, what then?" asked the girl, looking straight at him.

"I think he should be very distrustful, at any rate, of his conclusions, if self-interest was so wrapped up in them. But I don't profess to be a psychologist," he added, smiling.

Mr. Chomondeley might not believe everything or anything that the Catholic Church teaches. He does, however, know dishonesty when he sees it. He is also straightforward about "telling it like it is," or (as Benson put it), he is "rather like [Benson's impression of] an American," a people for whom (for all our faults) Benson seemed to have a great deal of admiration.

Naturally, in consequence of the minister's most unwelcome — if unintentional — perceptiveness, Marion isolates herself from Mr. Chomondeley: "I don't think I like Mr. Cholmondeley as much as I thought I did." — a sentiment that would probably have wounded Mr. Cholmondeley deeply, and rightfully so. When push came to shove, the minister of a very political, almost secular church came down on the side of truth and religion, and against the dictates of a very materialist society, perhaps the most materialist the world had seen up to that time. Not even his own admitted shallowness as a shepherd of his flock nor his discomfort with the question swayed him from what he believed to be right.

It becomes painfully clear to the reader (if nobody else) that Marion's choice is not between Catholicism and Protestantism. It is between religious belief of any kind and indifference. This is a question that every believer in every religion must face eventually. Benson's genius in putting "Catholic" principles in the mouth of a quintessentially, almost comically Protestant minister underlines their universality as nothing else could. The unusual nature of what Benson did could perhaps be better understood in our day if the plot had involved an orthodox Jew who receives a pointed (and very uncomfortable) lesson on the universality in the Law of Moses from an Islamic Imam.

As a somewhat obscure commentary on Marion's activities, she is "observed" in many important scenes by Rhadamanthus, a parrot belonging to Marion's friend and companion, Maggie Brent. A cursory reading might let the reader confuse this with "Radamanthus," a type of crow (and thus a suitable bird-name), or Rhadames, the hero in Verdi's *Aida*, and thus a suitable name for a pet associated with an opera singer.

Rhadamanthus, however, is a figure from Greek mythology, a brother of Minos and the son of Zeus and Europa, who ruled Crete before being driven out by Minos. A wise king, he was in some accounts made one of the judges of the dead after his death. The parrot's constant stream of profanity might be Benson's way of "warning" both the reader and Marion that something is definitely amiss in her behavior, and that she can expect a stern and terrible judgment unless she shapes up — "rhadamanthine" describes any just but inflexible judgment.[85]

What really starts Marion on the path to religious indifference, however, is not worldly pleasures *per se*, but a growing romantic attachment to Max Merival. Max is . . . well, Max isn't much of anything. He appears to be Benson's epitome of the shallow and purposeless member of the British upper class. P. G. Wodehouse's archetypical drone, Bertie Wooster, comes off well in comparison. While an inveterate and ineffectual boob, Bertie couldn't even imagine doing half the caddish things Max does as a matter of course, even if Jeeves would let him get away with it. Of course, the difference is that Bertie (somewhere deep inside) knows that he exists only to entertain the lower classes, while Max allows the lower classes to exist to entertain him.

This demand to be entertained is, in fact, the only thing that attracts Max to Marion. She, as a singer in Wagner, the grandest of all Grand Opera, is about as "high class" as it is possible for any stage-person to be . . . and still can't cross the invisible and obviously artificial barrier.

Max builds himself an imaginary Marion, based on her singing and her stage personae. Where another romantic aspirant would try to find out everything he could about the girl Marion — her birthday, her favorite food . . . espe-

---

[85] *Aeneid*, vi. 566.

cially her religion — Max buys a book about the characters she plays and studies it deeply. He never seems to find out anything about her life before they met, or her real life away from the theater. Even the one gift mentioned, a cat, is recognized instantly by Marion as being in fulfillment of some theatrical superstition. Marion simply does not exist to Max except as a creation of his own mind, extracted from the fictional characters she plays on stage and epitomized by her magnificent voice.

Max sees life and marriage as an adolescent fairytale. He goes to church as he does everything else, even his pursuit of Marion, as a pastime. He thinks vaguely of a remunerative position (regarding business in as fantastic a light as he does marriage), but it's clear that he would be living off his intended wife's money.

> One thing only had been insisted on, and that was that he should make himself acquainted with the working of estates. In this manner he would at any rate be a decent sort of landowner when the time came for him to take up his responsibilities. He had consented, because there was nothing else to do. And now he was to reopen the question and himself demand to be given what he did not want.
>
> Max, even now, had very vague ideas as to what his father could do for him. He supposed that just at first — say for six months — he would have to learn again the duties of a confidential clerk; and they appeared to him loathsome. However, it must be done.
>
> Then, say soon after the beginning of the new year, he would probably be promoted in some way; he did not know how; but he fancied that the sons of eminent financiers always are promoted very soon. Then his fortune would begin to have its foundations laid; in a year, even, he might be a director of a company; and directorships, he believed, carried large salaries, if the holders of them bore great names. Well; by then he would be independent; at least he would be independent enough to be able to marry Marion without actually going into the workhouse; her earnings, too, at Covent Garden would be an enormous

help, if only she wouldn't give away half of them in ridiculous charities. And all this was only if the worst came to the worst, and his father remained obstinate against the marriage, and behaved, indeed, like a stage-father. If not, the difficulty did not exist; if it did, well, it was surmountable, according to his program.

Benson saw the English upper class as being single-minded in pursuit of utter purposelessness and uselessness. They had been trained in this, as well as to reject anyone "not of their 'sort'," a point constantly raised against Marion by Max's family. In a supremely ironic sentence, Marion characterizes her co-religionists in words that applied much more to "society": "They just believe what's told them, like so many sheep." "Religion" is something in somewhat poor taste, as Benson makes clear is Max's chief religious tenet.

> Religion, to him, was not a practical thing at all; it was a particular kind of emotion which certain kinds of people had, and others had not. It was a matter of choice, or perhaps of temperament; and the amount of intellectual ideas that you held along with the emotion depended again on temperament, or perhaps education. Religion was like clear soup; you might like it, or you might not; it might be hot or cold or tepid; and its dogmas were like those little dough alphabets that float about in clear soup. If you were very much interested, and had a good many letters, you might even think they formed words. Catholics, as a class, he knew, had a great many dogmas and rules; he could not conceive how it was possible that they should really hold them, but some of them certainly appeared to do so. Very well, then, it was no affair of his. Live and let live. He had no objection.

Some readers more familiar with the typical sex-soaked modern novel might find *Loneliness?* a trifle anemic. This, however, would demonstrate an almost complete misunderstanding of what Benson was doing. The word "sex" might not appear too many times in Benson's fiction, but that doesn't mean it wasn't alluded to. In *An Average*

Man, for example, it's quite clear what is going on when a girl runs away with a man, without beating the reader over the head with it.

Benson was doing something different in *Loneliness?* He was not, I think, avoiding sex so much as using its absence to highlight the fact that Max and Marion are looking at life and marriage as pre-adolescents do — they are a virtual Ken and Barbie set half a century before those two dolls came on the scene. For all the scorn and derision heaped on the plastic pair, they epitomize the way many people today view "real" life when completely isolated from religious society (God), civil society (politics), and domestic society. Max and Marion, for example, mention children, but it's not altogether clear that they have any realistic idea how to go about the business of having them or raising them. Children are not a desired end of marriage, but a problem to deal with because of the religious issue, just as today they are seen as financial or social burdens.

Benson was constrained, of course, by the fact that decent authors didn't bring explicit sexual situations into their novels. A couple of writers (using rather mealy mouthed justifications) did: Grant Allen wrote *The Woman Who Did* (1895), about a woman who decides "for the highest and purest motives" to have an illegitimate child, while H. Rider Haggard (of *King Solomon's Mines* fame) tried to cash in on late Victorian England's sex obsession with his own rather flabby production, *Beatrice* (1890).

The effect of such novels — when taken seriously — is to undermine both religious and domestic society by making them completely individualistic and "personal," as typified by the utterance, "It's my life, body, company, money," whatever. Acts no longer have consequences, and the "artificial" consequences that society forces on people are to be condemned. Benson, however (like any true artist), used the "rules" to create his work of art, even to the point of using the rule itself to make a point.

Loneliness? could even be taken as Benson's answer to *The Woman Who Did* and similar works (parodied by P. G. Wodehouse as *Men Who Did And Women Who Shouldn't Have But Took A Pop At It*) by reinforcing the fact that acts have consequences. You don't mess around with the laws of religious, domestic, or even civil society with impunity. Marion loses her voice and her career by singing when she shouldn't in order to please Max, thereby losing the only thing that kept the relationship together.

Nevertheless, like all Benson's fiction, what at first glance appears to be a tragedy is actually a fulfillment of God's plan for what is best for us. "Society" was clearly ruining Marion, taking her away from God and what functioned as her family. Benson may even have selected grand opera instead of some other type of entertainment because it is the most artificial and removed from reality.

Marion and Max, however, constantly rave about how *real* the opera is, highlighting their construction of a relationship built on a fantasy. This is reminiscent of the names of the riverboats in *Huckleberry Finn* — *Lallah Rookh* and *Sir Walter Scott*, both symbolizing the decadent reliance of "southern aristocracy" on works of chivalric fantasy to form their outlook on life. Mark Twain was fully aware that much of the symbolism used by the Ku Klux Klan was taken from the works of Sir Walter Scott, notably the burning cross in *The Lady of the Lake*.

It is inevitable that Marion comes into conflict with reality. Out of pride or stubbornness (or naïveté) of course, Marion insists that it's all the fault of others, others who just won't see things her way: "'I mean that I shan't be able to live as a Catholic — or go to the sacraments; and that Catholics will believe — or pretend to believe —' (her voice shook a little, but with indignation) — 'will pretend to believe that you and I aren't married when we are.'" Truth is a "hateful system," and people who dare to tell her the truth are only saying "awful things" — obviously just to go along with a hateful system, and withholding their real opinion or beliefs because they (unlike her) have not liberated themselves from the artificial constraints "the system" imposes.

Marion turns into *The Woman Who Did*, but by giving up her faith instead of having an illegitimate child — in Benson's and God's eyes a much more serious thing (as it should be in ours). As she says to Max, "I'm not going to let it make any difference." Unfortunately for her, it is not her choice. Man is not an atomistic individual, but (at one and the same time) an individual and a member of society — a "political animal" who is a member of an almost unlimited series of overlapping groups, infinitely complex, institutions that determine how we live our lives in relationships with others. By constricting her world exclusively to her relationship with Max, Marion ignores (clearly at the peril of her soul), the vast network of institutions that comprise civil, domestic, and, yes, religious society. A human being is an individual creation . . . but the human person is a social, even political creature, a paradox that evades many people even today, and interferes with their understanding and acceptance of such basic concepts as social charity and social justice.

Marion thereby makes a life of loneliness with Max in the midst of society, then (paradoxically) is rewarded with solitude when it all falls apart — hence the question mark in the title. Which is the true loneliness? Was Marion lonely when she went counter to the rules of the institutions within which she was born and raised to please others, or was she lonely when those others abandoned her?

There is so much more in *Loneliness?* than could ever be covered in a brief essay like this. You would need an analysis many times longer than the novel itself to do it justice. Mr. Chomondeley, for example, almost demands a novel of his own, while treating Sir Robert Mainwaring as he deserves would be a delicate task without descending to spitefulness or unnecessary cruelty. Maggie Brent, Marion's friend and companion, is one of Benson's finest creations, and one of the few to receive an obvious reward in a Benson novel in the form of what Catholics call a "happy death" — having lived well, she dies well without fear, even with a solemn yet "terrible" joy.

Benson was probably well aware that *Loneliness?* would be his last novel. While the final version did not receive the same level of editorial scrutiny or rewriting as works published during his lifetime (there were some obvious and easy errors in the first edition that were not corrected), Benson seems to have put much more into this particular novel than into his others, more by intimation and subtle hint than by treating certain things explicitly.

The book is certainly enjoyable as a straight story, but each reading reveals another level, justifying many re-readings. Thus, in an ironic twist that might have delighted Benson, what ranks as one of his best efforts and greatest achievements is practically unknown even to his most devoted fans. It is only by chance that *Loneliness?* was the second Benson novel I read. I found a first edition hidden among even more obscure works for $3.00, less than a tenth of its value as I discovered much later, in a used bookstore specializing in cheap paperbacks and used magazines.

8. The Later Historical Novels

Come Rack! Come Rope! (1912)

Oddsfish! (1914)

Come Rack! Come Rope!

"*Come Rack! Come Rope!* is in a class by itself as a historical novel."[86]

That comment by the Reverend John A. Hardon, S.J., is pretty much the definitive statement about the wonderfully moving and powerful story related in *Come Rack! Come Rope!* Solidly fact-based, as are all of Robert Hugh Benson's historical novels (although he could always manage to find fault somewhere, having come short of the perfection he evidently desired), *Come Rack! Come Rope!* from 1912 is the second of Benson's two novels to feature the martyr Edmund Campion, "The Seditious Jesuit." The other is *By What Authority?* from 1904.[87]

It was the discovery that the copy of *Come Rack! Come Rope!* I purchased many years ago was an unacknowledged truncation of a much longer work that helped inspire the effort to republish all of Benson's fiction in consistent, newly formatted — and unabridged — editions (a project that we are slowly bringing to fruition). By an unusual coincidence, at about the same time I discovered that *Come Rack! Come Rope!* was an abridgement, I learned of the publication of a much-shortened version of *By What Authority?*

For some reason, virtually every mention of Campion was removed from the abridged edition of *Come Rack! Come Rope!* Since Benson took the title from Campion's reassurance to his friends that he would not betray them no matter what torture was applied, this made the title rather meaningless! Mary Stuart — "Mary Queen of Scots," a major character in the original — was also given short shrift. At the same time, a number of reviews on the internet expressing anger at the "surreptitious" nature of the abridgements of Benson's works — *Come Rack! Come*

---

[86] Rev. John A. Hardon, S.J., *The Catholic Lifetime Reading Plan*. New York: Doubleday, 1989,131-132.
[87] Once-and-Future Books, 2005, ISBN 97809729821XX

Rope! in particular — provided an added incentive to do something about the situation.

Such alterations, while no doubt well intentioned, do the author a great disservice. The vital question in *Come Rack! Come Rope!* is, as with all of Benson's fiction and much of his non-fiction, that of vocation — of "calling." How does God wish each individual to spend the life each of us is given?

That question seems almost to have consumed Benson, with the result that, coming from an eminently literary family (every one of his brothers and sisters was a published author[88]), he worked and struggled with that question principally through his novels and short stories. What does God want? Benson works out answers to that question in what his characters experience. He avoids the long introspective passages and lectures that seem to plague modern novels.

Cutting these episodes down to suit an editor's idea of what the modern reader wants, or in some cases eliminating them altogether removes most of the life and a great deal of the meaning from Benson's novels. Benson includes incidents and what might appear to the superficial reader to be long digressions for one very good reason: it advances the characters along their paths to God . . . or, in some of the novels, away from Him. (Ralph Torridon in *The King's Achievement* is particularly noteworthy in this regard.) While many of Benson's novels are lengthy, I believe I can honestly state that none of them is too long.

In *Come Rack! Come Rope!* we discover the simple answer that what God wants is complete surrender to His Will, something which all the major religions have been reminding us for thousands of years. Simple, yes — but never easy. Working through complex characterizations, intricate plots (especially in his historical novels, in which he had to make the fictional plot fit known facts) and a deep understanding of human nature, Benson told stories

---

[88] Benson's brothers in particular enjoy much more renown in certain circles than he does. Arthur C. Benson still has a small cult following for his horror and supernatural fiction, mostly short stories, while entire societies have been formed to promote and preserve the six "Lucia" novels of Edward F. Benson.

of individuals who gradually come to discover what the Divine Will means for them. As Father Hardon remarked,

> Everything he wrote was done with an avowed purpose and is marked by charm of style, subtle psychology, and appealing mysticism. Many of his novels are histories of a soul completely surrendered to God.[89]

It would have been more accurate to say that they are histories of a soul *surrendering* to God, but the point is well taken.

Come Rack! Come Rope! represents the culmination of a short lifetime of intense work and a project that Benson conceived as presenting the Catholic "side" of the English Reformation in fictional form. This was possibly intended to offset the frankly dreadful productions that the reading public in late Victorian and Edwardian times, as hungry for scandal and lurid sensation as today's television audiences, gobbled up with alacrity.[90] The result of Benson's efforts was a series of novels that were far removed from such polemics. Contrary to the usual presentation on the Catholic "side," he frequently depicted most Protestants and all Protestant clergy in very sympathetic, even attractive poses and roles. This resulted in a reasonable and balanced, albeit exciting picture of the period immediately following Henry VIII's "break with Rome."

Of course, being sympathetic towards and understanding of the Protestant position is not the same as accepting it. Benson could, and clearly did respect people for the fact that they believed in something. Even the atheist Oliver Brand in *Lord of the World*[91] believes in a god of sorts — humanity — and orders his life accordingly. The modern

---

[89] Hardon, *op. cit.*, 132.
[90] Edward Peters in *Inquisition* (Berkeley, California: University of California Press, 1988), makes a good case demonstrating his thesis that a lot of what people today believe about "the Spanish Inquisition" is derived not from historical fact, but from trashy Victorian and Edwardian novels. These could most charitably be described as soft-core pornography intended to titillate and shock audiences in much the same way as our modern "reality television."
[91] Once-and-Future books, 2005, ISBN 9780972982140.

phenomenon of people who believe in nothing would have been completely incomprehensible to Benson.

Not so much in *Come Rack! Come Rope!* as in other novels (although it is definitely there), Benson makes clear that — up to a point — it is belief itself that is important, not so much what a person believes. This is what Aristotle called the virtue of religion, a necessary part of what it means to be fully human. Religion and morality are not synonyms, contrary to what confused modern commentators, politicians and academics would have us believe. The virtue of religion is only a part of morality. Aristotle puts it under justice, the virtue that "renders to each his due," for religion means a relationship between man and God by which the individual human person is disposed to give to God the special honor that is His due.[92]

Benson therefore accepted the virtue of religion as a given in all his novels. It is very difficult to find a religious hypocrite in a Benson story. A character may be shallow, as many of them are in *The Conventionalists*. He may be mistaken, as with the condemned heretic in *The Dawn of All*. He can even be almost demonically evil, as with Topcliffe in *Come Rack! Come Rope!* They are all, however, sincere and convinced in their religious beliefs. As Benson related in his short autobiographical sketch, *Confessions of a Convert,*

> I understand now that there is coherence in all that God has made — that He has made of one blood all the nations of the earth; that there is not one aspiration out of the darkness that does not find its way to Him; not one broken or distorted system of thought that does not flash back at least one ray of eternal glory; not one soul but has her place in His economy.

The question then becomes *what* they believe — and how, for the reader, this creates the conflict that generates the plot. Benson was no fool, and was fully aware that there are many paths to God. He also knew that truth does not depend on who says it, but on how close it conforms to the natural law and to God's Nature on which the natural law is ultimately based. Thus while each of

---

[92] *Vide* St. Thomas Aquinas, *Summa*, IIa IIae, qq. 80-100.

his novels — *Come Rack! Come Rope!* in particular — tell the story of how someone in a specific set of circumstances surrenders himself to God, the plot is never a simple "true believers versus the satanic unbelievers." Even the diabolically sinister "Mr. Vincent" in *The Necromancers* is honestly convinced that he has found the right path.

Benson knew that each person is both an individual and a social being. He depicted, with a great deal of skill and sensitivity for all sides of the issue, the natural conflicts that arise when there is a lack of unity among members of a group — in this case the people of England. Lack of solidarity — acceptance and internalization by all members of the group of the principles and special characteristics that define a group as that particular group and no other — is clearly destructive of the social order as well as individual life. Benson depicts this issue with exemplary skill in his "semi-fictional" *The Religion of the Plain Man*.

The need for solidarity is critical whether we are looking at things from the level of single institutions, or groups ranging from small on up to the whole of the common good. As the common good in social terms is the entire network of institutions within which individuals "work out their salvation" — that is, surrender themselves to God and conform themselves to the natural law — solidarity must be achieved at all costs, or the social order is ultimately doomed.

The question is what the principles are in which people come together in solidarity — and the equally important issue of discerning the true principle and not mistaking a specific application of a principle for the principle itself. Benson's historical novels thus relate the struggle between two opposing groups seeking to define what it means to be "English," and, ultimately, "human" — and creating a great deal of confusion between principles and applications of principles as they go about the task.

This novel — the title comes from Saint Edmund's assurance to his friends that should he be arrested and tortured he would not talk (nor did he) — is the last and greatest of Robert Hugh Benson's historical novels. Technically, *Oddsfish!*, a "Restoration Adventure," followed this one, being the last novel published during Benson's lifetime, but had been written and rewritten several times before *Come Rack! Come Rope!* was begun.

Benson could have picked no better figure than Campion around which to build his story. Saint Edmund, in fact, appears to have exercised a fascination for Benson. His first historical novel, *By What Authority?*, seems to have been, at least in part, an attempt to make Campion better known,[93] and to highlight a conversion that, much more than Benson's own ever did Edwardian England, stunned and infuriated the Elizabethan establishment.

By Benson's day, it was generally recognized that a political unit had to make room for people of different religious beliefs. An established church is, as Mark Twain remarked, an established crime. Making non-conformity to a State religion a civil crime violates both free will and the correlative freedom of association that Pius XI stressed so much as a necessary part of the restructuring of the social order — not to mention the little matter of individual conscience!

The worst that could happen to Benson when he converted to Catholicism, as he knew full well, was the relatively minor matter of social ostracism. As "the priest" relates to "John" in *The Religion of the Plain Man,*

> Three hundred years ago we could have offered you great things: the hatred of all who heard your name; the contempt of those who were loudest in their love for England. We could have offered you the Tower as your prison, chains, stinking dungeons, the rack, the whip, the gallows, the hangman's cauldron. Now we have no more than the chips of Christ's cross to tempt you with; a little sneering and lifting of eyebrows; a little good-humored laughter; a few remarks about 'intellectual servitude'; a little smiling pity over your medievalism, your materialism, your lack of the sturdy British spirit, your superstition and your fear of the priest.

---

[93] Evelyn Waugh, a great admirer of Benson, may have been inspired by Benson's regard for Campion in writing his own famous biography of the saint.

Benson, however, was spared even that. As he related in *Confessions of a Convert*,

> I must acknowledge with the greatest gratitude that the charity with which I was treated by members of the Anglican communion in general simply astonished me. I did not know that there was so much generosity in the world.

That was not the case with Edmund Campion. In his day non-conformity to the Church of England, whether you were a "papist" or a member of another sect of Protestantism, was a civil crime: high treason. Anabaptists, for example, at times suffered worse persecution than Catholics.

The only perceived difference (the actual ones were many) on the part of most Englishmen of Campion's day between "papists" and "loyal Englishmen" was the matter of the pope's authority. That being so, those "papists" were just being stubborn and disloyal not to surrender their allegiance to some foreign prince and come over to the "right" side. As the idea of the Nation-State took root and ultra-nationalism grew in prominence, especially during the reign of Elizabeth I, so grew the fervor with which non-conformists were persecuted. Thus Campion, more than most people, could expect death or worse should he convert — hence his assurance to his comrades that nothing would move him, come rack or rope.

This is easy to understand once we realize just who this man Campion was.[94] Edmund Campion at the time of his conversion had already been ordained a deacon in the Anglican communion. He was considered the foremost Latin orator at Oxford, making presentations before Queen Elizabeth herself. Campion was also, oddly enough, a leader of fashion. Groups of students and young townsmen copied him the way Elvis impersonators used to emulate "the King," calling themselves "Campionists." Had he remained in the Church of England, Campion could rea-

---

[94] The outline of Saint Edmund's career given here is taken largely from the sketch in Leo Knowles' excellent book, *The Prey of the Priest Catchers: The Lives of The Forty Martyrs*. St. Paul, Minnesota: Carillon Books, 1980.

sonably have expected to rise to the highest level, even to the Archbishopric of Canterbury, a position in the kingdom second only to that of Elizabeth.

Nevertheless, Campion seems to have been tormented, as was Benson himself (perhaps the reason for the apparent affinity) with the question of vocation. In 1573 Campion was selected to defend the Established Church in an open-air gathering in London, initiating what promised to be a brilliant public career to match his amazing achievements at Oxford. In a surprising move, however, he escaped to Ireland. Ireland in the sixteenth century was considered a wild and savage country and certainly no place for the most learned scholar any English University had turned out in a generation. While there he converted to Catholicism, wrote a history of Ireland, and attempted to found a university.

Soon, however, Edmund had further struggles with his conscience, with the result that he made his way to Douai, where English Catholics had established a college, by way of London. While in London, suitably disguised, he attended the trial of Reverend John Storey. Father Storey was an elderly priest against whom Elizabeth's advisors harbored a special animus. Storey had been kidnapped from Antwerp, was tried, and then executed with singular ferocity.

Father Storey's passion and death seems to have affected Edmund deeply. He became a Jesuit and spent his "novitiate" — the years of study and preparation to enter the Order permanently — in many parts of Europe. Ordained a priest in 1578, he was appointed to the faculty of the Jesuit college in Prague, where his immense learning was seen as most usefully employed. Barely a year later, however, the call went forth for volunteers to go to England. Campion was among the first chosen.

Campion's adventures during his nearly two years on the "English Mission" have achieved the status of near-legend. In *Come Rack! Come Rope!*, while relating only a tiny fraction of all that Campion accomplished and experienced, Benson drew a masterful portrait of the martyr in strokes nearly as bold as the man himself. I do not know whether the incident that Benson related of Campion's meeting with Topcliffe in the Tower of London was an invention, but it was quintessentially Campion. The "Brag" to which Benson referred was an astounding proposal circulated throughout England that, if he would be granted safe conduct, Campion challenged any or all of the best scholars in the Church of England to a debate — to which he made a point of inviting Elizabeth!

Nor was Elizabeth immune to such courage. Despite her own weakness of character and her life as a virtual prisoner of her "advisors," she seems to have made a genuine and honest effort to save Campion after his arrest and four days of torture in the "Little Ease." The "Little Ease" was a cell in the Tower in which it was impossible either to stand or lie at full length. Prisoners incarcerated there frequently went insane. Unfortunately the conditions attached to the offer — recantation of his Catholic faith and an assured career at the highest levels of the Church of England — were too high a price. Campion politely refused. He was returned to the Tower and "put to the question" — the standard euphemism for torture.

After three sessions on the rack the torturers asked Campion how he felt. He replied, "Not ill, because not at all." Soon after he was finally granted his chance to debate with the chief theologians of the Church of England. In crippling pain and denied access to books or even writing materials, he refuted their arguments by quoting long passages in Latin and Greek from memory, demonstrating where they had twisted or misinterpreted the original. The only point scored against him was a minor grammatical error in Greek.

Campion managed to defend himself so ably at his trial (without benefit of counsel or access to law books) that the jury — specially selected to convict him, regardless of the evidence — took over an hour to come to a decision concerning him and his companions. This was after they had been instructed to find the defendants guilty — with a damoclean "or else" implicitly hanging over their heads. On the day of Campion's death, Elizabeth sent a message to Tyburn, the usual place of execution, that he would be spared up to the moment he was hanged if he would but recant. Again he refused — although urging everyone to pray for the Queen, as did he.

In *Come Rack! Come Rope!* Benson clearly intended Campion's career both as an inspiration for and a mirror to that of his fictional hero, Robin Audrey of Matstead, one of those houses to which Benson gave nearly as much life as his human characters. That, and if I were to explain Robin's own struggles, both internal and external, in any but the broadest terms I would necessarily reveal "spoilers" for which a reader of the novel would scarcely thank me.

Suffice it to say, then (in the most general terms, of course), that the real point in *Come Rack! Come Rope!*, as with all Benson's fiction and most of his non-fiction, is very straightforward. As Evelyn Waugh remarked, "He worked without thought of posterity, as though Doomsday were imminent, using all his talents lavishly to draw as many souls as possible among his immediate neighbors to their true end in God."[95] As Benson himself concluded in *Confessions of a Convert*,

> And through all this ruined wilderness He has brought me, of His infinite goodness, to that place where Jerusalem has descended from on high, which is the mother of us all; He has brought me out of the mire and clay and set my feet upon the rock; He has lifted me from those straying paths that lead nowhere, on to the broad road that leads to Him.
>
> What yet lies beyond I do not know: the towers of this City of God rise immediately into the clouds that are about His Throne; the City is too vast, its streets too glorious, its houses too stupendous for any soul to dream that she knows them all or understands their secret. In this world, at least, not even the saint or the theologian, or the old man who has lived all his days within her walls, can dare to think that he has advanced more than a few steps within her heavenly gates. He stands within her, and, thank God, I stand there with him, as

---

[95] Evelyn Waugh, "Preface" to Robert Hugh Benson's *The History of Richard Raynal, Solitary*. Chicago, Illinois: Henry Regnery Company, 1050, xii.

does every soul to whom God has shown this great mercy. But all of us together are but as a party of children wandering in from the country, travel-stained, tired, and bewildered with glory. About us are the great palaces, where the princes dwell; behind us that gate of pearl which, somehow, we have passed; the streets before us are crowded with heavenly forms too bright to look upon; and supremely high above us rises that great curtained stairway that leads to the King.

Oddsfish!

On November 20, 1903, Robert Hugh Benson wrote his mother a letter from Rome in which he noted that, even before his first novel *By What Authority?* had been accepted by a publisher, he was already devising the plot of another, this one to take place in the time of Charles II Stuart, the "Merry Monarch." Work on the book proceeded with extreme rapidity, and by Trinity Sunday of 1904 he was able to write,

> The book is FINISHED. I do wonder whether it is any good at all. I shall love to read it aloud. And now comes the labour of rewriting it; there are endless things to do at it. All kinds of people have to planed down and carved and re-grouped. But I shall reserve the general re-editing until I come home. . . .
>
> P.S. — Nell Gwyn is at this moment bowing on a platform, and I must rush and let her sit down.

With that tantalizing glimpse of a literary "might have been," work on the novel that Benson insisted must be called *A Seminary Priest of the Seventeenth Century* would proceed by fits and starts over the next decade until it was completely rewritten — down to changing the names of virtually everyone in the book except for known historical personages. From being — very nearly — the second novel Benson wrote, the story that eventually came (thankfully) to be titled *Oddsfish!* was the last published in the author's lifetime.

What happened?

Martindale made note of several letters through the years in which Benson lamented his inability to finish the book. Possibly this was due to the fact that the original work was drafted while he was in the process of becoming a full member of the Catholic Church, and some of his attitudes (though not his basic convictions) were in a state of flux. The attempt to rewrite it may have meant — essentially — that he was taking the work of a different literary self and updating it to reflect a deeper understanding of Catholicism made possible from his new vantage point.

The possibility also exists that Benson was disappointed in the effect that his historical fiction was having. His historical novels were written to counter the execrable productions so popular at the time projecting an image of the Catholic Church that was largely the product of Tudor propaganda. Benson's novels were successful as marketable products, but clearly were not having the desired effect on the popular mindset. The Catholic Church remained, and is still depicted in a great deal of modern entertainment as a subversive organization bent on enslaving the human race in one form or another.

As I have pointed out a number of times already, this presumed disappointment may have led to Benson focusing on extremely heavy-handed satire holding Edwardian English society up to a very unflattering mirror. Unfortunately, his efforts in this line (while recognized today as classics . . . for all the wrong reasons) were also short of the mark. In 1910 Benson once again appears to have changed direction, and concentrated on much more subtle satire embodied in "mainstream" contemporary fiction. In this he was stunningly successful, although attitudes among the general public remained unchanged.

There were, however, some slight digressions along the way. In 1912, for example, Benson turned out *Come Rack! Come Rope!*, a novel covering much of the same material as *By What Authority?* Far from being an old plot in thinly disguised new clothes, however, *Come Rack! Come Rope!* managed to be a completely new and different work.

The success of *Come Rack! Come Rope!* may finally have provided Benson with whatever it was he needed to finish *Oddsfish!* It was rewritten to the point that the final product bears virtually no resemblance to the references and descriptions of the early drafts in the author's letters. (Nell Gwyn, for example, disappeared almost completely.) While not up to the stratospheric standard of *Come Rack! Come Rope!*, *Oddsfish!* is well worth reading, and has maintained a level of popularity through the years, even suffering the indignity of coming out in a heavily abridged paperback version in the 1950s (presented as a romance), as well as more entertaining full editions.

Nevertheless, I have a serious criticism to make of *Oddsfish!*, albeit one that shouldn't interfere with anyone's enjoyment of the novel. This might strike the reader as too esoteric a point to raise, were it not symptomatic of much of what passes for political philosophy these days. Since at least part of Benson's purpose in his fiction was to educate people about the truth to be found in the Catholic Church and to encourage understanding of the institution to counter centuries of lies and misunderstandings, however, it is appropriate to point out that Benson's own understanding of the political philosophy of the Catholic Church was not entirely accurate.

Briefly, despite the availability of the encyclicals of Pope Leo XIII, the philosophy of Saint Thomas Aquinas, and the work of Saint (then Venerable) Robert Cardinal Bellarmine, Benson appears to have accepted a belief in the "Divine Right of Kings" as somehow consistent with the social and political teachings of the Catholic Church. Algernon Sidney — whose *Discourses on Government* had heavy influence on the Founding Fathers of the United States — is portrayed in *Oddsfish!* as a consummate villain and rogue for his opposition to Charles II's philosophy of government.

Ironically (unlike John Locke, who presented a distorted and uncredited version of Catholic political philosophy in his *First Treatise on Government*), Sidney actually defended Catholic social teaching against attacks by Sir Robert Filmer in *Patriarcha* and a number of tracts and pamphlets by James I Stuart. Filmer, the chief theologian of James I, "accused" Catholics of being democratic at a time when Divine Right was the up-and-coming philosophy of government. In the first chapter of *Patriarcha*, for instance, Filmer wrote,

> In a commonwealth all men are born naturally free; consequently, the people themselves, immediately and directly, hold the political power so long as they have not transferred this power to some king or ruler. This tenet was first hatched in the schools [*i.e.*, by

Scholastic philosophers such as Aquinas] and hath been fostered by all succeeding papists.

The upshot for loyal English Catholics was that, in order to demonstrate that a "good Catholic" could at the same time be a "good citizen" — a presumed dichotomy that still suffuses the popular mindset — they felt they had to accept a political theory directly at odds with Aristotelian and Thomist philosophy, as well as contrary to that which prevailed in England before Henry VII Tudor became king.

The situation became even more confused when France — "The Eldest Daughter of the Church" — espoused a version of Divine Right theory in order to bolster the State absolutism of Louis XIV, while Spain subverted Church institutions (notably the Inquisition) in an effort to become "more Catholic than the pope" and impose its vision of what form the Catholic Church should take as the idea of the Nation-State took hold throughout a formerly politically homogenous Europe.

Ironically it was during the seventeenth century, the time of the setting of *Oddsfish!*, that the Polish-Lithuanian Commonwealth, the most powerful nation in Europe, achieved its preeminence on the strength of its elective kingship and democratic institutions. Flaws in the application of democratic principles would result in "the Deluge" that ultimately destroyed the Commonwealth. The fact remains, however, that Poles and Lithuanians credit democracy resting on Catholic principles with making the Commonwealth great.

As if to ensure a permanent state of confusion among Catholics and non-Catholics alike, the revulsion against the atrocities of the French Revolution allowed the reactionary political philosophies of such people as Joseph-Marie, Comte de Maistre (1753-1821), who promoted yet another version of Divine Right theory in contradiction to Thomism, to achieve credibility among conservative Catholics.

So deep-rooted did this belief become that every encyclical or allocution of Pius IX and Leo XIII that attempted to set the record straight seemed to many people to be, on the contrary, supporting Divine Right theory instead of democracy! One example of this is the egregious misinterpretation of *Testem Benevolentiae*, Leo XIII's "Apostolic Letter" to the American bishops in 1899.

The letter, which gave a virtual endorsement of and high praise to the American political system, condemned the application of those same democratic principles to Church administration, practice, and the determination of religious truth. In other words, civil political theory applies to civil society, while religious political theory — a horse of a different color — applies to religious society. Consequently, it is inappropriate to apply civil theory to religious society, and *vice versa*.

Nevertheless, in a stunning example of human contrariness, many well-intentioned individuals have misinterpreted (and continue to misinterpret) *Testem Benevolentiae*. They interpret it as condemning democracy and the American political system, rather than as a restatement of the traditional Catholic doctrine of the separation of Church and State . . . another doctrine that has been grossly distorted and misused against religion in general and the Catholic Church in particular, both by the Church's friends and its enemies. Thus, while the Catholic Church was attacked in the sixteenth and seventeenth centuries for promoting democracy, today it is excoriated for a presumed condemnation of democracy and promoting the divine right of kings.

To make absolutely certain everyone is confused, you had people such as John Locke and Algernon Sidney espousing "Catholic" political philosophy (with certain critical omissions that don't concern us here), at the same time they advocated a most un-Catholic violent opposition to the legitimate government. On the other hand, Catholics (in order to prove that they could be both good citizens and good Catholics) were supporting the legitimacy of the government by advocating non- or un-Catholic political philosophy!

Thus, the reasoning for an English "good Catholic" since the Reformation would run along these lines: "I am — or at least am trying to be — a good Catholic. I am also a loyal citizen of my country, despite the fact that I am not a member of the established State church, and accept the civil legitimacy of the government. Because I am loyal to both my Church and my State, the prevailing philosophy that supports the legitimate government must, therefore, be consistent with that of the Catholic Church."

The fact that the Catholic Church has throughout history had to reach an accommodation with a significant number of governments that are actively hostile to the Catholic Church and even religion in general obviates this line of reasoning does not occur to most people. Acquiescence to a deplorable situation that cannot at present be changed due to political factors (such as abortion or slavery) constitutes neither an endorsement of the situation, nor absolve anyone from the responsibility to work peacefully to change the situation through acts of social justice.

The whole situation — and, of course, the plot of *Oddsfish!* itself — adequately demonstrates the confusion rampant during times when people mix politics and religion, ending up with little regard for either. Thus, Benson probably could not have picked a better way to illustrate the political problems for both Catholics and Protestants that came out of the Reformation, and the difficulties this has caused for the whole of human society ever since . . . even if that was not his conscious intention!

Index

"Out of Depth," short story by Evelyn Waugh, 152, 153
Act of Union, 12
Adler, Mortimer J., 199
Allen, Grant, 231
American Civil War, 62
Americans, 34, 35, 136, 219, 220
An Average Man, novel by Robert Hugh Benson, 135, 143, 182, 196, 203-211, 224, 231
Anglican Church (Church of England), 1, 12, 20, 25, 39, 56, 57, 59, 63, 65, 70, 79, 122, 159, 181, 207, 209, 224, 225, 243
Apologia Pro Vita Sua, John Henry Newman, 23, 32, 61, 62, 71
Aquinas, St. Thomas, 2, 4, 5, 9, 10, 16, 109, 111, 121, 157, 162, 225, 240, 251, 252
Aristotelian philosophy, 10, 39, 252
Aristotle, 2, 5, 110, 141, 225, 240
Augustine, St., 32, 122, 157
Austin, Jane, 55, 60, 62
Awful Disclosures of Maria Monk, The, 51
Bagehot, Walter, 37, 38, 96
Baker Street Irregulars, 90
Barbie doll, 231
Battle of Dorking, The, novella by Sir George Chesny, 39, 134

Beatrice, novel by H. Rider Haggard, 231
Bellarmine, St. Robert, 157, 251
Belloc, Hilaire, 95
Ben Hur, A Tale of the Christ, novel by Lew Wallace, 53
Benedict XVI, 23, 32
Benson, Arthur Christopher, 40, 41, 42, 43, 77, 116, 122, 196, 238
Benson, E. F., brother of Robert Hugh Benson, 40
Benson, Margaret, sister of Robert Hugh Benson, 83, 96
Benson, Monsignor Robert Hugh, 2, 11, 12, 13, 15, 16, 33-43, 63, 73-254
Bible, 5, 97, 162
Billy the Kid, 66
Binary Economics, 199
Branch Theory, 58
Brownson, Orestes, 26
Bulwer-Lytton, Edward, 49, 65, 66, 70
By What Authority?, novel by Robert Hugh Benson, 89-93, 98, 135, 160, 179, 180, 237, 242, 249, 250
Caldwell, Taylor, 85
Callista, novel by John Henry Newman, 29, 30, 31, 32, 51, 60, 63, 65-72
Camm, Dom Bede, 89, 91
Campion, St. Edmund, 92, 160, 237, 242, 243, 244, 245, 246

Canterbury Tales, 84
Capital Homesteading, 200
Capital, Karl Marx, 59, 60
Catholic Church, 11, 13, 15, 16, 17, 19, 20, 23, 24, 32, 39, 42, 48, 49, 50, 51, 52, 55, 56, 57, 58, 62, 65, 66, 79, 90, 108, 109, 110, 120, 135, 148, 152, 153, 156, 161, 162, 165, 179, 180, 181, 191, 192, 197, 198, 199, 204, 205, 206, 208, 210, 227, 249, 250, 251, 252, 253, 254
Catholic Crusade (Anglo-Catholic), 59
Catholic emancipation, 11
Catholic fiction, 1, 47
Catholic Relief Act, 12, 18, 57
Catholicism, 1, 11, 12, 13, 17, 18, 21, 23, 24, 27, 29, 36, 39, 42, 49, 50, 51, 57, 58, 63, 65, 89, 104, 112, 139, 153, 156, 183, 196, 205, 207, 209, 227, 242, 244, 250
Center for Economic and Social Justice (CESJ), 200
Cervantes, Miguel de, 61
Charles II, 90, 99, 249, 251
Chesny, Sir George, 39, 134
Chesterton, Gilbert Keith, 4, 6, 9, 95, 110, 111, 121, 162, 187
Christ, 6, 15, 23, 92, 113, 121, 169, 208, 209, 213, 242
Christian Social Union, 59
Christianity, 3, 6, 10, 11, 16, 20, 26, 39, 53, 58, 63, 66, 68, 110, 167, 168, 169
Church of England, 11, 17, 19, 20, 28, 32, 42, 49, 50, 55, 56, 58, 79, 207, 243, 245
Cobbett, William, 95, 96, 161, 204
Colonel Blimp, 195
Come Rack! Come Rope!, novel by Robert Hugh Benson, 99, 180, 187, 211, 237-247, 250
Communist Manifesto, The, Karl Marx, 59
Confessions of a Convert, short memoir by Robert Hugh Benson, 42, 122-126, 209, 240, 243, 246
Confessions of St. Augustine, 32
Conventionalists, The, novel by Robert Hugh Benson, 131, 132, 139-143, 180, 203, 240
Corelli, Marie, 119, 147, 148, 159, 181, 206
Coward, The, novel by Robert Hugh Benson, 135, 182, 183, 195-201
Crimean War, 62
Curtain, Jeremiah, 70
Dawn of All, The, novel by Robert Hugh Benson, 41, 112, 125, 139, 151-158, 177, 181, 197, 240
Diary of a Nobody, novel by George Grossmith, 149
Dickens, Charles, 32, 60, 61, 92, 99, 205
distributism, 95
Douglas, Lloyd C., 66
Doyle, Sir Arthur Conan, 80
Dublin Review, 17
Duke of Wellington, Arthur Wellesley, 12
Duns Scotus, 7, 111
Easter Rising, 156

Elizabeth I, 90, 92, 101, 104, 243, 244, 245
Emerson, Ralph Waldo, 26
England, 11, 12, 13, 15, 17, 18, 19, 20, 21, 24, 29, 30, 34, 35, 36, 37, 38, 39, 48, 49, 50, 51, 52, 55, 60, 89, 90, 91, 92, 93, 95, 96, 98, 101, 104, 113, 133, 135, 137, 147, 151, 152, 156, 157, 160, 161, 166, 171, 172, 173, 180, 181, 183, 184, 187, 195, 197, 203, 204, 208, 209, 216, 225, 231, 241, 242, 244, 245, 252
English Constitution, The, political philosophy by Walter Bagehot, 37, 96
Essay on Population, An, Thomas Malthus, 60
Essay on the Development of Christian Doctrine, John Henry Newman, 59, 61, 71
ethics, 8
Everyman, Medieval morality play, 193
Fabiola, novel by Cardinal Wiseman, 16, 21, 30, 47-54
faith, 5, 8, 9, 13, 14, 16, 33, 37, 42, 69, 110, 112, 124, 130, 136, 162, 170, 188, 193, 207, 208, 211, 224, 232, 245
Father Dowling mysteries, 1
Fighting Gladiator, The, film version of *Fabiola*, 54
Filmer, Sir Robert, 11, 251
Four Feathers, The, novel by A. E. W. Mason, 195
Froude, James Anthony, 24, 57

Gibson Girl, 219
Gibson, Charles Dana, 219
Gilbert, William Schwenk, 129, 130, 148, 187
Grand Opera, 224, 228
Grandmother and the Priests, short story collection by Taylor Caldwell, 85
Grenville, Lord, 12
Grossmith, George, 148
Haggard, H. Rider, 231
Hardon, Rev. John A. (*Catholic Lifetime Reading Plan*), 23, 71, 79, 80, 237, 239
Henry II, 157, 159, 160, 171
Henry VI, 113
Henry VII, 96, 158, 160, 204, 252
Henry VIII, 97, 159, 160, 161, 171, 204, 239
High Church, 56, 57
Hill of Trouble, The, short story collection by Arthur C. Benson, 77
History of Richard Raynal, Solitary, The, novel by Robert Hugh Benson, 33, 78, 99, 107-117, 120, 159, 246
Hobbes, Thomas, 11, 37
Holy Blissful Martyr, Thomas à Becket, The, historical monograph by Robert Hugh Benson, 159-173
Hopkins, Gerard Manley, 57
Horace, Roman Poet, 2
Huckleberry Finn, novel by Mark Twain, 232
Hugh: Memoirs of a Brother, memoir by Arthur C. Benson, 16, 40, 77, 78, 89, 116, 119,

122, 133, 136, 159, 197, 209, 213, 246
Hypatia, novel by Charles Kingsley, 20, 30, 31, 49, 51, 65
Industrial Revolution, 59
Ingenioso Hidalgo Don Quixote de la Mancha, El, novel by Miguel de Cervantes, 61
Initiation, novel by Robert Hugh Benson, 34, 123, 182, 183, 184, 196, 213-221
Intellect, God's, 1, 5, 7, 8, 9, 11, 37, 108, 111, 162
Ireland, 12, 57, 92, 95, 137, 156, 161, 204, 244
Islam, 1, 3, 10
James I Stuart, 11, 251
Judaism, 1, 3, 10, 168, 190
Keble, John, 57
Kelso, Louis O., 199
Khaldûn, Ibn, 2, 10
King's Achievement, The, novel by Robert Hugh Benson, 95-99, 160, 180, 238
Kingsley, Rev. Charles, 20-32, 49-65
Ku Klux Klan, 232
Lady of the Lake, The, epic poem by Sir Walter Scott, 232
Lallah Rookh, epic poem by Thomas Moore, 232
Last Days of Pompeii, The, novel by Edward Bulwer-Lytton, 49, 65
Leo XIII, 16, 34, 198, 205, 251, 252
Lever, Charles, Anglo-Irish novelist, 32, 60
Leviathan, political philosophy by Thomas Hobbes, 37

Lewis, C. S., 1, 9, 10, 17, 39, 67, 97
Liberal Party, 21
Light Invisible, The, short story collection by Robert Hugh Benson, 77-81, 85, 89, 123
Locke, John, 251, 253
Lombard Street, financial theory by Walter Bagehot, 37, 38, 96
Loneliness?, novel by Robert Hugh Benson, 143, 182, 196, 210, 211, 223-234
Lord of the World, novel by Robert Hugh Benson, 39, 40, 41, 105, 112, 124, 133-137, 139, 141, 151, 152, 156, 177, 179, 180, 181, 187, 197, 239
Loss and Gain, novel by John Henry Newman, 29, 32, 51, 55-63, 70, 93
Love Among the Ruins, novella by Evelyn Waugh, 40
Low Church, 56
Macmillan's Magazine, 24, 25, 27, 29
Magna Charta, 38, 173
Maimonides, Moses, 2, 10
Malthus, Thomas, 60
Malthusian scarcity, 59
Man for All Seasons, A, play by Robert Bolt, 97
Manichaean, 4, 5, 9, 10, 11, 20, 31, 108
Manichaeism, 3, 6, 11, 35
Manichees, 3
Manzoni, Allesandro, 60
Martindale, Rev. C. C., Robert Hugh Benson's biographer, 43, 78, 79, 80, 83, 84, 85, 89, 92, 97, 101, 103, 104, 113, 116,

117, 119, 120, 136, 137, 139, 140, 142, 146, 151, 152, 156, 159, 196, 197, 198, 199, 203, 213, 214, 220, 249
Marx, Karl, 59, 60, 205
Mary Queen of Scots, 92, 185, 237
Maslow, Abraham, 220
McInerny, Dr. Ralph, 1
Mirfield Community, Anglo-Catholic religious community, 77, 78
Mirror of Shalott, A, short stories by Robert Hugh Benson, 40, 83-85
Modernism, 6, 108, 109, 110, 111, 112, 114
More, St. Thomas, 27, 97, 108, 109, 133, 157, 158, 160, 162
Mrs. Grundy, 195
Nation-State, 11, 37, 92, 93, 243, 252
Natural Law, The, H. Rommen, 7, 112
natural moral law, 1, 2, 5, 6, 7, 8, 9, 11, 21, 35, 36, 37, 39, 69, 108, 111, 112, 126, 163, 198, 205, 240, 241
nature, divine, 2
Nature, God's, 1, 2, 5, 9, 10, 33, 37, 108, 111, 162, 240
nature, human, 1, 2, 5, 10, 92, 162, 204, 238
Necromancers, The, novel by Robert Hugh Benson, 139, 145-149, 180, 241
Newman, Blessed John Henry Cardinal, 2, 11, 12, 13, 17, 18, 23-32, 33, 51, 55-71, 93

None Other Gods, novel by Robert Hugh Benson, 16, 182, 187-194
O'Connell, Daniel, 11
Oates, Titus, 90, 99
Oddsfish!, novel by Robert Hugh Benson, 89, 90, 99, 102, 135, 180, 241, 249-254
opera, 223, 224, 228, 232
Oriel College, 56
Oscott, English Catholic college, 18, 89
Oxford Movement, 17, 18, 19, 20, 28, 32, 55, 56, 57, 59, 200
Oxford University, 56
Palmer, Sir William, 57
Papers of a Pariah, novella by Robert Hugh Benson, 119-122, 124, 139
Pascal's Wager, 68
Patriarcha, treatise on political theory by Sir Robert Filmer, 251
Paul Kelver, novel by Edward Bulwer-Lytton, 66
Peel, Sir Robert, 12
Pesch, Rev. Heinrich, S.J., 151, 152
Pharisees, 190
Pius IX, 18, 19, 252
Pius X, St., 108, 112, 114, 155, 198
Pius XI, 157, 165, 169, 198, 205, 242
Polish-Lithuanian Commonwealth, 252
Poor Laws, 59
Popular Catholic Library, 48, 49
positivism, 7, 111, 112
Pride and Prejudice, novel by Jane Austin, 55

private property, 9, 35, 38, 59, 95, 109, 133, 158, 161, 162, 163, 164, 170, 171, 204
Promessi Sposi, I, novel by Allessandro Manzoni, 61
pursuit of happiness, 5, 9, 109
Pusey, Edward Bouverie, 56
Queen's Tragedy, The, novel by Robert Hugh Benson, 99, 101-105, 160, 180
Quo Vadis, novel by Heinryk Sienkiewicz, 48, 70, 97
Quran, 5
rack-renting, 59
reason, 5, 6, 7, 8, 10, 11, 16, 33, 37, 39, 63, 110, 112, 120, 162
reasoning, deductive, 8
reasoning, inductive, 8
Reformation, 36, 37, 38, 52, 59, 69, 95, 96, 99, 160, 161, 162, 170, 180, 184, 189, 190, 199, 204, 239, 253, 254
Religion of the Plain Man, The, semi-fictional apologetics by Robert Hugh Benson, 43, 120-122, 124, 208, 209, 241, 242
Rerum Novarum, 34
Rhadamanthus, 228
Robe, The, novel by Lloyd C. Douglas, 66
Rolfe, Frederick ("Baron Corvo"), 119, 120, 147, 148, 159, 181, 206, 214
Roman law, 2, 53
Rommen, Dr. Heinrich, 6, 7, 111, 112, 163
Roosevelt, Theodore, 35
Sadducees, 190

science fiction, 39, 41, 99, 102, 134, 135, 151, 154, 181, 182, 187, 223
Scott, Sir Walter, 32, 61, 63, 99, 103, 177, 232
Sentimentalists, The, novel by Robert Hugh Benson, 129-132, 139, 140, 141, 142, 143, 148, 180, 211
Sheen, Bishop Fulton, 15, 60
Sidney, Algernon, 183, 184, 251, 253
Sienkiewicz, Heinryk, 47, 70, 97
Siger of Brabant, 110
Slaughterhouse Five, novel by Kurt Vonnegut, Jr., 152
Smith, Adam, 60
social doctrine, 109
social encyclicals, 198
Society for Creative Anachronism, 61
Spain, 12, 185, 252
Storey, Father John, 244
Sullivan, Arthur Seymor, 148, 187
Testem Benevolentia Nostrae, 35
Testem Benevolentiae, 253
Thackery, William Makepeace, 32, 60, 61
That Hideous Strength, novel by C. S. Lewis, 39, 97
Thirty-Nine Articles, 28, 58
Thoreau, Henry David, 26
Torah, 5, 190
Tract 90, John Henry Newman, 28, 58, 59, 61, 71
Trollope, Anthony, 32
Twain, Mark, 147, 232, 242
United Kingdom, 11, 54

United States, 6, 21, 34, 35, 157, 165, 173, 251
Upper Ten Thousand, 36, 37, 225
virtue, 5, 10, 12, 24, 25, 48, 62, 68, 99, 101, 102, 109, 113, 137, 145, 155, 158, 190, 198, 199, 225, 240
vocation, 9, 29, 33, 34, 36, 39, 41, 78, 79, 80, 81, 99, 107, 112, 113, 114, 115, 117, 137, 142, 143, 181, 182, 185, 189, 192, 201, 220, 221, 224, 238, 244
Wagner, Richard, 223, 228
Wallace, General Lew, 66
Walsh, Bishop Thomas, 18
Water Babies, The, fable by Charles Kingsley, 30
Waugh, Evelyn, 33, 40, 78, 119, 120, 143, 152, 153, 159, 160, 177, 181, 184, 242, 246
Wealth of Nations, The, Adam Smith, 60

Westward Ho!, novel by Charles Kingsley, 30
What, Then, Does Dr. Newman Mean? Kingsley's attack on Newman, 27
Wilberforce, Robert, 57
Will, God's, 1, 7, 8, 9, 11, 33, 36, 37, 108, 111, 162, 188, 193, 218, 238, 239
William of Occam, 7, 112
Williams, Isaac, 57
Winnowing, A, novel by Robert Hugh Benson, 177-186
Wiseman, Nicholas Patrick Cardinal, 2, 11, 12, 13, 15-21, 30, 33, 47, 48, 50, 51, 52, 53
Wodehouse, P. G., 135, 142, 177, 228, 231
Woman Who Did, The, novel by Grant Allen, 231, 232

Robert Hugh Benson Titles from Universal Values Media

A WINNOWING

Mixing such seemingly incongruous elements as social satire, near-slapstick, and obsession with death, *A Winnowing* flays Edwardian society in terms that bring to mind the comedy of P. G. Wodehouse, and the black humor of Evelyn Waugh.

ISBN 978-1-60210-005-3   224 pp. $20.00

NONE OTHER GODS

This gentle, yet profound satire relates the story of Frank Guiseley, a young man who drops out of college and tries to force God to instruct him personally on what God wants him to do. People of all faiths can appreciate the growing frustration and bafflement Frank experiences until he finally stops trying to make God listen to him, and starts listening to God.

ISBN 978-1-60210-006-0   312 pp. $20.00

THE COWARD

A young man is faced with challenges and manages to fail at every step. He becomes convinced he is an irredeemable coward, and only then begins to find courage. In a damning indictment of close-minded Edwardian society, a supreme act of courage on the young man's part is mistaken for yet one more craven act.

ISBN 978-1-60210-007-7   312 pp. $20.00

AN AVERAGE MAN

Possibly Benson's finest achievement, *An Average Man* rips to shreds the assumptions on which Edwardian upper class society believed civilization itself was built. Worldly success destroys one "average man," while it presents another, afflicted with seemingly endless and crushing defeats, with the opportunity of practicing virtue of a heroic stature.

ISBN 978-1-60210-008-4   340 pp. $20.00

INITIATION

Initiation explores the different types of pain with which people are afflicted, spiritual, psychological, and physical, none of it deserved, yet all of it leading to greater self-awareness and growth in understanding of what it means to be human. Despite the theme, the novel is both entertaining and profound.

ISBN 978-1-60210-009-1   360 pp. $22.00

LONELINESS?

Loneliness? examines the life of a woman who sacrifices everything to be accepted by people who can see her only in terms of her singing ability and the roles she plays on the stage, and who is abandoned by them when she can no longer fit into their preconceived ideas. *Loneliness?* may be Benson's least known, yet one of his most insightful — and entertaining — novels.

ISBN 978-1-60210-010-7   298 pp. $20.00

www.ingramcontent.com/pod-product-compliance
Lightning Source LLC
Chambersburg PA
CBHW031138160426
43193CB00008B/177